IT'S ALL ABSOLUTELY FINE

IT'S ALL ABSOLUTELY FINE

LIFE IS **COMPLICATED** SO I'VE DRAWN IT INSTEAD

RUBY ELLIOT

Andrews McMeel
Publishing®
a division of Andrews McMeel Universal

For Nina and Harry and Miranda, just . . . yes?

For Mum and Dad, who I've known pretty much all my life and have, despite everything, always kept the house filled with so much laughter and nuttiness and love and pens. You're alright I guess.

And also for Sam, who we miss very much.

THIS IS A MAGICAL EDITH.
WE DON'T KNOW WHY,
BUT SHE IS.

CONTENTS

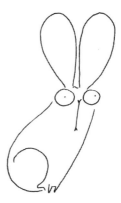

INTRODUCTION BIT

Hello, my name is Ruby and that's about as far as I can get before I start worrying about what to say next. To give you a bit of context, here are some other names I go by:

RUBY: EMOTIONAL CESSPIT, THE 9TH WONDER OF THE WORLD

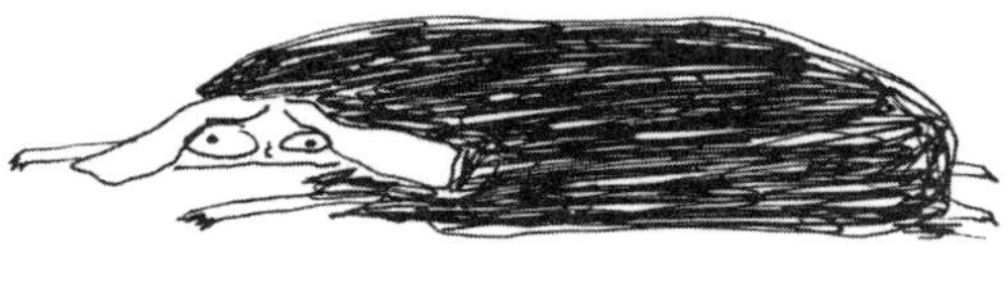

BIG BAG OF TEARS

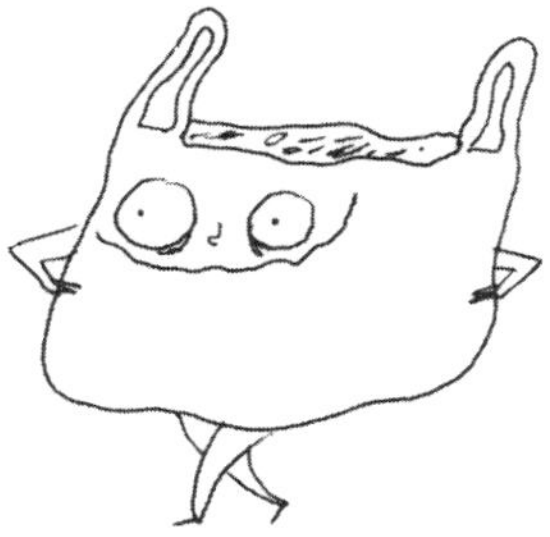

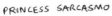PRINCESS SARCASMO

NO REALLY,
THAT'S GREAT

A POTATO

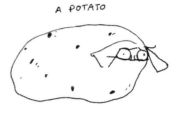

So yes, I'm a pretty versatile disaster as you can see. What I've essentially done for this book is draw about the stuff that goes on in my head, and stuff that goes on outside of my head, and how those things mush together in a bit of a strange and confusing way. They are drawings about me, but I hope that some of them may be about you, too. And if not, that's fine; the book will work nicely as a sort of deluxe rectangular coaster. Everyone's a winner.

IT'S A BEAUTIFUL DAY FOR DON'T

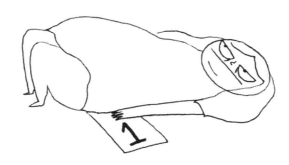

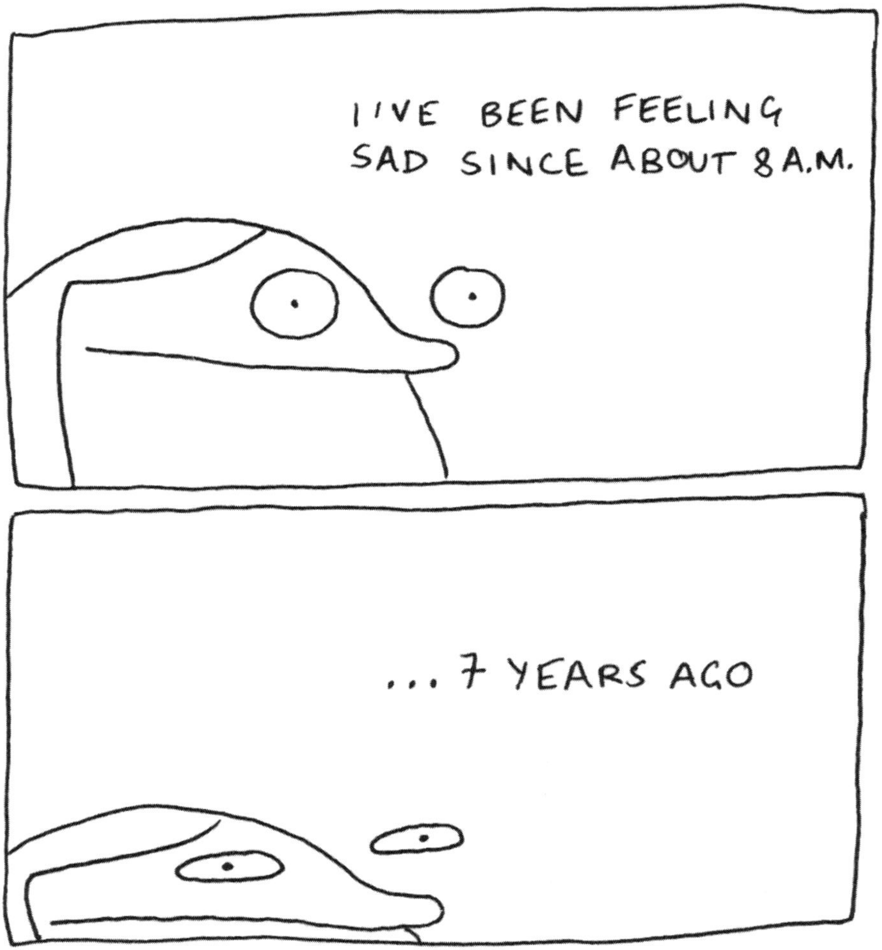
I'VE BEEN FEELING SAD SINCE ABOUT 8 A.M.
... 7 YEARS AGO

I am sitting on the floor next to the bed waiting for nothing to happen. The blinds are closed because I cannot stand the light and the way it makes people want to be outside doing talking and laughing and interesting things with their lives. The last activity I did was dragging myself on all fours, slug-like, to the kitchen and sprinkling sugar straight out of the bag onto a piece of old bread, then standing by the counter cramming it into my face like I was a VHS on fast-forward. If I don't feel real then why would I bother feeding myself as if I were? I've been wearing the same pajamas for years, centuries, well, a week really but the level of stale is probably sufficient for them to be sealed in a glass case and put on one of those little plinths in a museum. I imagine tour guides pointing out the various unidentifiable stains (a mixture of snot, tears, and canned soup) to a group of confused tourists taking polite photos—"And here we have a garment dating back to a four-year-long depressive episode." There could be a little plaque. And a gift shop selling postcards, except they're just bits of old pizza box torn up into postcard size with UGH scribbled on them in crayon.

The first time I experienced major depression was age sixteen. I'd already been very unwell for a couple of years with an eating disorder that had left me miserable and often hospitalized. But this was different; this was as if an actual steamroller driven by a crazy grinning idiot had trundled through the door and flattened my entire life into a sad pancake of nothingness. It wasn't that I stopped caring about life, but I stopped being able to care. My brain, having been suspended in a state of hypervigilance for such a long time, just packed in and said, "No more, your job now is to lie on the sofa incredibly still and just work on evaporating, you useless trowel." And so I did.

For months and months I spent all day and all night curled up in a variety of mildly uncomfortable positions on my parents' sofa, creating a small arse-shaped dent in one of the seat cushions and wearing the others down until they looked as deflated and sad as I felt. And you know what? It was shit. It was very shit for a long time. No one wants to be lying there at 3:30 a.m. reciting the entirety of a PedEgg commercial verbatim as it plays for the fifth time in a row because you haven't had the energy to change the channel. No one wants to be permanently on the edge of bawling because their reality is one of life being utterly futile and pointless. No one wants to feel so desperate that they end up in a psychiatric ward being asked to rate their mood on a scale of 1–10 as they watch their laces being yanked out of their shoes and taken somewhere out of reach. But these were all things that happened to me because I was depressed.

My dog was the first person to get me out of the house during the sofa months. I mean, there are only about two things in the world that can make me go outside when I am at my most dysfunctional—the first of which came to light when I was living alone and had run out of toilet paper (doesn't matter how low I felt, at some point I was going to have to pee) and the second was my woofular unit needing a walk. At age sixteen I was acutely insecure and paranoid about other people seeing me, but clipping the dog's leash on and having her bounce along beside me sniffing the pavement and pissing on trees distracted me from the crushing weight of my own negative thoughts. She was like a mobile security blanket except better and funnier, with barking, and a brilliant reminder that it is possible to just "be." It's for this reason that animals are excellent to have around, particularly when you're feeling shit, because they are so untroubled by existence and unwaveringly confident in their ability to enjoy stuff (even if that stuff is rolling in fox poo). When I was unwell, all the care and kindness I wasn't able to offer myself I could defer onto the dog, and it was in loving the very simple, very stupid, incredibly happy ball of fur and ears I could find just a little bit of point in the pointless.

That's what you need sometimes, whether it's a dog or a cat or a jazzy lizard or something else entirely that provides you with some emotional respite when it's all too messy—a tiny yet significant port in an almighty storm.

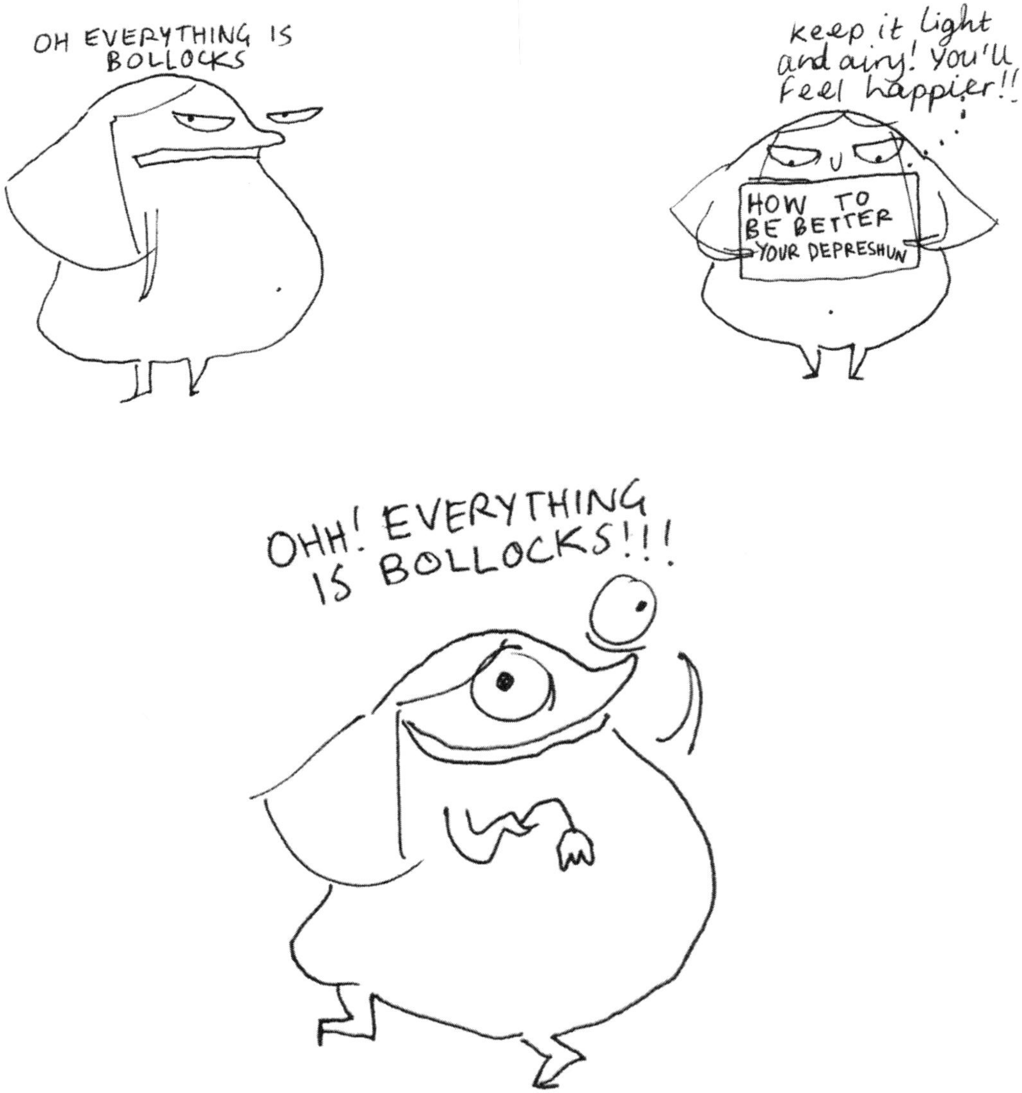
OH EVERYTHING IS BOLLOCKS
keep it light and airy! You'll feel happier!!
HOW TO BE BETTER YOUR DEPRESHUN
OHH! EVERYTHING IS BOLLOCKS!!!

EAU DE DEPRESSION
NOTES OF YET ANOTHER LONELY MICROWAVE MEAL
WHY
HINTS OF PANIC PERSPIRATION
SNOT-INFUSED TEARS
DON'T
SCENTS OF I HAVEN'T WASHED IN WEEKS
NO

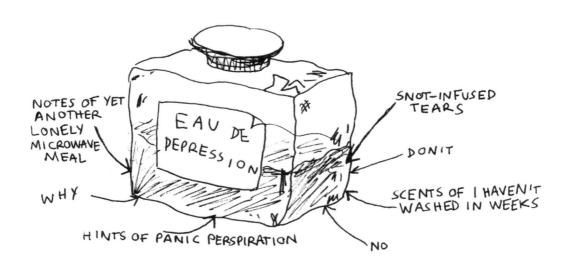

WALKIN' WALKIN'... STROLLIN' STROLLIN'... SUDDENLY REMEMBERING THAT THIS IS ALL PRETTY POINTLESS AND WE ARE JUST BLIPS IN TIME RUNNING FROM THE INEVITABILITY OF DEATH...

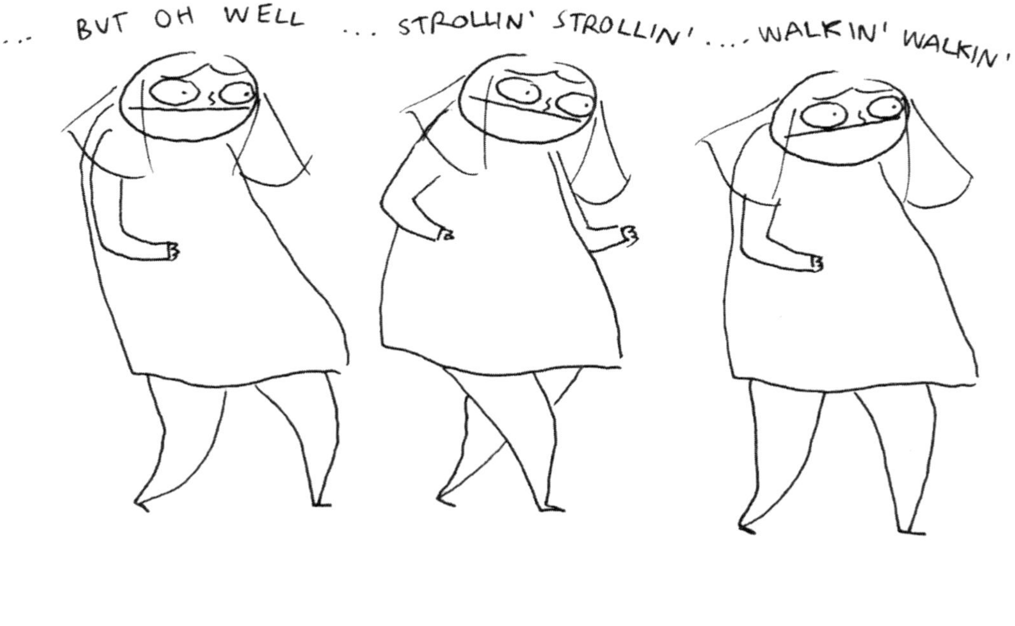
... BUT OH WELL ... STROLLIN' STROLLIN' ... WALKIN' WALKIN'

TODAY I FEEL LIKE A VERY
TERRIBLE PEBBLE

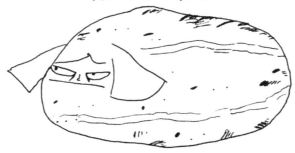

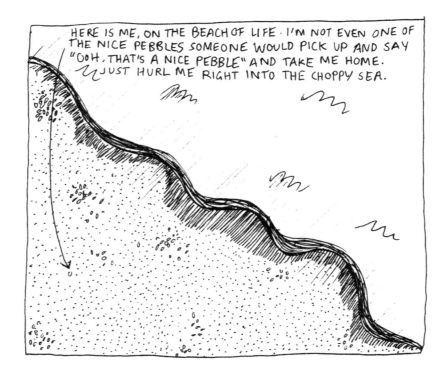

HERE IS ME, ON THE BEACH OF LIFE. I'M NOT EVEN ONE OF THE NICE PEBBLES SOMEONE WOULD PICK UP AND SAY "OOH, THAT'S A NICE PEBBLE" AND TAKE ME HOME. JUST HURL ME RIGHT INTO THE CHOPPY SEA.

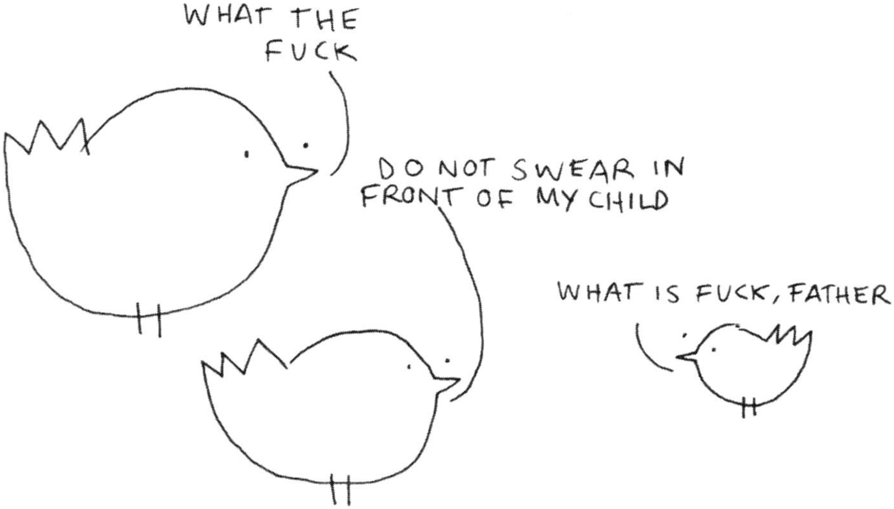
WHAT THE FUCK
DO NOT SWEAR IN FRONT OF MY CHILD
WHAT IS FUCK, FATHER

EMOTIONAL SMOOTHIE RECIPE

INGREDIENTS:

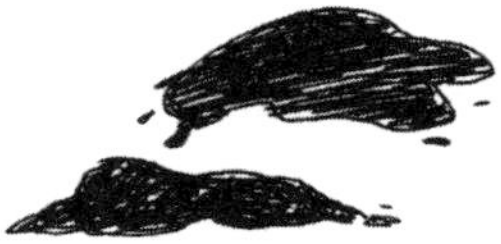

COUPLE GLOBS OF UNSPECIFIED YET WEIGHTY SADNESS

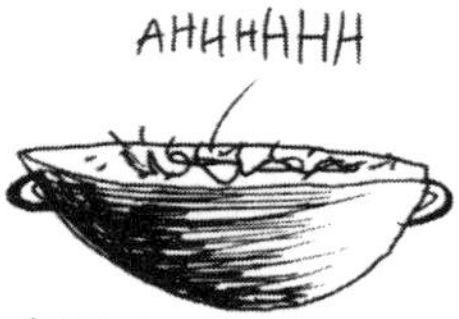
AHHHHHH

A GOOD WOK'S WORTH OF FEAR & CONFUSION (WHY IS IT A WOK? NOBODY KNOWS, THAT'S PART OF THE TERRIBLE MYSTERY)

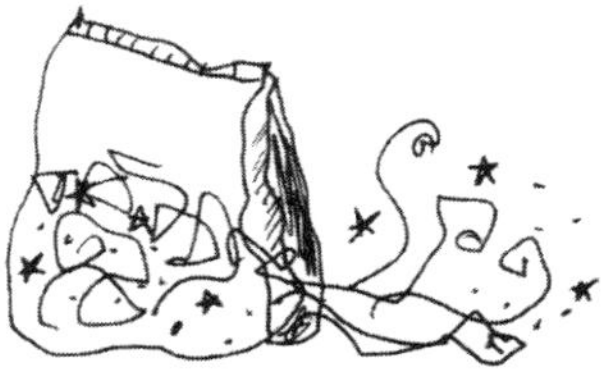

BAG OF ANXIOUS EXCITEMENT THAT'S ALL SPLIT DOWN THE SIDE AND SPILLING EVERYWHERE

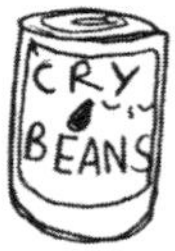
CRY
BEANS

CAN O' EXHAUSTION INDUCED TEARS

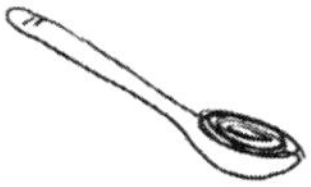

LONELINESS MEASURED OUT IN THAT ONE WEIRD SPOON EVERYONE HAS THAT DOESN'T MATCH THE REST OF THE CUTLERY

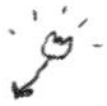

ONE VERY TINY TENTATIVE PINCH OF HAPPINESS AND HOPE (OR HOWEVER MUCH YOU CAN TOLERATE)

METHOD:

CRAM INGREDIENTS INTO BLENDER

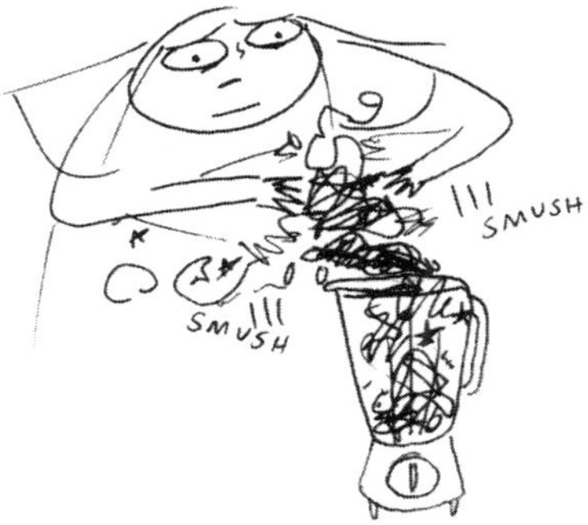
SMUSH
SMUSH

BLEND UNTIL GRITTY AND WEIRD. YOU'RE AIMING FOR A TEXTURE THAT'LL STICK IN YOUR THROAT AND MAKE YOU FEEL LIKE YOU'RE VAGUELY SUFFOCATING

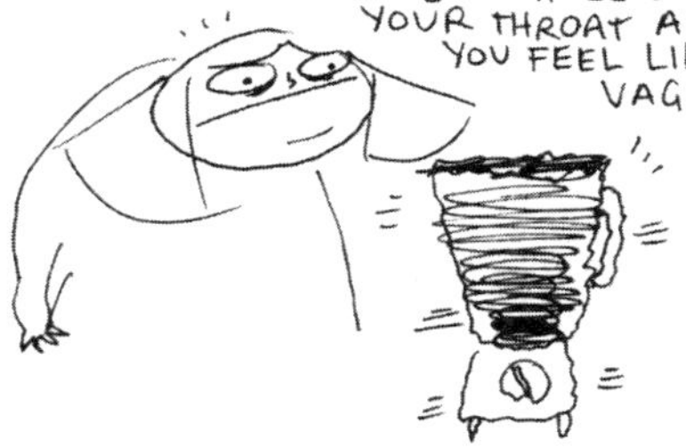

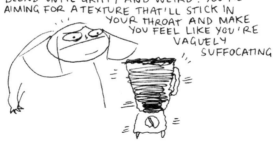

POUR INTO A GLASS AND ADD ONE OF THOSE STUPID TINY UMBRELLAS, FOR STYLE

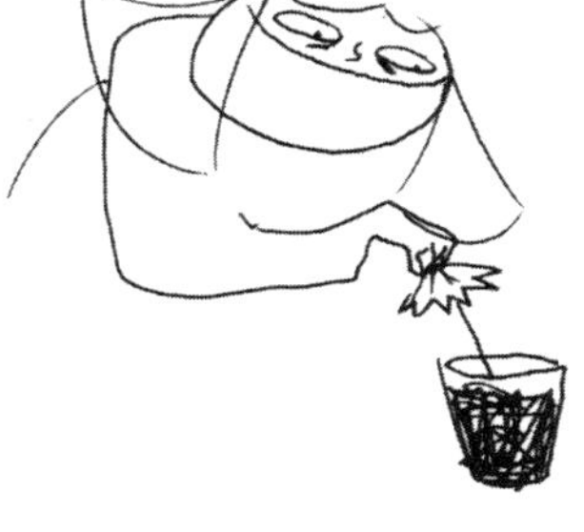

ENJOY!

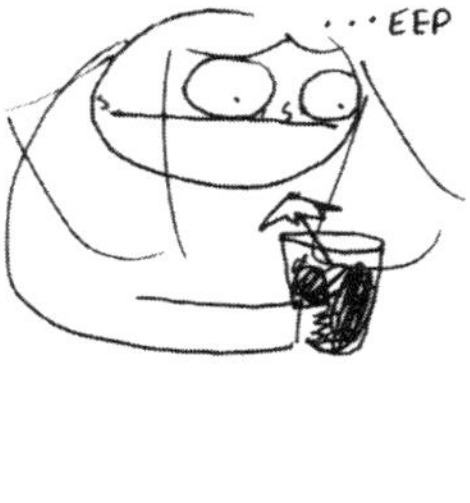
...EEP

I DON'T WANT TO HEAR IT

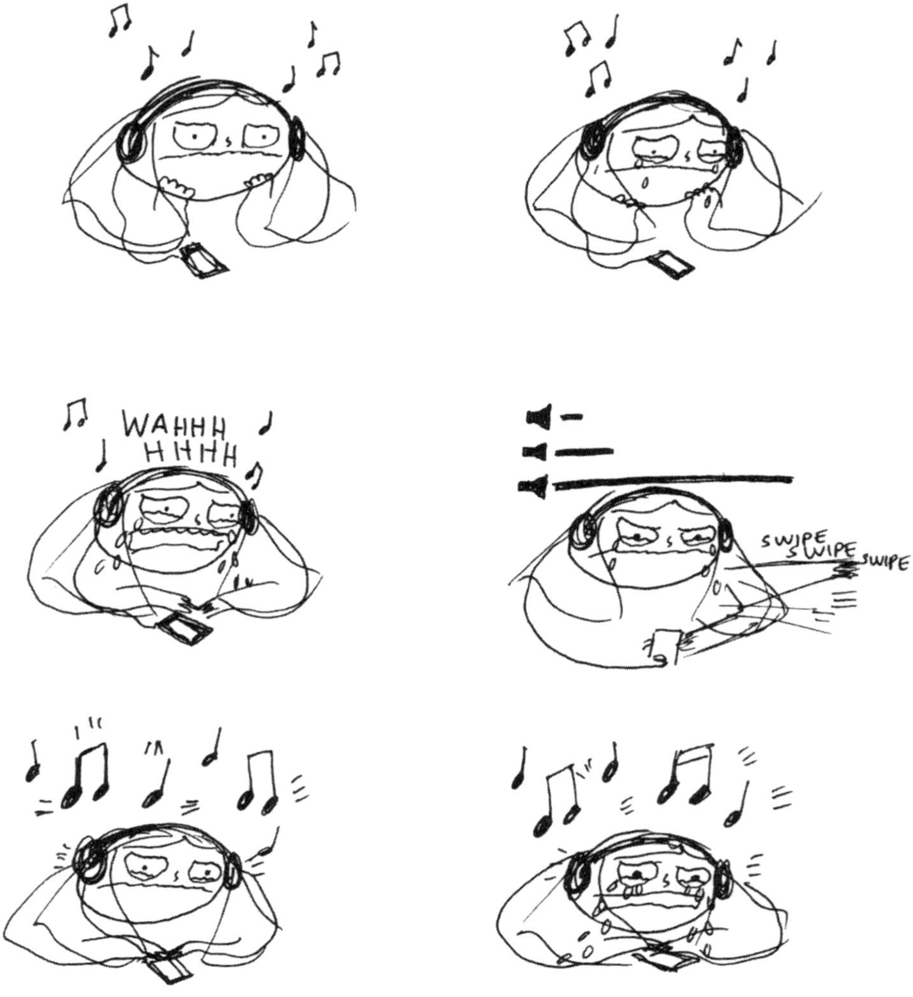

WAHHH
HHHH
SWIPE
SWIPE
SWIPE

FOR THE LAST TIME THESE AREN'T **TEARS**,
THEY ARE **GLAMOUR BEADS** THAT JUST
HAPPEN TO BE FALLING FROM MY EYES IN MY FACE

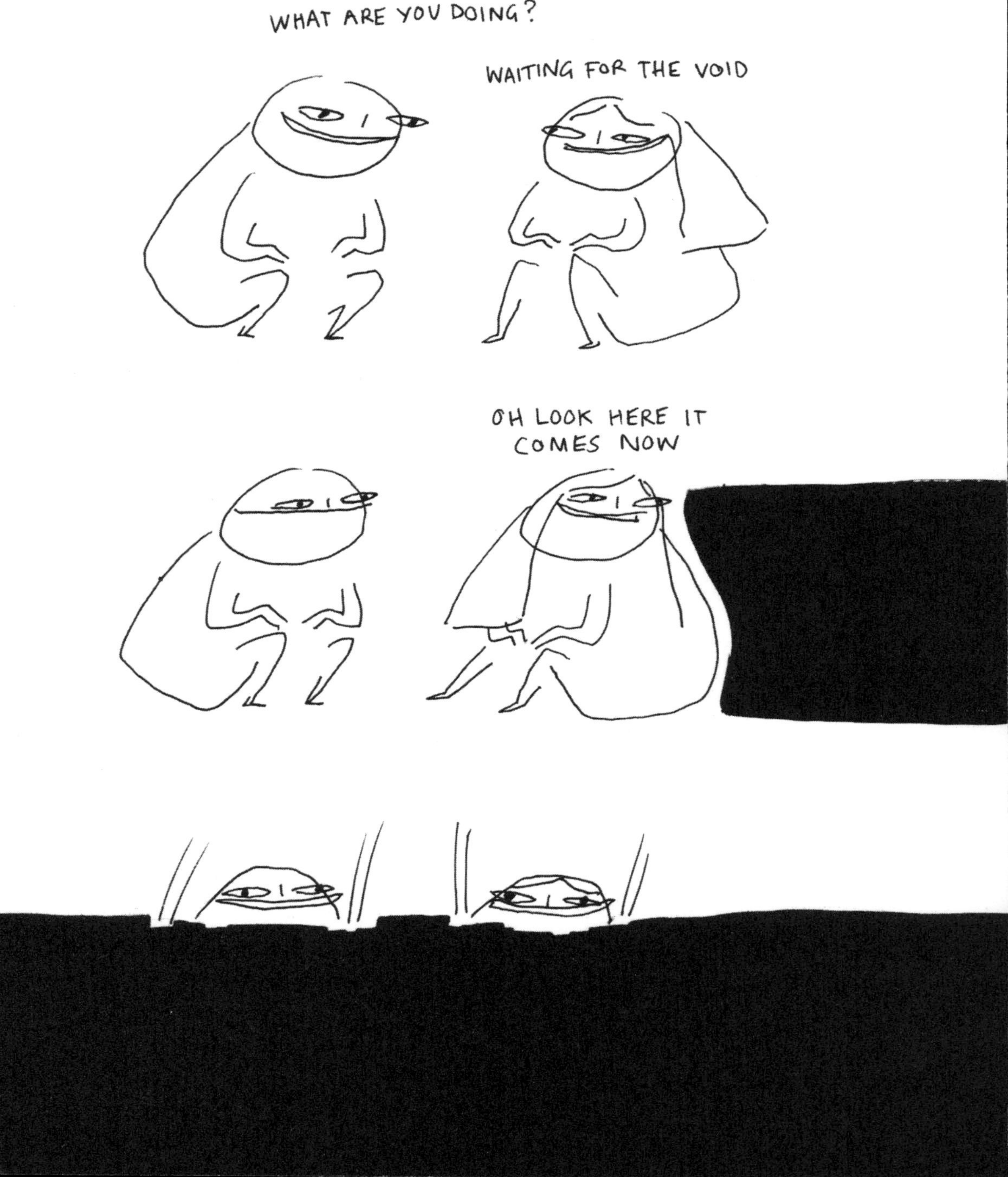
WHAT ARE YOU DOING?
WAITING FOR THE VOID
OH LOOK HERE IT COMES NOW

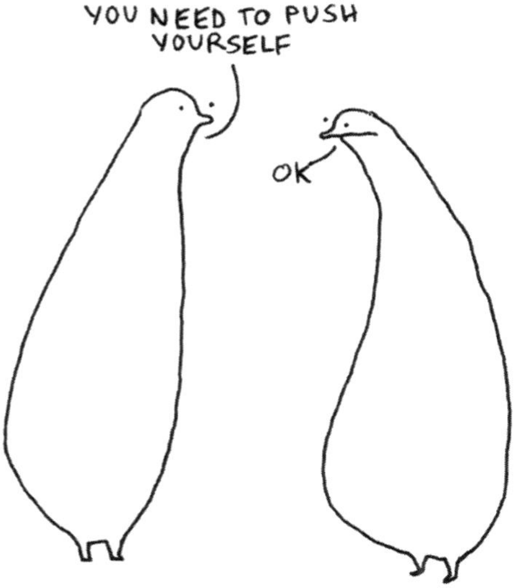
YOU NEED TO PUSH YOURSELF
OK

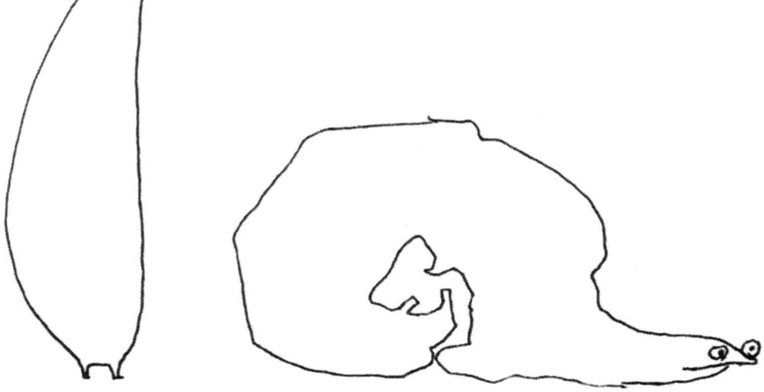
WHY ARE YOU DEAD NOW?

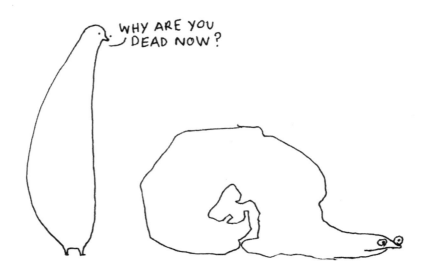

TURN THAT FROWN

SIDEWAYS

GO OUTSIDE

TERRIFY THE PEOPLE

THE SOUNDTRACK TO MY LIFE

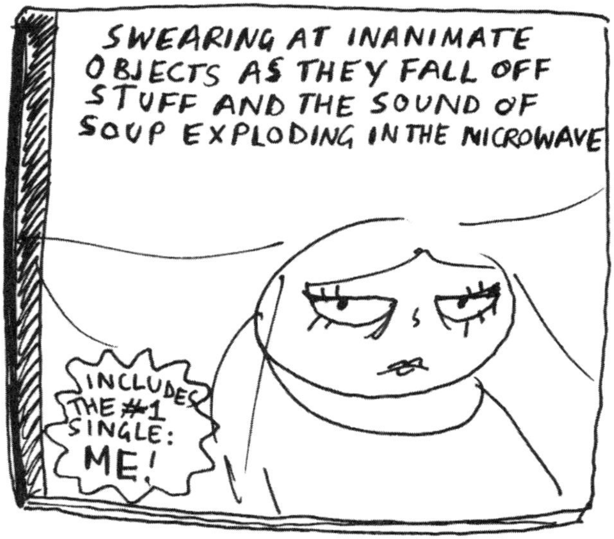
SWEARING AT INANIMATE OBJECTS AS THEY FALL OFF STUFF AND THE SOUND OF SOUP EXPLODING IN THE MICROWAVE
INCLUDES THE #1 SINGLE: ME!

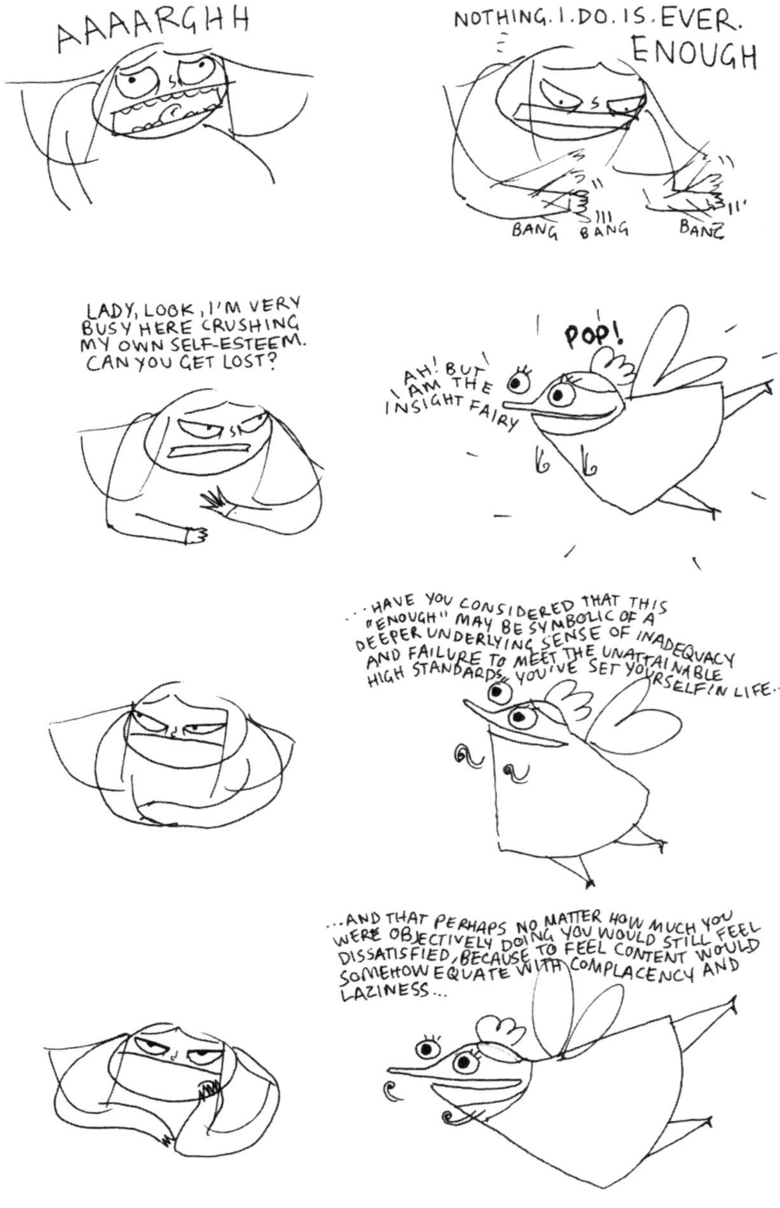
AAAARGHH
NOTHING. I. DO. IS. EVER. ENOUGH
BANG BANG BANG
LADY, LOOK, I'M VERY BUSY HERE CRUSHING MY OWN SELF-ESTEEM. CAN YOU GET LOST?
POP!
AH! BUT I AM THE INSIGHT FAIRY
...HAVE YOU CONSIDERED THAT THIS "ENOUGH" MAY BE SYMBOLIC OF A DEEPER UNDERLYING SENSE OF INADEQUACY AND FAILURE TO MEET THE UNATTAINABLE HIGH STANDARDS YOU'VE SET YOURSELF IN LIFE...
...AND THAT PERHAPS NO MATTER HOW MUCH YOU WERE OBJECTIVELY DOING YOU WOULD STILL FEEL DISSATISFIED, BECAUSE TO FEEL CONTENT WOULD SOMEHOW EQUATE WITH COMPLACENCY AND LAZINESS...

I DON'T THINK YOU EVEN KNOW WHAT "ENOUGH" IS. I THINK YOUR PERCEPTION OF ACHIEVEMENT IS SO SKEWED BY YOUR LOW OPINION OF YOURSELF THAT YOU FIND IT EASIER TO STAY SUSPENDED IN A STATE OF MILD TO MODERATE DISCONTENT BECAUSE AT LEAST THEN YOU CAN PRETEND YOU HAVE ANY IDEA OF WHAT IS GOING ON

TICKLE TICKLE

I'M GOING TO LIE DOWN. PLEASE WAKE ME UP IN A COUPLE OF DON'T

YOU KNOW WHEN PEOPLE SAY "THEY'VE THROWN ME IN AT THE DEEP END"?

YEH

AND IT'S MEANT TO BE SCARY? BUT IF YOU WERE THROWN IN AT THE SHALLOW END

YOU'D PRETTY MUCH JUST SMACK YOUR HEAD AND DIE!

ARE YOU OKAY?

YES, PROBABLY NO

WE ARE GOOD AND WE ARE OKAY YES SIR

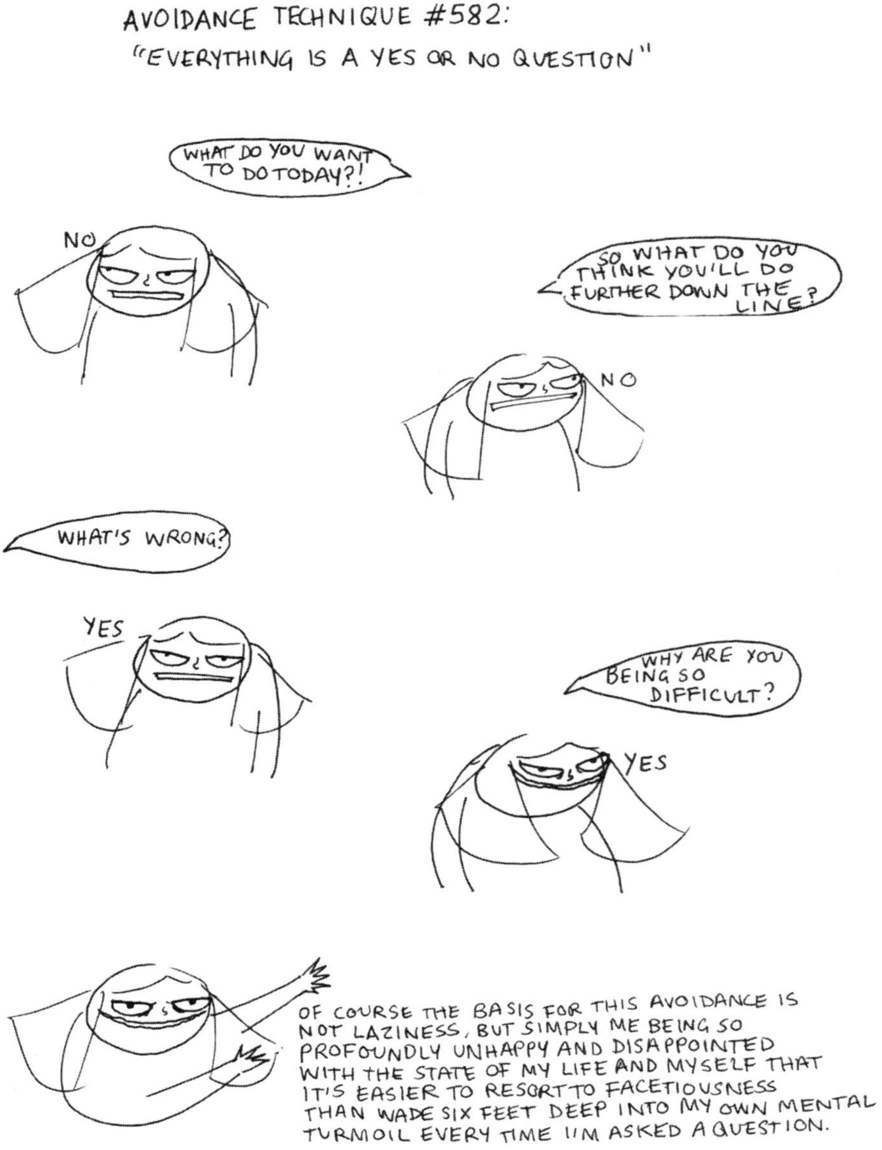
AVOIDANCE TECHNIQUE #582:
"EVERYTHING IS A YES OR NO QUESTION"
WHAT DO YOU WANT TO DO TODAY?!
NO
SO WHAT DO YOU THINK YOU'LL DO FURTHER DOWN THE LINE?
NO
WHAT'S WRONG?
YES
WHY ARE YOU BEING SO DIFFICULT?
YES
OF COURSE THE BASIS FOR THIS AVOIDANCE IS NOT LAZINESS, BUT SIMPLY ME BEING SO PROFOUNDLY UNHAPPY AND DISAPPOINTED WITH THE STATE OF MY LIFE AND MYSELF THAT IT'S EASIER TO RESORT TO FACETIOUSNESS THAN WADE SIX FEET DEEP INTO MY OWN MENTAL TURMOIL EVERY TIME I'M ASKED A QUESTION.

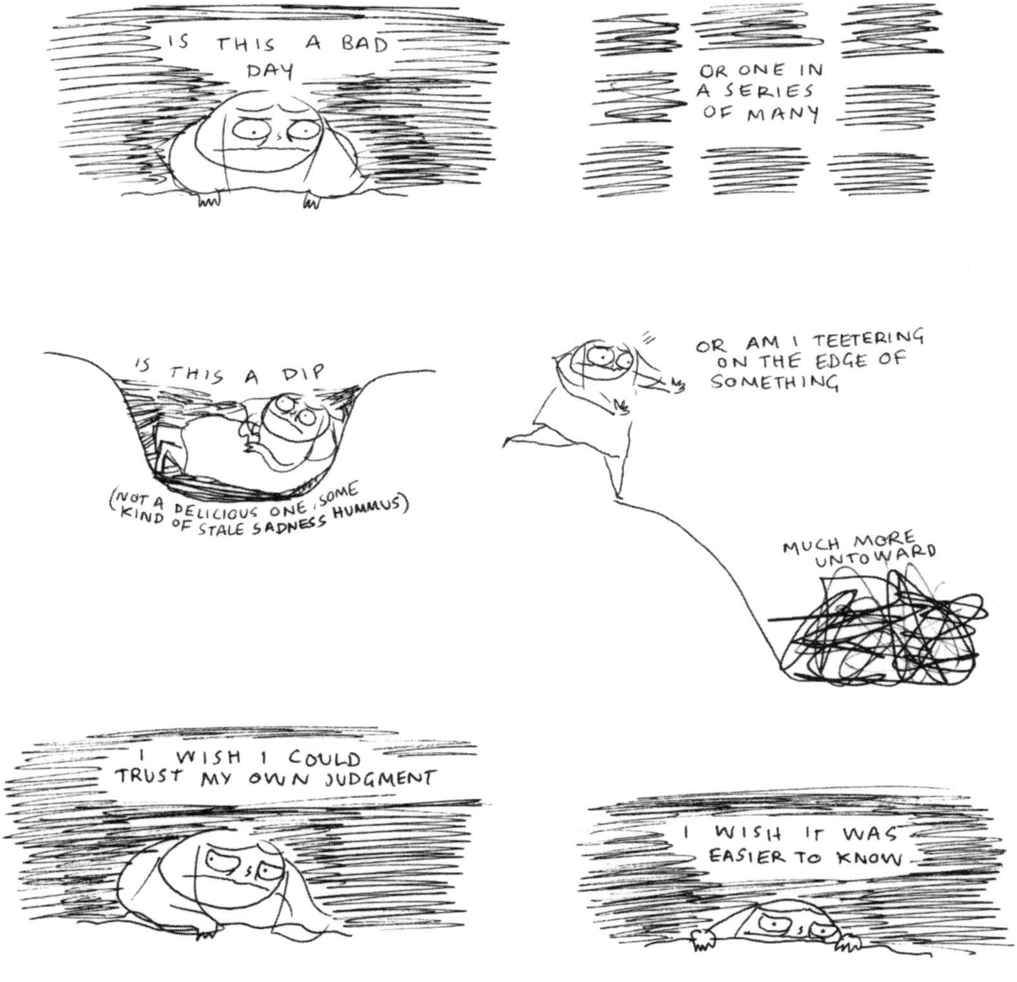
IS THIS A BAD DAY
OR ONE IN A SERIES OF MANY
IS THIS A DIP
(NOT A DELICIOUS ONE; SOME KIND OF STALE SADNESS HUMMUS)
OR AM I TEETERING ON THE EDGE OF SOMETHING
MUCH MORE UNTOWARD
I WISH I COULD TRUST MY OWN JUDGMENT
I WISH IT WAS EASIER TO KNOW

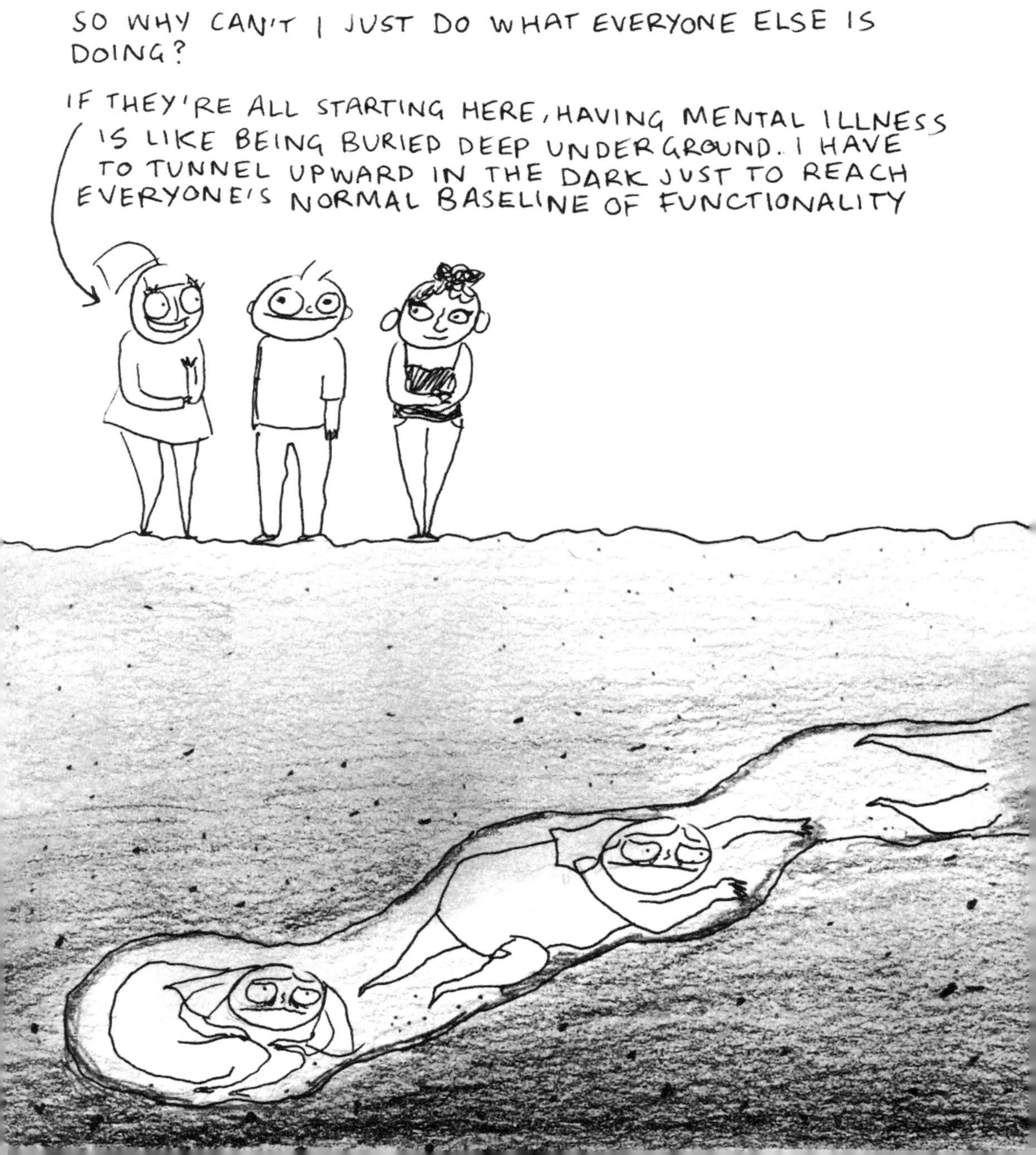

SO WHY CAN'T I JUST DO WHAT EVERYONE ELSE IS DOING?
IF THEY'RE ALL STARTING HERE, HAVING MENTAL ILLNESS IS LIKE BEING BURIED DEEP UNDERGROUND. I HAVE TO TUNNEL UPWARD IN THE DARK JUST TO REACH EVERYONE'S NORMAL BASELINE OF FUNCTIONALITY

IT'S SO FRUSTRATING, HAVING TO LIE THERE WIPED OUT AND COUGHING UP SOIL WHILE EVERYONE ELSE DANCES OFF INTO THE WORLD

I'VE BEEN DIGGING AND DIGGING, BUT I CAN STILL FEEL LIKE A FAILURE. I CAN STILL FEEL LEFT BEHIND.

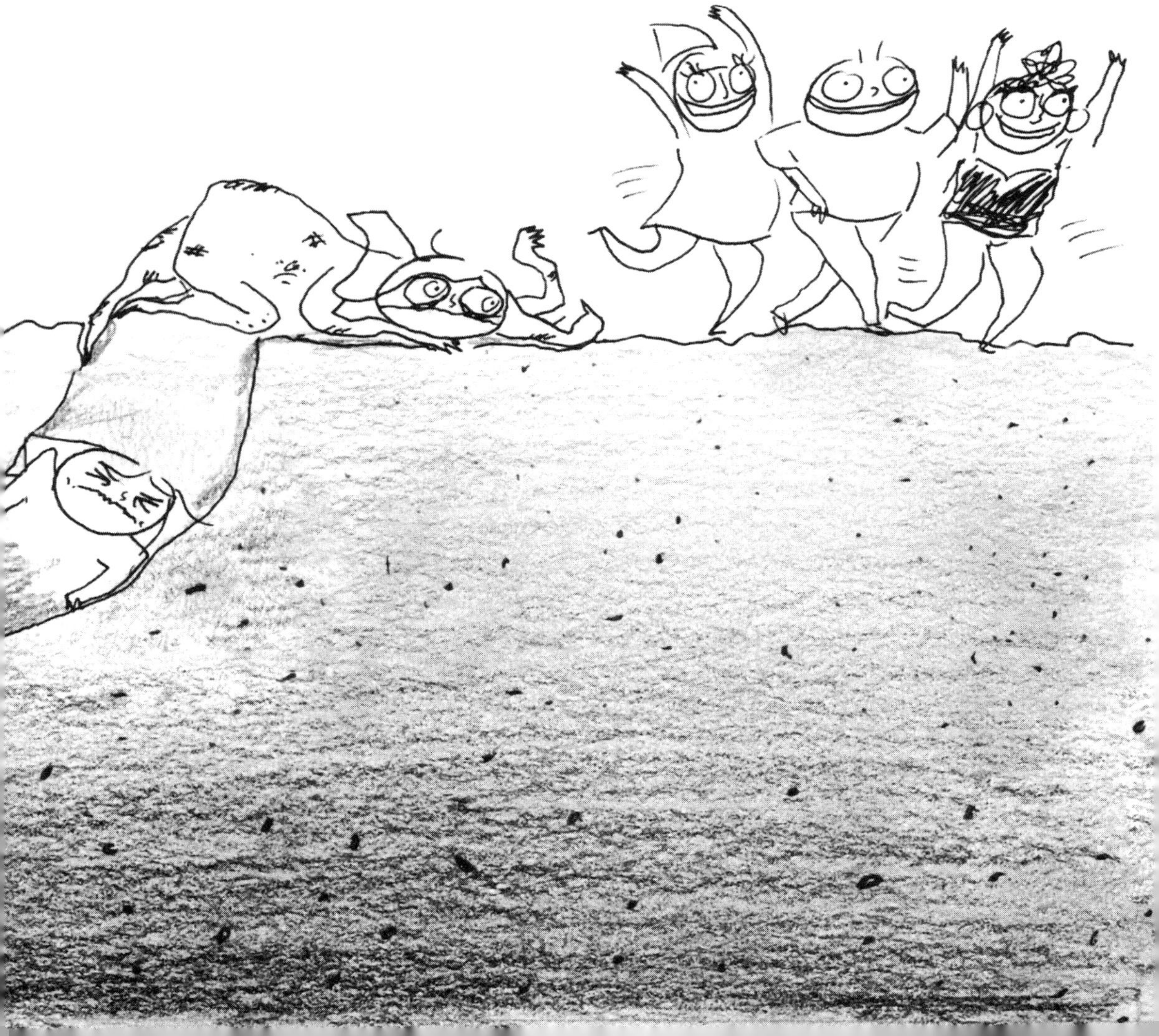

GET IN TOUCH WITH YOUR FEELINGS
THERE THEY ARE
BLIP
HERE I GO, I'M DOING IT, I'M BREAKING THE RECORD FOR FASTEST MOST
IT'S ALL HERE, I'M ALL HERE, LOOK HOW MUCH!

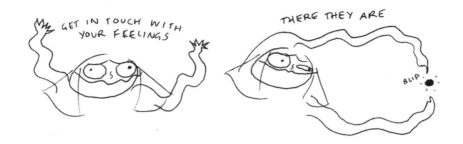

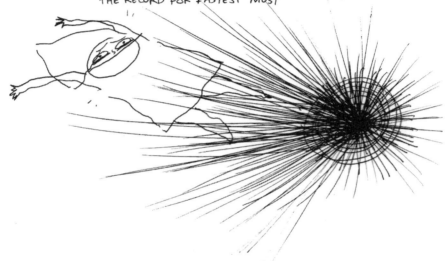

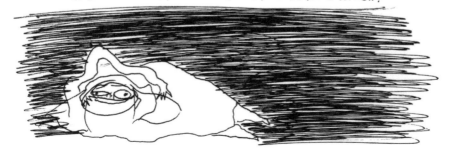

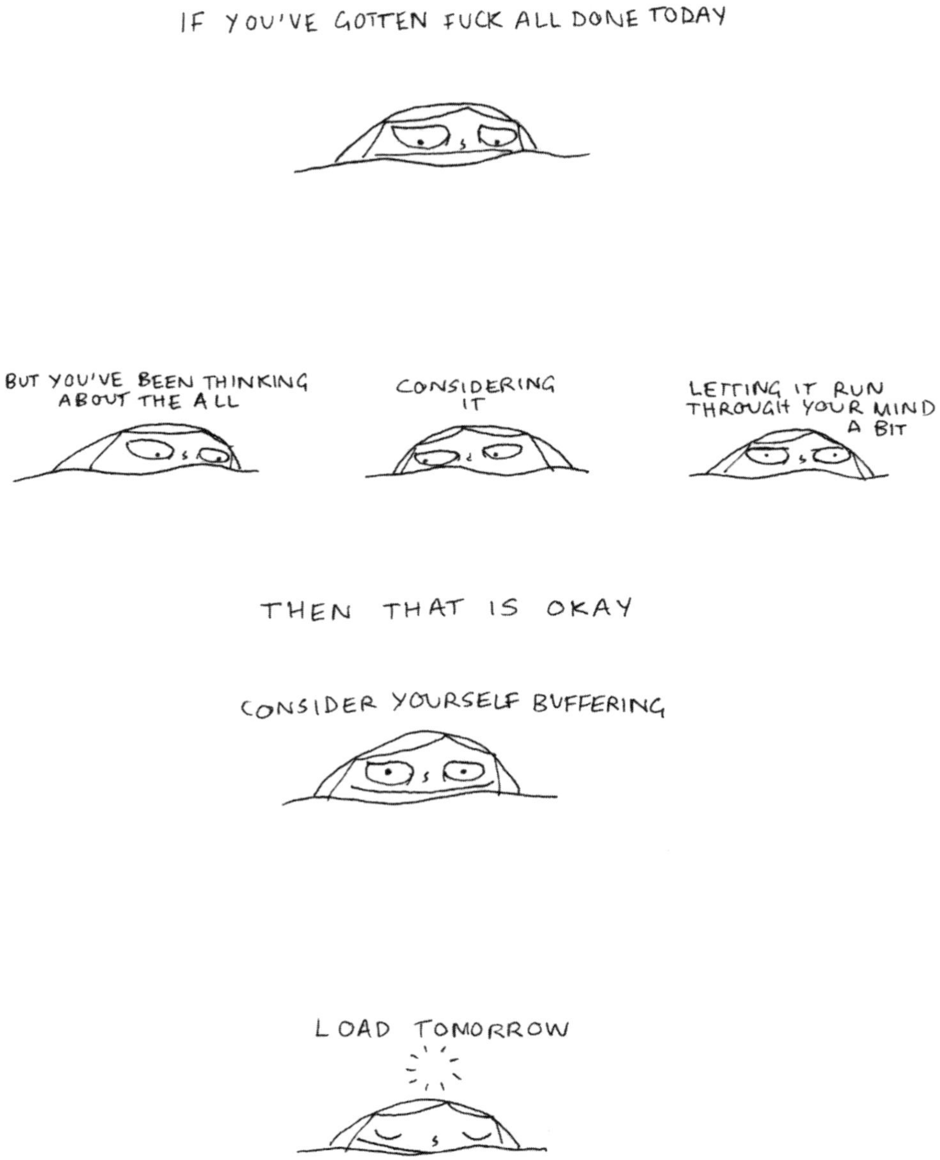
IF YOU'VE GOTTEN FUCK ALL DONE TODAY
BUT YOU'VE BEEN THINKING ABOUT THE ALL
CONSIDERING IT
LETTING IT RUN THROUGH YOUR MIND A BIT
THEN THAT IS OKAY
CONSIDER YOURSELF BUFFERING
LOAD TOMORROW

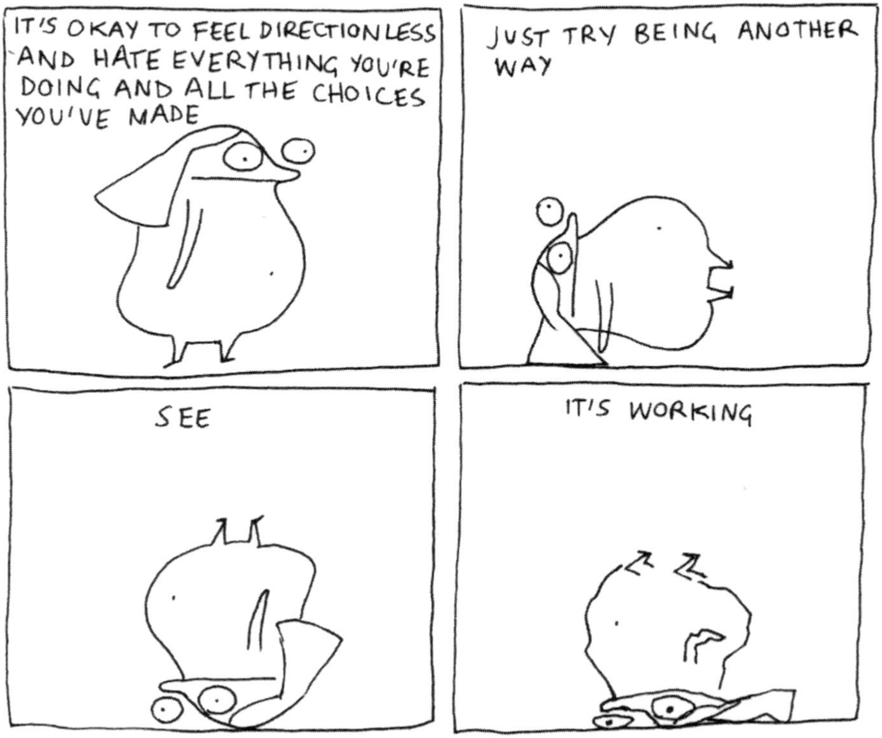
IT'S OKAY TO FEEL DIRECTIONLESS AND HATE EVERYTHING YOU'RE DOING AND ALL THE CHOICES YOU'VE MADE
JUST TRY BEING ANOTHER WAY
SEE
IT'S WORKING

A NICE DRAWING OF WELL-MEANING ME DRAGGING RELUCTANT, DESPONDENT ASSHOLE ME EVERYWHERE

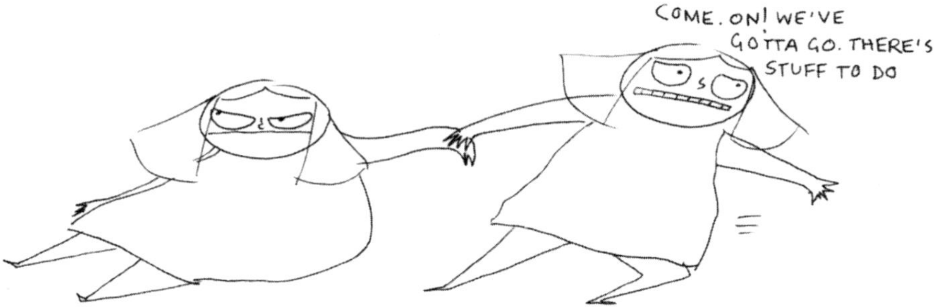
COME. ON! WE'VE GOTTA GO. THERE'S STUFF TO DO

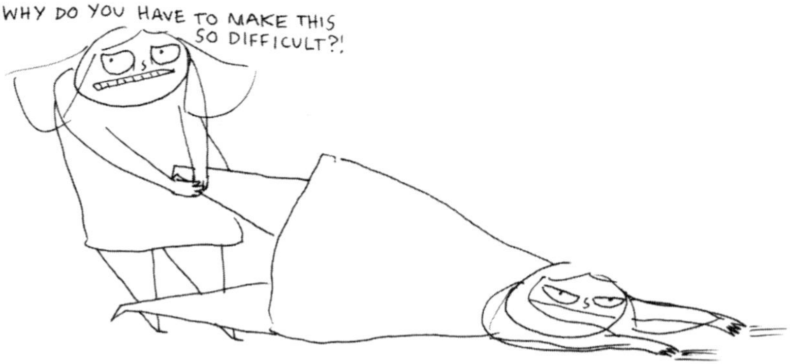
WHY DO YOU HAVE TO MAKE THIS SO DIFFICULT?!

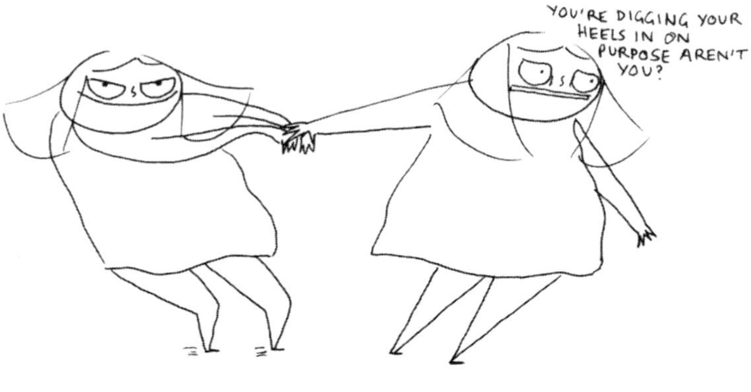
YOU'RE DIGGING YOUR HEELS IN ON PURPOSE AREN'T YOU?

MY HAPPY CORNERS

FOAMY COFFEE WITH THE CHOCOLATE NONSENSE

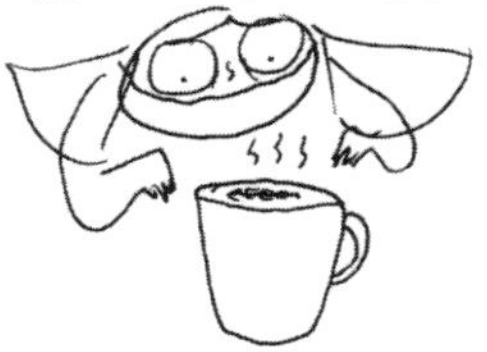

A PARK BENCH WHEN IT'S COLD AND BRIGHT

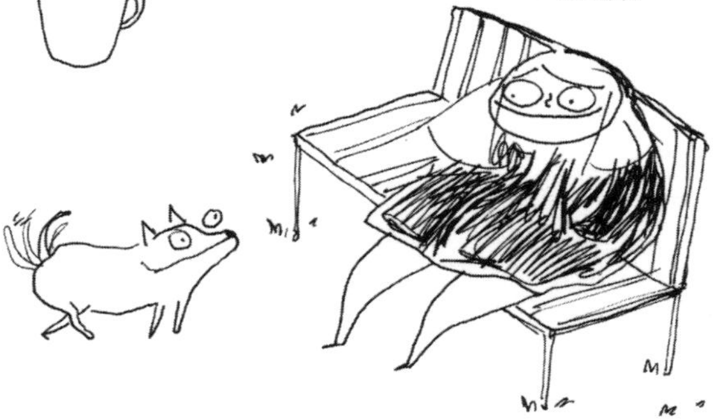

DRAWING SOMETHING SILLY WHILE I SING AND DO A LITTLE DESK WIGGLE DANCE TO A WHOLE KATE BUSH ALBUM

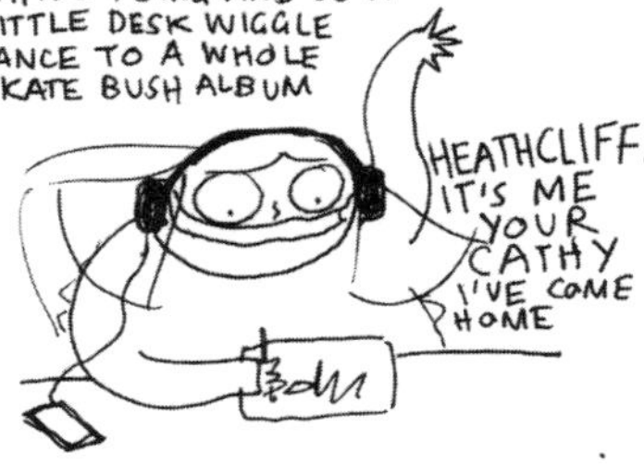
HEATHCLIFF! IT'S ME YOUR CATHY I'VE COME HOME

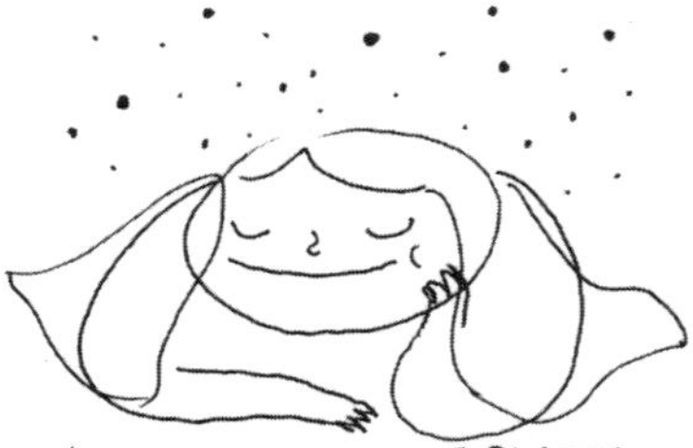

I KNOW THESE ARE PLACES I CAN GO WHEN I'M NOT OKAY. THESE ARE MY SAFE SPACES; MY HAPPY CORNERS

HOW TO BE

① FROWNY

② HELLO

③ WHAT?

④ IT IS SIMPLE

HEY, YOU ARE BRILLIANT.
KNOW THIS.

MAKE THINGS

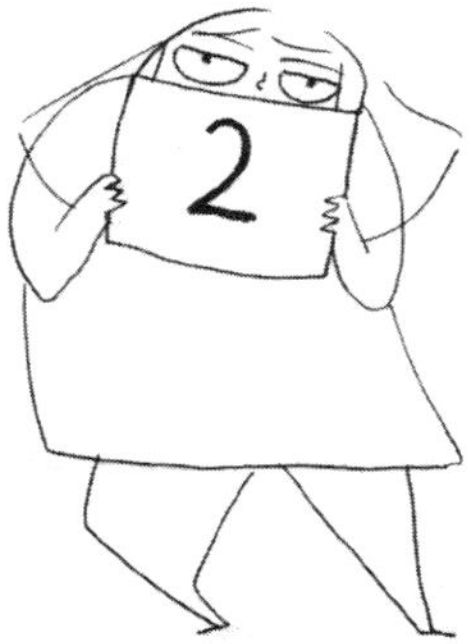
2

EXCUSE ME WHILE I RUIN EVERYTHING ACCIDENTALLY ON PURPOSE

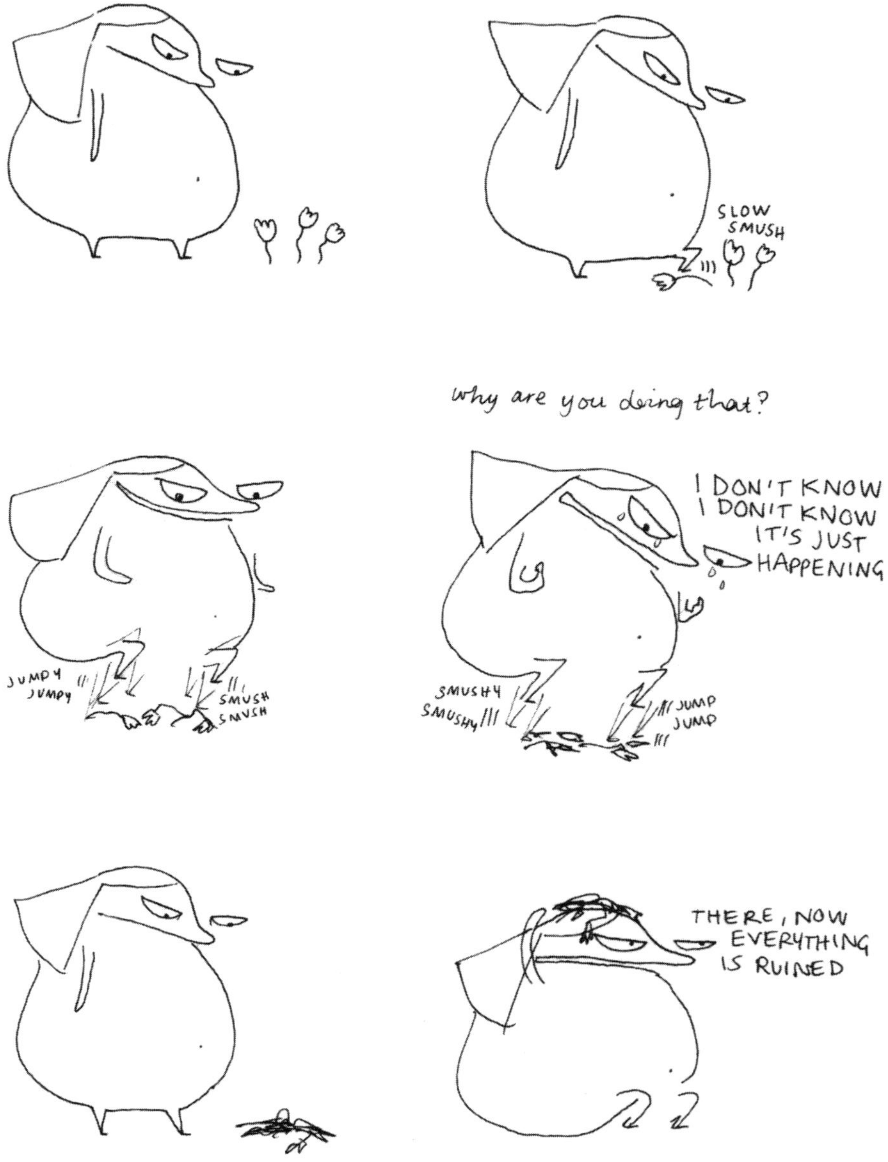
SLOW
SMUSH
JUMPY
JUMPY
SMUSH
SMUSH
why are you doing that?
I DON'T KNOW
I DON'T KNOW
IT'S JUST
HAPPENING
SMUSHY
SMUSHY
JUMP
JUMP
THERE, NOW
EVERYTHING
IS RUINED

I DO NOT

PARTICULARLY UNDERSTAND

WHY IT IS
NECESSARY

FOR ME, MYSELF

TO BE SUCH AN
ALMIGHTY SHIT

MNEH

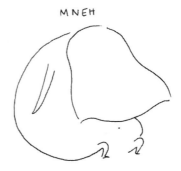

GOT ME A NICE PRESENT
FOR ME!

HMM...I COULD ACKNOWLEDGE THE THINGS I'VE ACHIEVED AND THE STUFF THAT'S GONE WELL...YES...

OR!

I CAN USE THIS UNDERMINEOSCOPE TO MAGNIFY ALL MY SHORTCOMINGS ANDS THINGS I COMPLETELY FUCKED UP ON

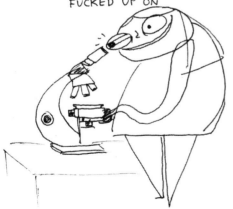

A DELIGHT

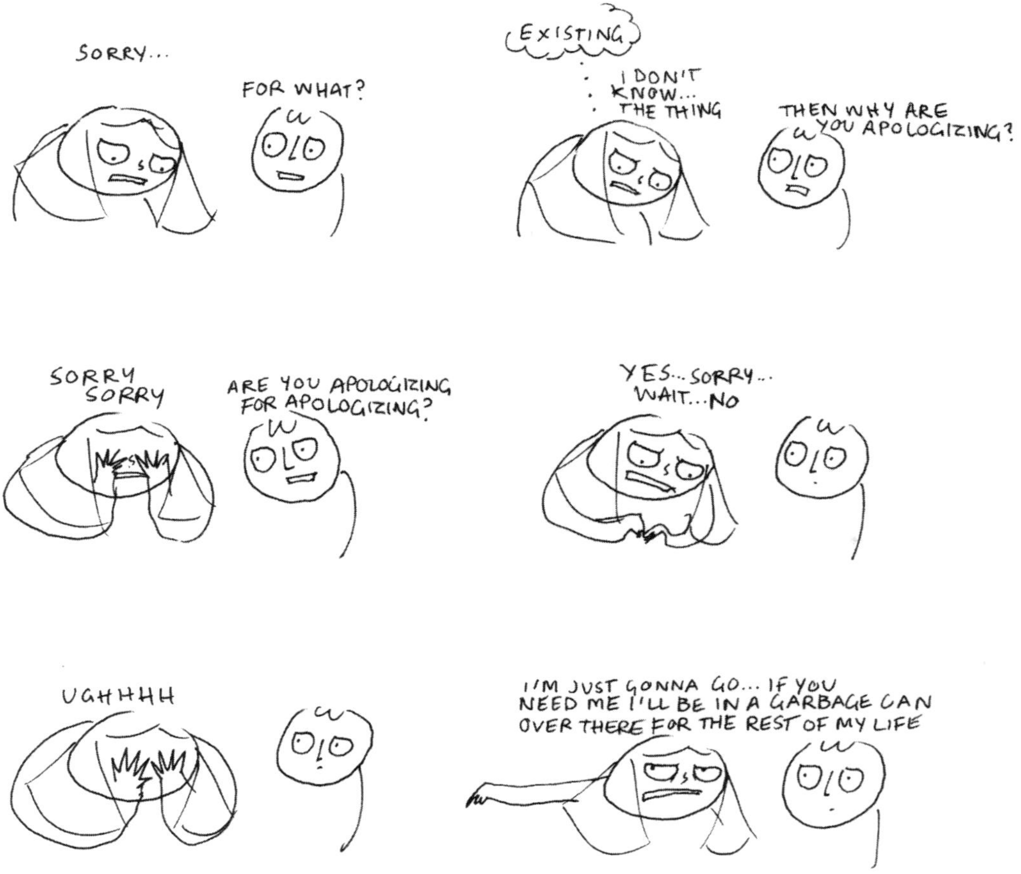
SORRY...
FOR WHAT?
EXISTING
I DON'T KNOW... THE THING
THEN WHY ARE YOU APOLOGIZING?
SORRY SORRY
ARE YOU APOLOGIZING FOR APOLOGIZING?
YES... SORRY... WAIT... NO
UGHHHH
I'M JUST GONNA GO... IF YOU NEED ME I'LL BE IN A GARBAGE CAN OVER THERE FOR THE REST OF MY LIFE

DENIAL
DENIAL
DENIAL
LALALALALALA

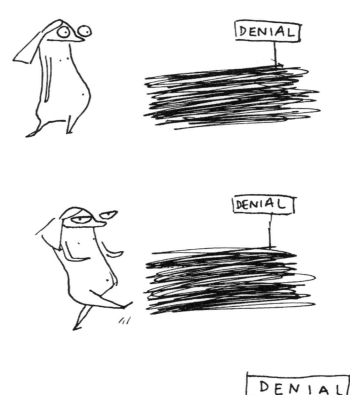

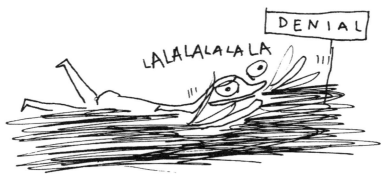

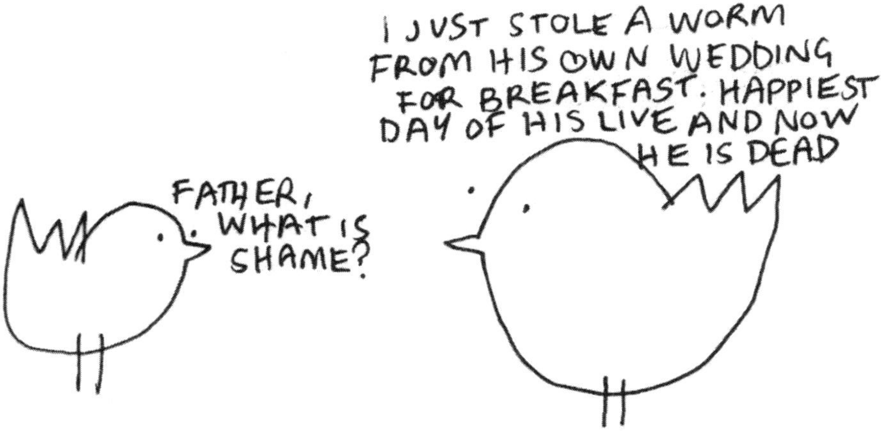
FATHER, WHAT IS SHAME?
I JUST STOLE A WORM FROM HIS OWN WEDDING FOR BREAKFAST. HAPPIEST DAY OF HIS LIVE AND NOW HE IS DEAD

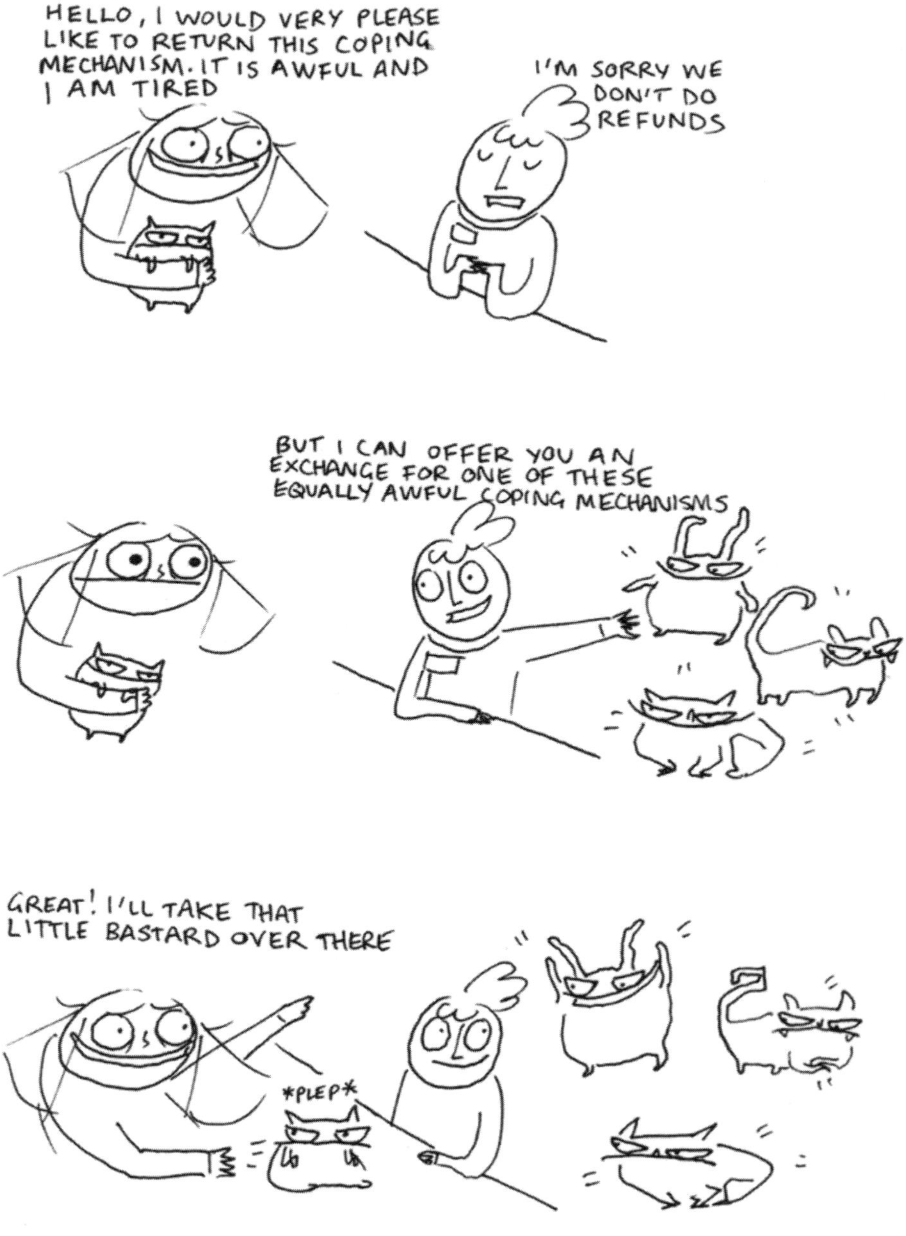
HELLO, I WOULD VERY PLEASE LIKE TO RETURN THIS COPING MECHANISM. IT IS AWFUL AND I AM TIRED
I'M SORRY WE DON'T DO REFUNDS
BUT I CAN OFFER YOU AN EXCHANGE FOR ONE OF THESE EQUALLY AWFUL COPING MECHANISMS
GREAT! I'LL TAKE THAT LITTLE BASTARD OVER THERE
PLEP

WAIT... NO...

HEY!

POOF!

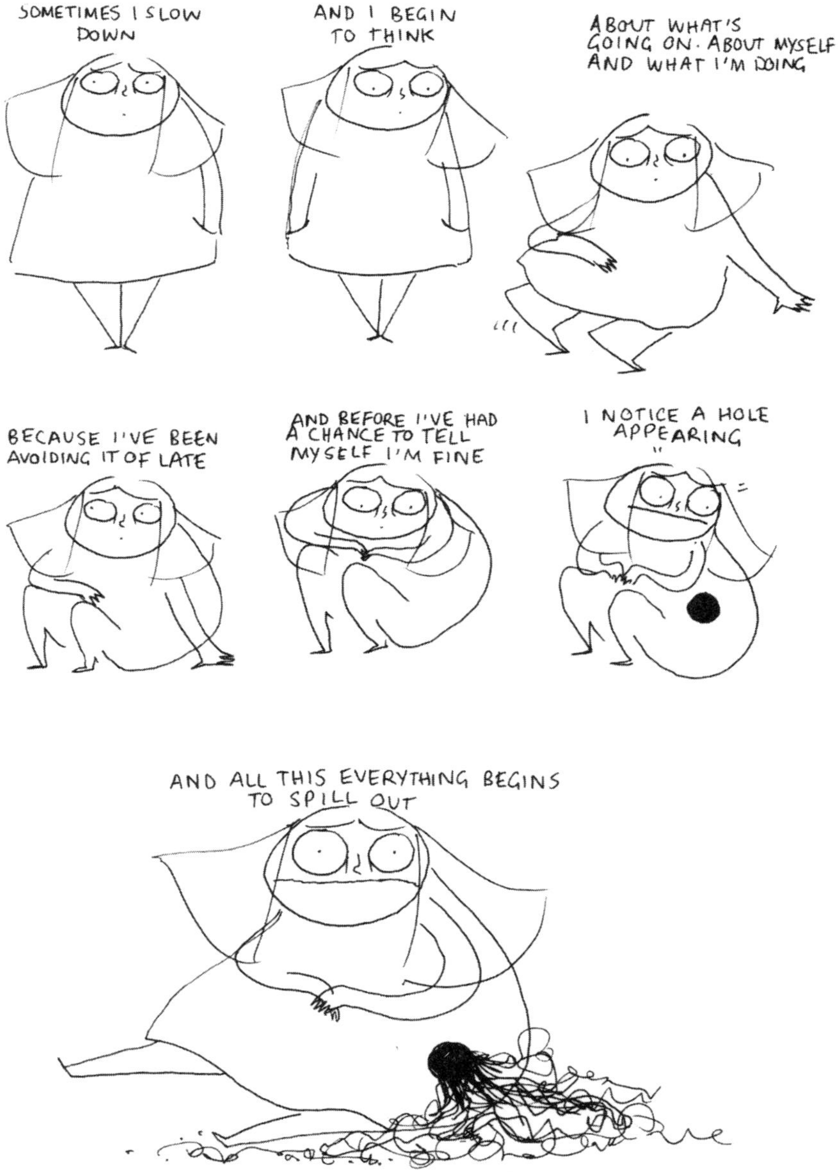
SOMETIMES I SLOW DOWN
AND I BEGIN TO THINK
ABOUT WHAT'S GOING ON. ABOUT MYSELF AND WHAT I'M DOING
BECAUSE I'VE BEEN AVOIDING IT OF LATE
AND BEFORE I'VE HAD A CHANCE TO TELL MYSELF I'M FINE
I NOTICE A HOLE APPEARING
AND ALL THIS EVERYTHING BEGINS TO SPILL OUT

GOD THERE IS SO MUCH

I FEEL SO SMALL IN THE FACE OF IT

AND INSTEAD OF GATHERING IT
ALL UP

HURRIEDLY STUFFING IT BACK IN
SO NOBODY, INCLUDING MYSELF,
HAS TO SEE IT

. . . FUUUUUCK

STUFF "IN" STUFF

I LET IT HAPPEN

I FEEL

AND I AM VULNERABLE NOW

SOMETHING'S BEEN PUNCTURED

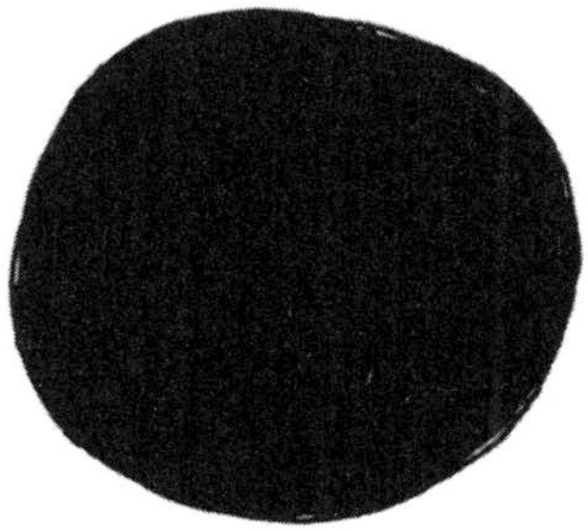

EVERYTHING'S SURFACING

IT HURTS

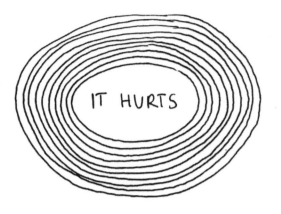

AND I DON'T

I DON'T WANT

TO GET RID OF IT

I DON'T WANT TO
RUN

I WANT TO RIDE
THIS OUT

I'M GOING TO RIDE THIS OUT BUT IT'S SCARY

AND I'M SO SCARED

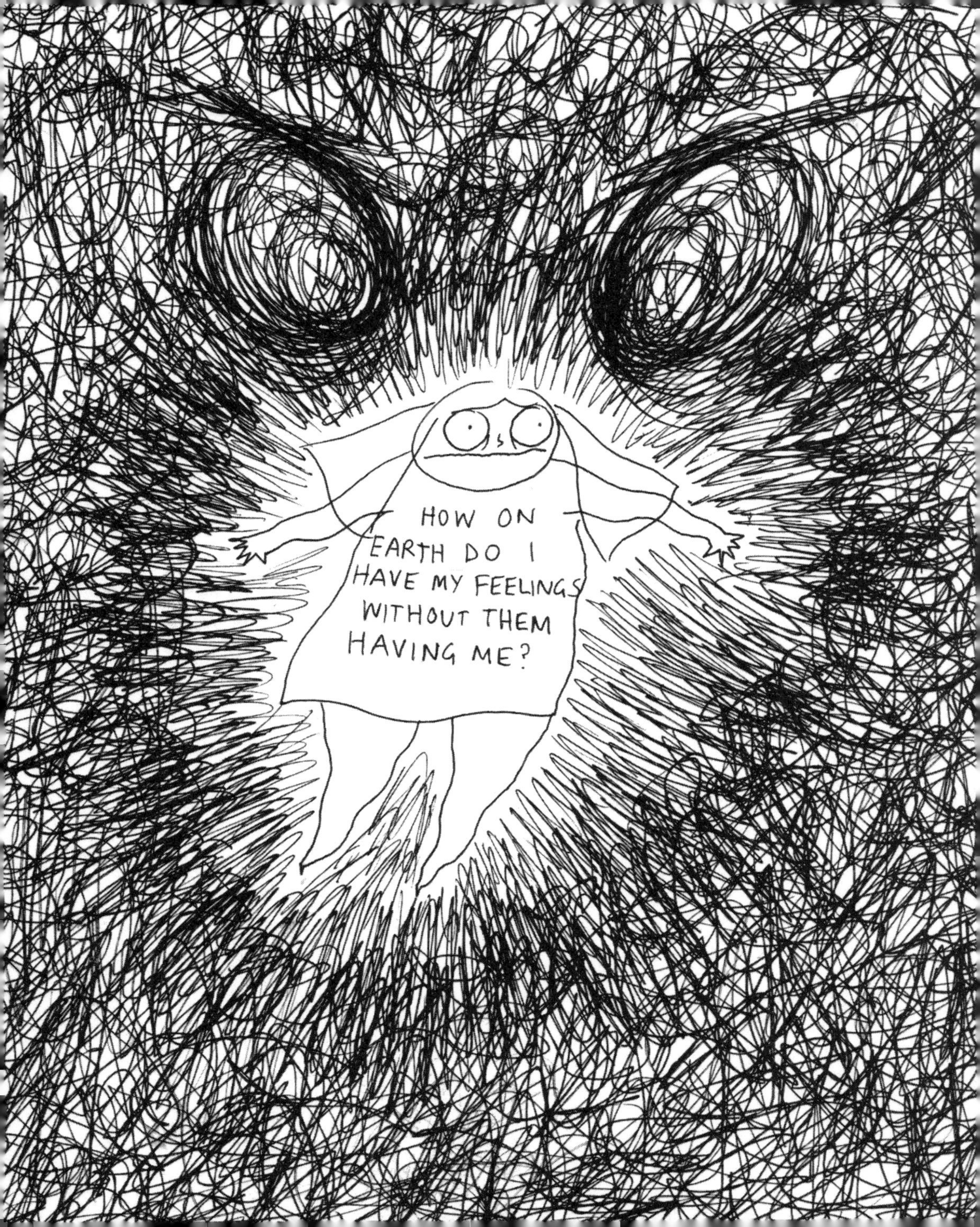
HOW ON EARTH DO I HAVE MY FEELINGS WITHOUT THEM HAVING ME?

TODAY'S LOOK

NOT STRONG ENOUGH TO DEAL WITH
MY OWN INEPTITUDE

I am well practiced in the art of fucking myself over. If self-sabotage were an exam I'd pass with flying colors and then stare at my result blankly for seven minutes before scrunching it up and throwing it in the garbage because UGH, I should have passed with colors more flyingly and it doesn't change the fact I'm a terrible person and in fact everything about me is wrong please excuse me while I leave town to go and live in a cave.

You know the thing—those moments where something goes mildly wrong in the day so you think "bollocks to this" and cancel plans you were looking forward to in order to sit at home feeling miserable; receiving a compliment that you don't feel you deserve so you either deny it profusely or grit your teeth and smile while it is filed away under "things I can use to beat myself up with later." Then there's neglecting to shower or eat or go to bed before 5 a.m. because you can't quite bring yourself to look after you properly even though you *know* it's what is good for you. The tendency to do things that might sabotage us physically or emotionally exists to one degree or another within a lot of people I reckon.

So what gives then? One of the reasons I've struggled so much with this has been due to an inability to tolerate uncertainty and the "gray areas" that life is full of. My brain used to say that if things weren't going to go ***absolutely perfectly***, and if I wasn't ***absolutely perfect,*** then they were destined to be a **total disaster** and **so was I**. Any perceived threats to this state of "perfection" would cause me to shut down and instantaneously commit to things being awful. There was no middle ground—no concept that things could be kinda alright and a little bit shitty at the same time. And crucially, my brain said if they were definitely going to be awful anyway then fuck it, *I might as well launch myself there headfirst before anything out of my* *control has the chance to do it.* That's self-sabotage: undermining yourself because at least then the outcome is predictable—bad, but in my control.

Combine this with terrible self-esteem and mental illness and we've arrived at one of the tabooiest of taboos—self-harm. A lot of people will never come close to experiencing anything like it, but a lot of people, including myself, will. It's one of the aspects of mental health people find "unpalatable" and uncomfortable to consider, and so discussion around it is often silenced, or else reduced to misrepresentative media depictions of teenage "cries for help" with all the attendant implications that it is an attention-seeking or selfish behavior; nothing more than a phase (I need to employ a proxy to do my eye rolling for me whenever I hear that stuff being said because my face is too exhausted at this point). Yes, it is baffling trying to get to grips with how anyone could possibly override the need to self-preserve in order to voluntarily cause themselves pain, but this should not be more important than the suffering of those who feel they have to spend years concealing that pain while they become experts in thinking up creative answers for "What are those marks on your arm?" This is why I talk openly about what I've been through. Because the silence is exhausting and isolating in a way it needn't be.

Self-harm is not an uncommon experience, nor is it a shameful defect or personal failure; it happened to me because I wasn't able to manage intense emotional distress. It had the very specific function of turning an intangible and relentless mental pain into an acute and quantifiable physical one, which temporarily (because it was always temporary) alleviated some of the distress I was in. And frankly, given the levels of shitstorm going on in my mind at the time, I held on to any relief I could, even if it was via self-sabotage. There were logical reasons to my illogical behavior, based on feelings about myself and my situation that may not have been the reality, but were incredibly real and scary to be experiencing.

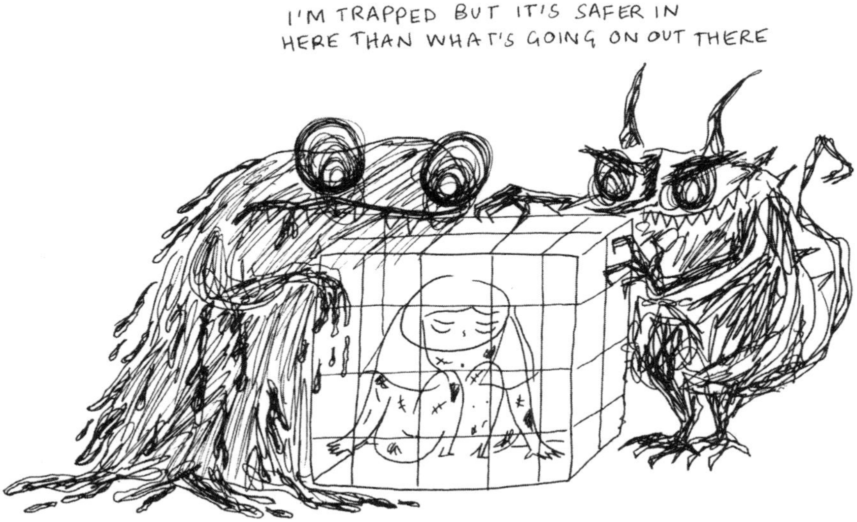
I'M TRAPPED BUT IT'S SAFER IN
HERE THAN WHAT'S GOING ON OUT THERE

There is no neat little paragraph for how I broke the cycle of punishing myself for my brain punishing me—I wish there was. It's actually been pretty messy and boring. It took a long time to arrive at a place where I even wanted to take an active role in my existence, let alone work through enough stuff in my own mind and in therapy to feel I might deserve something other than self-destruction. But the point is that you can arrive at that place. I'm not going to use the phrase "finding alternative healthy coping mechanisms," not because it's untrue, but because it's one of those things that's been said at me by professionals so many times it makes me want to scream just a tiny bit a lot.

Preventing self-sabotage is a very personal act, and I had to develop my own ways of doing this. Some came about organically over time and others were hops and leaps of faith I had to trust might work and be more sustainable than the trauma I was putting my brain and body through (even if in the short term they felt rubbish and difficult to tolerate). So here are some bits of that; a few of my routes out:

- It's unrealistic to expect myself to go from "I loathe myself beyond words" to "I love and value me 'cuz I'm worth it *hair swish*" overnight. I can take jazzy little lizard steps toward compassion at my own pace.

- Self-soothing takes work, but it doesn't have to be outrageously positive or anything. Sit-down-'n'-cry-in-the-dark showers are surprisingly effective.

- As is painting my nails obnoxious colors.

- And listening to very loud music through headphones while I do my best and most stunning fetus impression under the duvet.

- And hugging the dog, because she is a dog.

- Whichever form of potential self-sabotage I'm up against, putting distance between me and the act is important. In a very practical sense, not having the means to wreck things available to me or removing myself from the immediate situation if it's getting dodgy gives me a bit more breathing space.

- Because urges do pass. They do. They pass.

- If I've written the word "fuck" all over a piece of paper then scribbled it in black, I feel a bit better.

- I don't have to view my experiences in any way I don't feel is right for me. I don't choose to put any quasi-positive spins on self-harm like it "made me a stronger person" or think of my scarring as beautiful "signs of survival." I'll be indifferent about it if I want. I'll be sad about it if I want. I'll place focus on it when I want to and not when I don't.

- Similarly—I don't apologize. I don't owe anyone an explanation or justification and if people have a negative opinion or issue with scar tissue then they can piss off really.

- Reminder that if I am going to punch the wall I need to put a pillow between it and my fist before doing so (swollen bruise hands and scrapey knuckles are not a great look).

- Horrible times or feelings don't have to be counteracted with more horrible, and I can't always contain it on my own. **It's okay.** And I am allowed to text/call/e-mail/fax/send a messenger pigeon to someone and ask for help before it all goes completely to piss. That is a good thing to do.

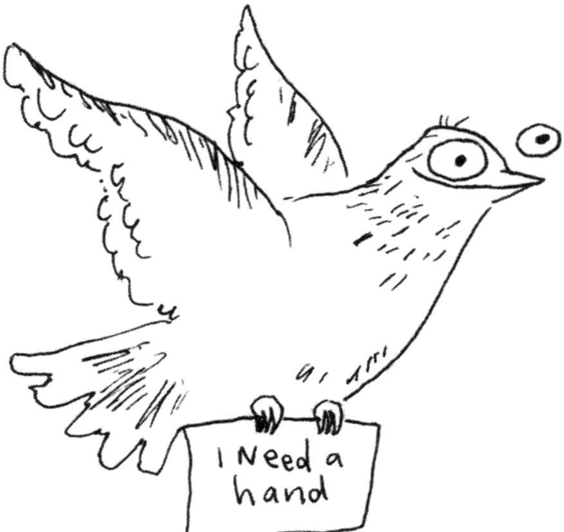
I Need a hand

- There is very little in life that is All or Nothing, and I'll learn to tolerate gray areas; it's possible but it just takes bloody ages (I've made it through this whole piece without using the word bloody for obvious reasons but I've caved here because it's a good word and I like it).

- It can be the end of the world, sure, but it won't be this way forever.

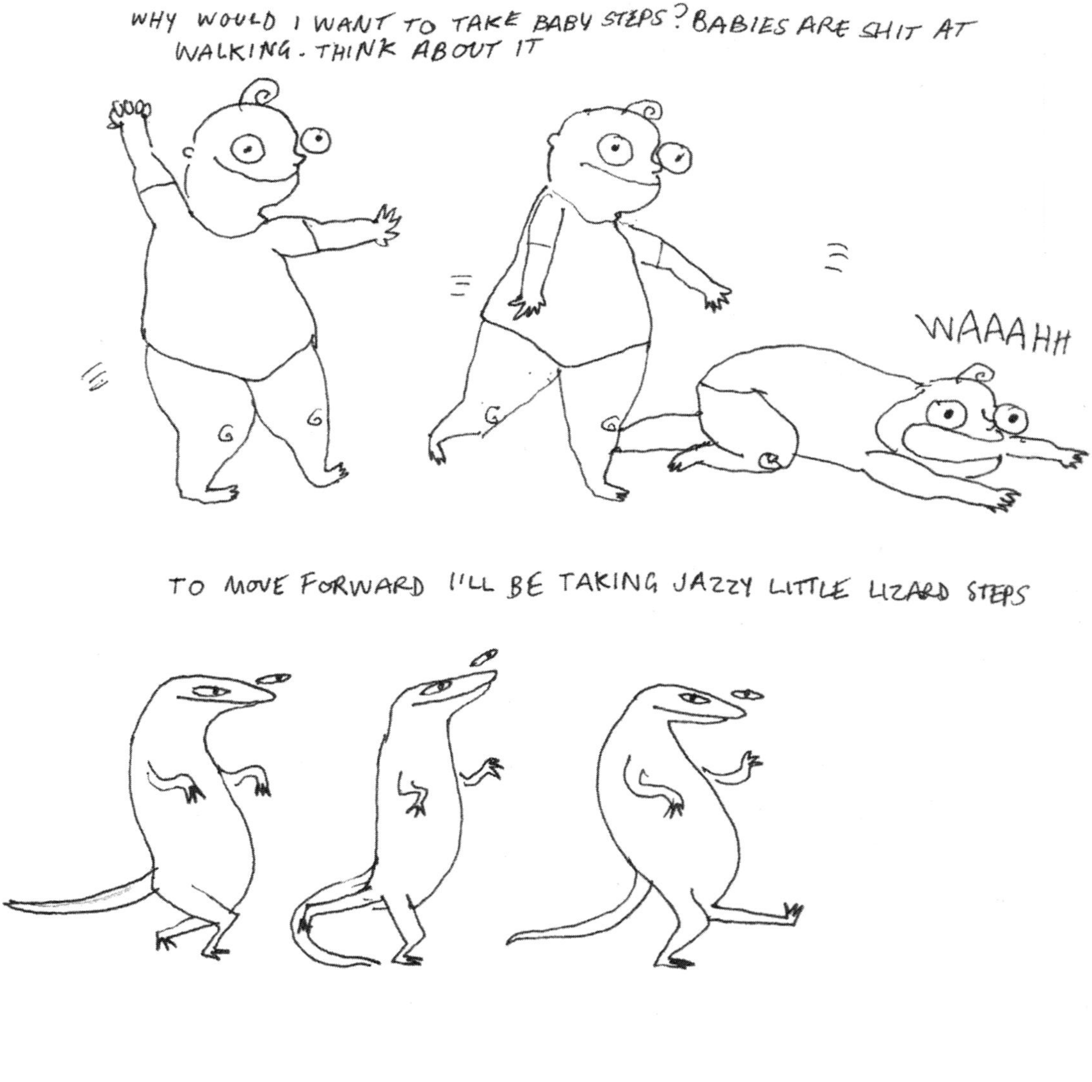
WHY WOULD I WANT TO TAKE BABY STEPS? BABIES ARE SHIT AT WALKING. THINK ABOUT IT
WAAAHH
TO MOVE FORWARD I'LL BE TAKING JAZZY LITTLE LIZARD STEPS

TOGETHERNESS

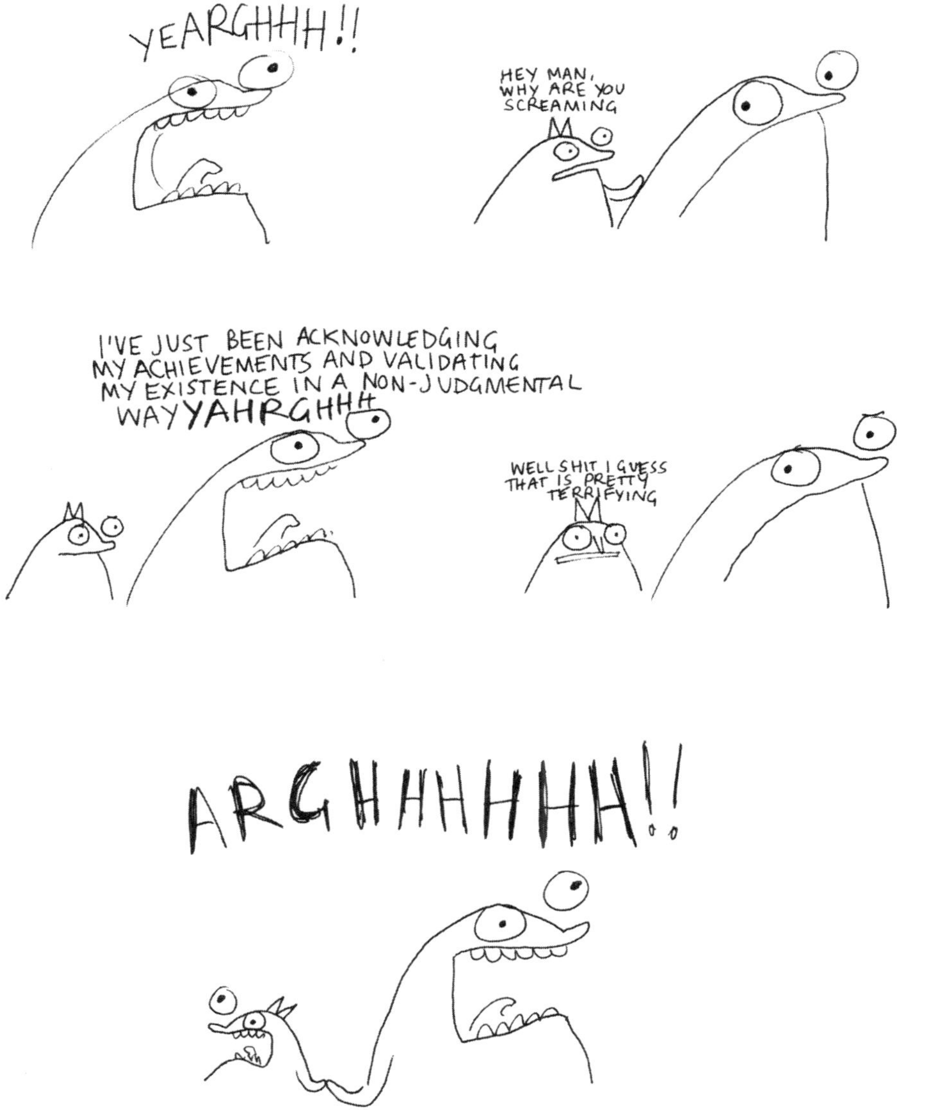
YEARGHHH!!
HEY MAN, WHY ARE YOU SCREAMING
I'VE JUST BEEN ACKNOWLEDGING MY ACHIEVEMENTS AND VALIDATING MY EXISTENCE IN A NON-JUDGMENTAL WAY YAHRGHHH
WELL SHIT I GUESS THAT IS PRETTY TERRIFYING
ARGHHHHHH!!

ALTERNATIVE SELF-CARE

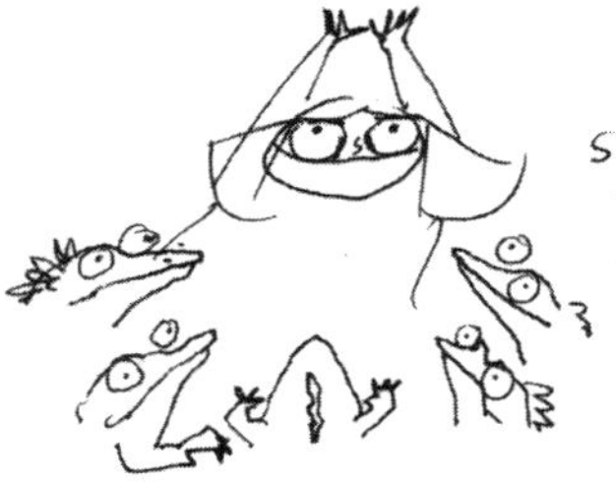

SURROUND YOURSELF WITH LIZARDS; YOU ARE THE QUEEN NOW

SMASH A CROISSANT INTO A WALL

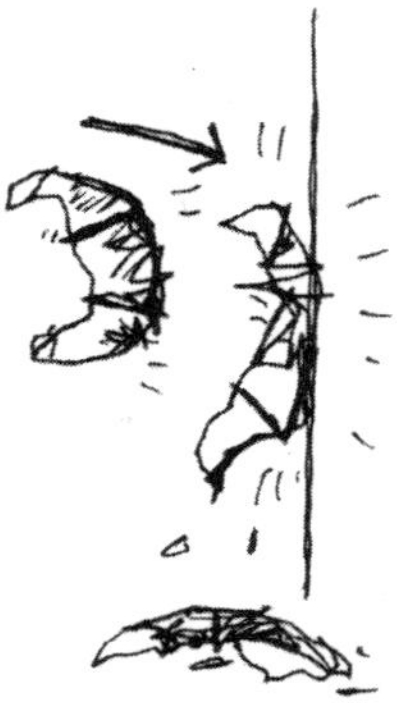

DIP YOUR ELBOW IN CANDLE WAX AND RUIN ALL THE CANDLES AND NOW THEY LOOK HOW YOU FEEL AND IT IS A FUN TIME

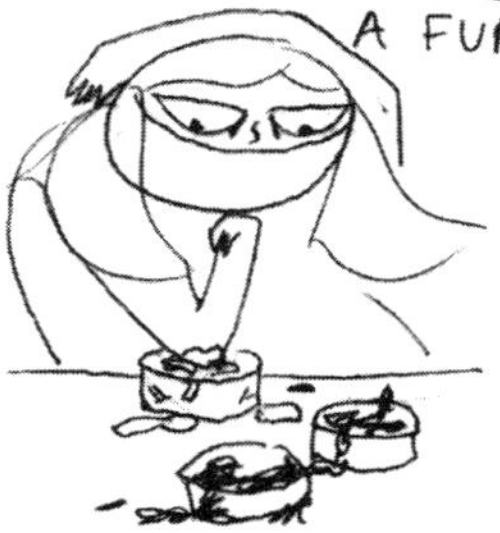

IT IS IMPORTANT TO
NOTICE WHAT YOU HAVE
DONE WELL

IT IS ALSO IMPORTANT TO
NOT LET THINGS YOU
MESSED UP UNDERMINE
THE THINGS YOU DID DO WELL

THE TWO CAN COEXIST

HOLD ON TO YOUR
ACHIEVEMENTS

ARTICULATE DOG

YOU DON'T NEED HIM SHARON. IT'S TIME TO FOCUS ON YOUR NEEDS AND LOVING YOURSELF AGAIN
NOW TAKE ME FOR A FUCKING WALK

SELF-
CONFIDENCE
SLAP
SLAP
SLAP
SLAP
SLAPPY
FEAR OF
EGOTISM
AND ARROGANCE

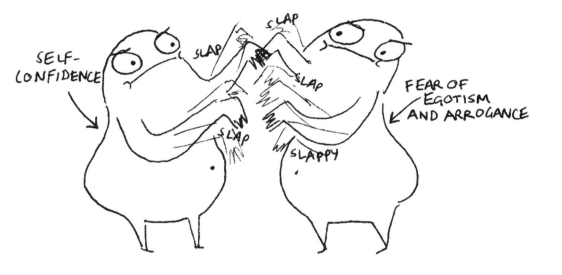

GOOD DAY

GOOD DAY AFTER A
STRING OF BAD DAYS

MAYBE I <u>AM</u> CAPABLE

HAHAHA

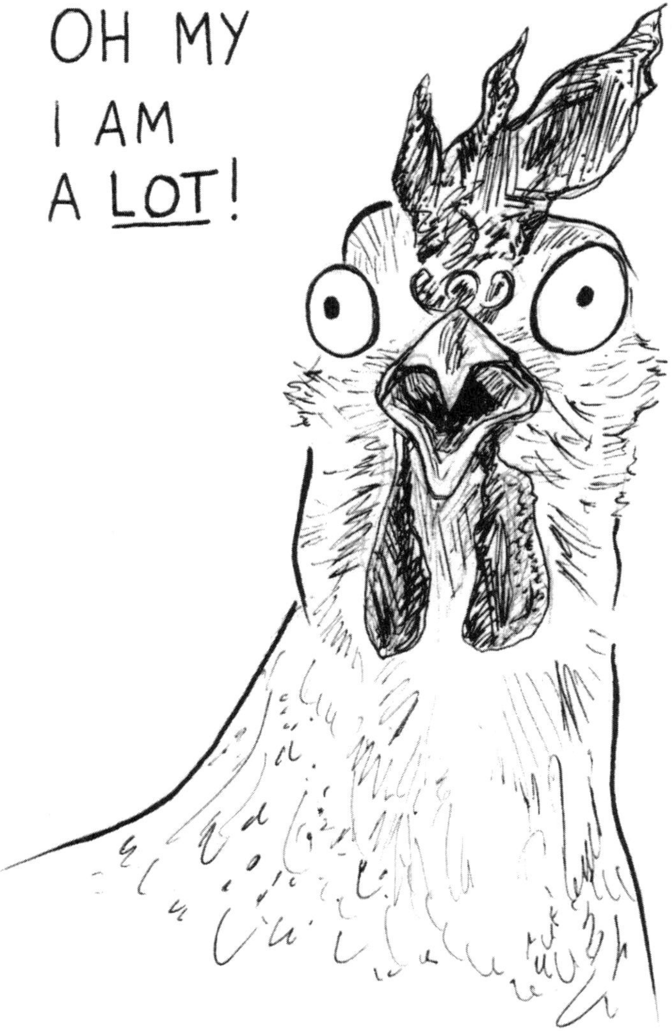
OH MY
I AM
A LOT!

5 GOOD THINGS ABOUT ME

I.   I LIKE DOGS

b)   SOMETIMES MY EYEBROWS LOOK NICE

iii   THIS ONE TIME I WALKED HOME
      WITHOUT A SINGLE BUS GOING PAST
      WHICH MEANS I WON

IV   DOGS LIKE ME

Fig5 I HAVE ALLTWO OF MY ELBOWS

6.   I AM EXCELLENT AT COUNTING
     AND STUFF

PEP TALK

HEY
YER DOING ALRIGHT, DID YOU KNOW THAT?
PEP
PEP PEP
THANK YOU
THAT IS A NICE

I'M DOING MY STUFF
EVERYONE ELSE'S STUFF
CAN FUCK OFF

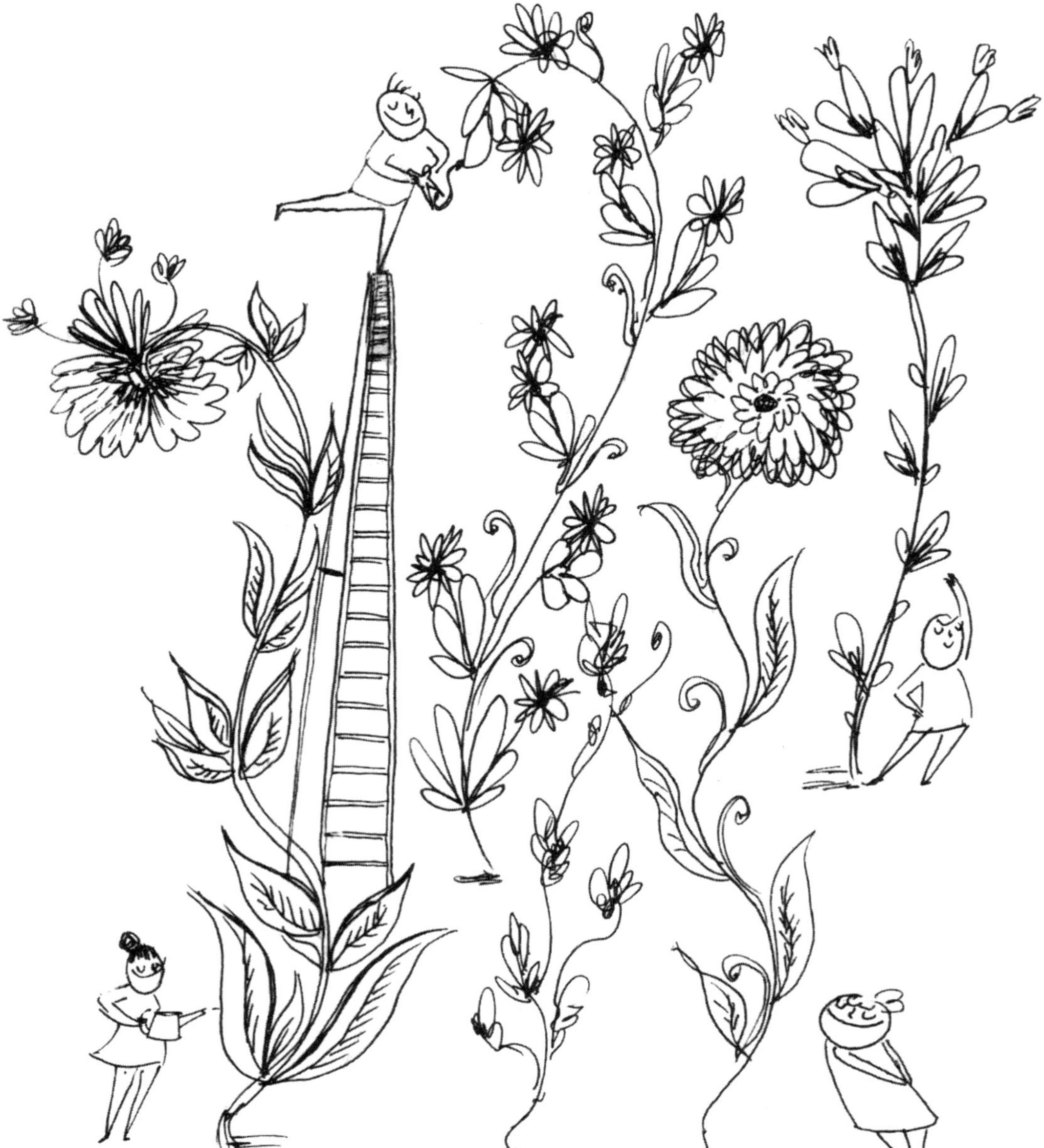

MAGICKEN

SEE THE MAGIC
SPARKLE IN HER
BEAUTY EYE

SO,
HOW ARE YOU
FEELING
TODAY?

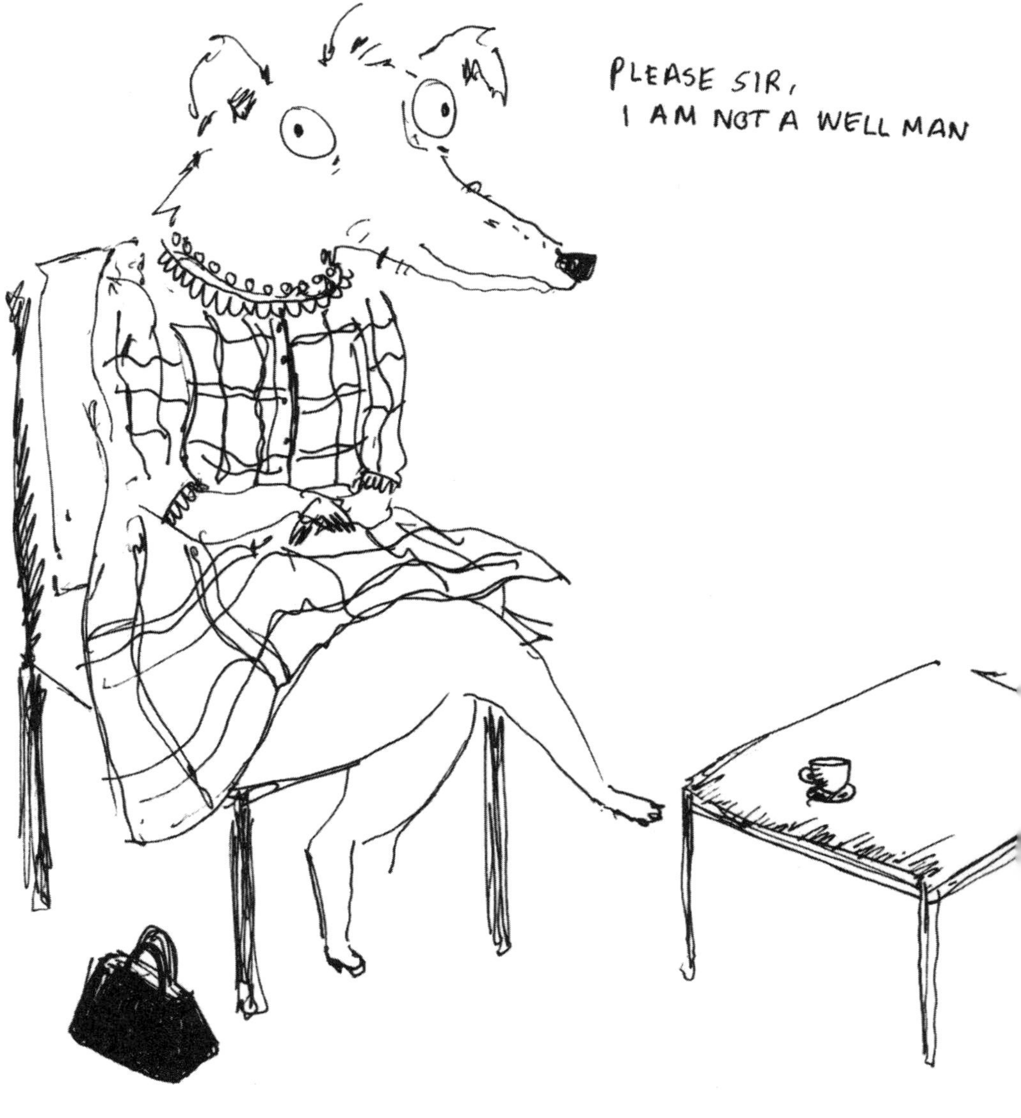
PLEASE SIR,
I AM NOT A WELL MAN

USEFUL VISUAL INDICATORS OF HOW
I'M FEELING WHEN WORDS WON'T HAPPEN

THE RAIN

MOLDY OLD
BREAD

SHITTY CHILD'S DRAWING
OF A HUMAN

BAD SOCK DRAPED
OVER THE BACK OF
A RADIATOR

BALLOON UNKNOWINGLY
WAFTING TOWARD SOMETHING
POINTY

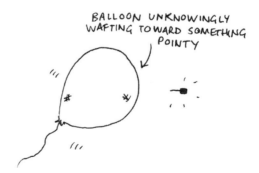

RUBY, ARE YOU ALRIGHT?

YESSSSS, I GOT THREE HOURS OF
SLEEP LAST NIGHT BECAUSE MY
BRAIN HATES ME AND IS SLOWLY
BECOMING SOME SORT OF TERRIBLE
ANXIETY-BASED FONDUE BUT LOOK
WHAT I CAN DO WITH MY LEG?!!

I THINK WHAT WE KNOW IS THAT YOU HAVE THE TENDENCY TO BE QUITE IMPULSIVE...

I WAS WONDERING WHETHER YOU HAD ANY THOUGHTS ON THAT?

MMM?!

UNNECESSARY SHOPPIN'

MORE UNNECESSARY SHOPPIN'

YOU ARE HAVING
AN ILLNESS

OK, SO HOW LONG
WILL THIS GO ON
FOR?

 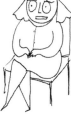

MEHDUNNO...COULD
BE ANY TIME BETWEEN
NOW AND WHENEVER
IT ENDS

BUT THERE'S A
TREATMENT?

YESS

BUT ITS EFFECTIVENESS ISN'T
GUARANTEED AND IS ALSO LARGELY
DEPENDENT ON HOW MUCH WORK
YOU PUT IN

BUT I'M SO TIRED FROM
HAVING THE ILLNESS AND
NOW I HAVE TO WORK?!
FOR SOMETHING THAT
MAY NOT WORK?

OH! THERE
ARE ALSO
SOME
PILLS

FANTASTIC!
GIMME GIMME GIMME

BUT AGAIN, THERE IS NO REAL GUARANTEE THESE WILL WORK OR BE WORTH THE MANY POSSIBLE SIDE EFFECTS - INCLUDING WORSENING OF YOUR EXISTING SYMPTOMS...

TAKE ALL THESE NICE LEAFLETS WITH YOU!

UNHELP FUL BULL SHIT

SEE YOU IN 3 MONTHS!

UNHELPFUL BULLSHIT

Right, let's get over this fear of talking about Going To Talk To Someone; because that's what therapy is by and large. When we are worried, miserable, or frustrated about relatively everyday things, we may speak to someone we know, love, and trust to try and alleviate the stress. But what about when you find yourself awake at 3 a.m. every night sobbing and wishing you weren't alive? Or your body feels like it's about to crumple under the weight of your own anxiety every time you leave the house? Maybe you're having weird thoughts that don't make sense and they're so loud and constant you can't really understand what's going on outside of your head. You know, stuff that is really beginning to fuck shit up. Collectively, our mental health relies heavily on supporting one another, but sometimes that's not enough. On a basic level, I think therapy is a slightly more structured way of getting what we probably all need when we are struggling, which is to talk and to be heard. So let's do away with stereotypes of shrinks and couches (I've only ever seen one once in a lifetime of therapy, and I wasn't even allowed to lie on it; it was just there like some sort of weird ornament covered in uncomfortable looking cushions). Needing therapy in itself is not that big of a deal.

A misconception that really pisses me off is that therapy is a hippy-dippy cop-out for those who are too weak to deal with their problems. Nothing could be further from the truth. Being unwell is not a choice and neither is the resultant isolation, shame, guilt, and conviction that you are undeserving of help that often accompany it. So actually, scraping yourself up off the floor and asking for some assistance even when every inch of your brain is screaming at you to lie there alone in your pile of brain melt is BLOODY HARD and the act of someone who is brave. It takes enormous amounts of

THERAPEST

THERAPSSHT

THERAPISS OFF

FREUD
SAYS
RELAX

THE ONE WHO ACTUALLY GETS
IT, BUT WILL INEVITABLY GO ON
LEAVE OR GET PREGNANT
BECAUSE OF COURSE

mental effort to arrive at a place where you can ask for help, and even more to believe your problems are valid and warrant being taken seriously by a third party. I need to lie down.

I've been having therapy on and off for most of my life. And I've been through the lot in terms of therapists—the good, the bad, the ones who opt to do most of their communication through the medium of concerned eyebrows. I often consider what I could have done with the cumulative number of hours I've spent scowling on buses as I travel to and from appointments (they must be well into their hundreds). Probably could have scaled a few mountains. Or learned to play the bassoon. Or done the two simultaneously while training an antelope to crochet.

I digress . . . Therapy has acted as a lot of different things for me at different times in my life. Sometimes it's been a pressure valve, other times it's been a genuine lifeline. More than once I've struggled to see what its function is beyond being a giant aggravation. But for the most part it's been my fifty minutes out of the 10,080 in a week (which, by the way, is why I get so stressed about being on time) where I get to slump in a chair and let everything unceremoniously spill out, knowing that I won't have to sit there and look at it alone.

Sure, working through the things I was in therapy for has been an integral part of the process, but actually one of the most important things I've taken away from therapy is how to use therapy and, by extension, how to allow myself to be helped. I'll explain.

I never had a problem talking about my issues (although I know this is a struggle for a lot of people); I would talk and talk until the misery cows came home about how much I loathed myself and didn't want to be here. As a teenager I would storm into the therapist's room every week like a thundercloud on angry legs and erupt with self-effacing commentary. So opening up was not the problem; knowing what to DO once I'd done that was. I remember a specific occasion when I was in a right old state— catastrophically depressed and agitated, and so immeasurably fed up with it all that I didn't want to be here anymore. This was not an unfamiliar scenario; I'd been dipping in and out of these sorts of crises for years, and doing my best to ask for help before self-obliterating. One of the most painful things about feeling very depressed and suicidal for me was the total lack of control I felt over my situation. The only thing I felt I DID have control over was my own exit strategy, and that's a pretty terrifying place for anyone to be.

So I sat opposite my therapist in floods of tears, yanking tissue after scratchy tissue out of the box between us and wishing she would take con-trol. I mean she was the therapist after all and therapists are meant to fix you, right? Surely they have some kind of magic therapists' repository where they can scoop up and take people's distress so that they can skip out of the room afterward, smiling and laughing and pissing rainbows? That's how it works, right? RIGHT? OH FOR THE LOVE OF GOD PLEASE MAKE THIS GO AWAY! That was the gist of the situation.

And then something hit me slightly like maybe, 1/80th of a ton of bricks: No one and nothing is going to take this away right now. What's happen-ing is real and it's there and it's shit and I can't really control it, and wishing someone else would take it away in the knowledge they can't really do that was only making me feel more trapped and desperate. What I have got a shot at controlling is the way I manage what's happening. And that's what I was in therapy for; not to be fixed, but to facilitate and support me finding some sort of way through my difficulties. Cuz you know, I can sit there in the chair for fifty minutes, but I will always have to go away and deal with the other 10,030. Those minutes are mine. And I have the capacity, if not to be a shiny happy people, to cut myself some slack when I'm suffering. And to allow the help and support in, rather than just dismiss it because I want evaporation of the ocean, not what feels like drops. Those are my minutes, my time, and even if I'm not interested in having them right now I will hold on, because the little bit of me that drags myself out of the house and makes substantial dents in the therapist's tissue supply may want that later. That bit of me may grow. That bit of me has grown.

SOMETIMES I FEEL SO **BIG** AND FULL OF **STUFF**, LIKE THERE'S NO WAY ON EARTH I COULD POSSIBLY BE CONTAINED

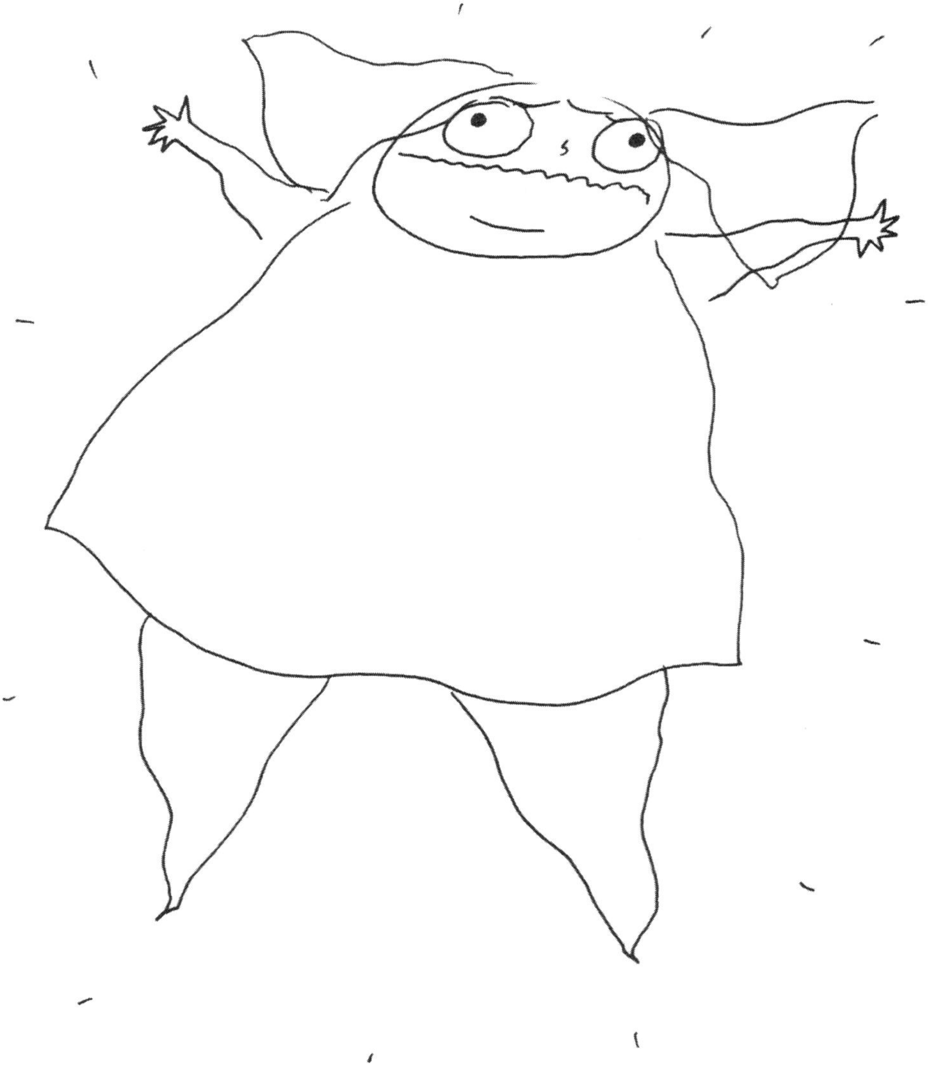

OTHER TIMES IT'S THE WORLD THAT
FEELS TOO BIG AND I FEEL TINY.
 EXPAND, CONTRACT, EXPAND,
  CONTRACT, EXPAND, CONTRACT, EXPAND

IT'S NOT THAT I DON'T HAVE
ANY IDEAS

I'VE GOT A TON FLYING AROUND

BUT THEY'RE EVASIVE
LITTLE BASTARDS

SWIPE

SWOOSH

AND WHEN I DO GRAB ONE

IT'S SO HARD TO HOLD ON TO

BKAAWK
FLAP
FLAP
FLAP

FLAP
FLAP
FLAP
EXCESSIVELY LOUD BIRD CHIRPS
FLAPPITY FLAP

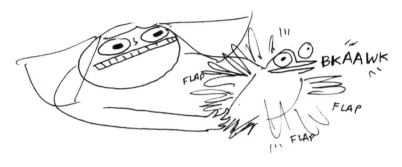

SO I'M STUCK WITH THIS NOISE OF ALL THE BLOODY BUGGERING BIRDEAS

I CAN'T PIN ANYTHING DOWN

MY EATING PATTERNS

MY SLEEPING PATTERNS

YOU SEE BECAUSE THEY ARE NOT PATTERNS AT ALL THEY ARE JUST A BIG LOAD OF STUPID

I worry about everything. Sometimes I think if I was put in a safe cube filled with only pillows and Thin Mints I'd still whip myself up into a total frenzy and end up on fire or something. My brain is wired to run on tangents and "what ifs," and has a horrible habit of taking something small and snowballing it around the insides of my skull until it's twelve times its original size. That in itself is enough to be grappling with, but because this is my default setting, it means that when there ARE actually things to worry about it goes "ALRIGHT THEN let's turn this one-tier classic sponge cake of worry into a giant eighteen-tier Tower of Pisa style anxiety wedding cake with elaborate piping and sparklers topped with little fondant people screaming," except actually there is no cake, there's just me curled up on the floor hyperventilating because I have to go and do something that involves talking to real people and the world is almost certainly ending.

your ANXIETY CARD
HAVE 9 PANIC ATTACKS AND GET A FREE MELTDOWN!
REALLY? THIS IS WHAT WE'RE DOING?

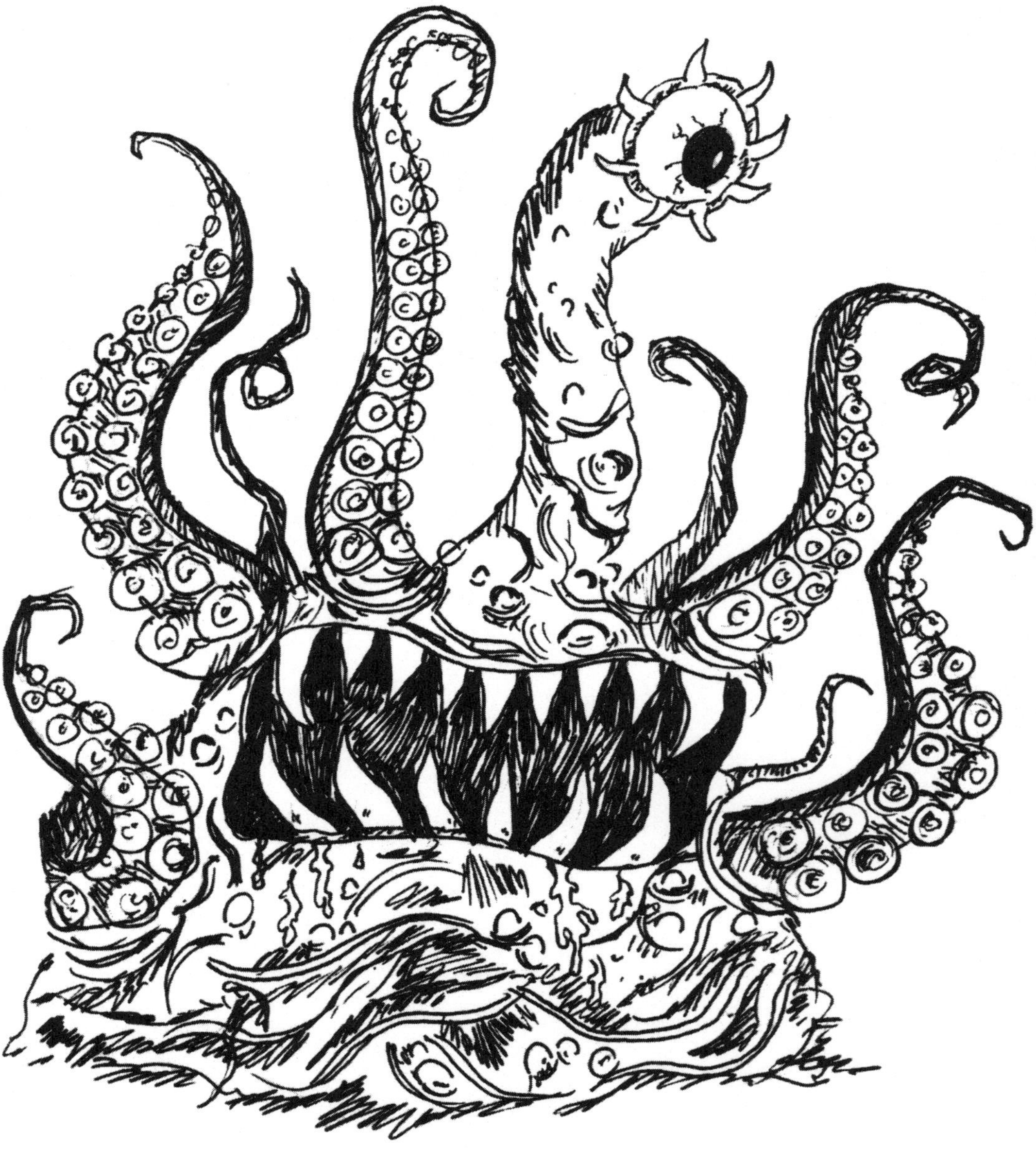

PLEASE, I AM
ONLY SMALL

GIANT TURD MOUNTAIN,
OF MENTAL ILLNESS
BULLSHIT PAST AND
PRESENT

PHEW
ALRIGHT, LETS SORT
THIS OUT

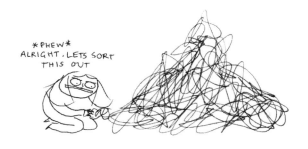

. WEEKS/MONTHS OF LABORIOUS PROCESSING.
LATER

HAH! TAKE THAT
YOU TURD STACK

SLIGHTLY LESS GIANT
TURD MOUNTAIN OF
MENTAL ILLNESS BULLSHIT
PAST AND PRESENT

(EXHAUSTED)

RESOLVED
ISSUES

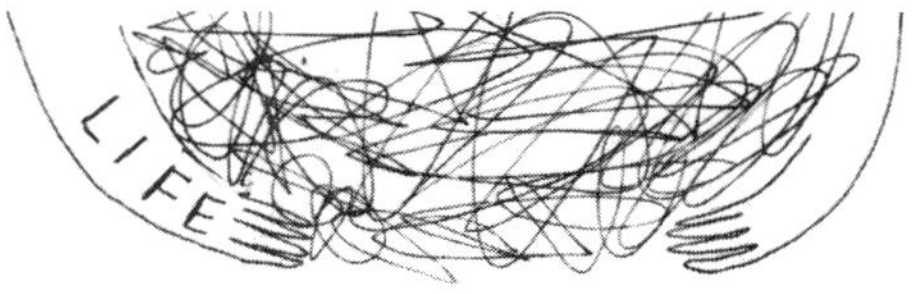
LIFE

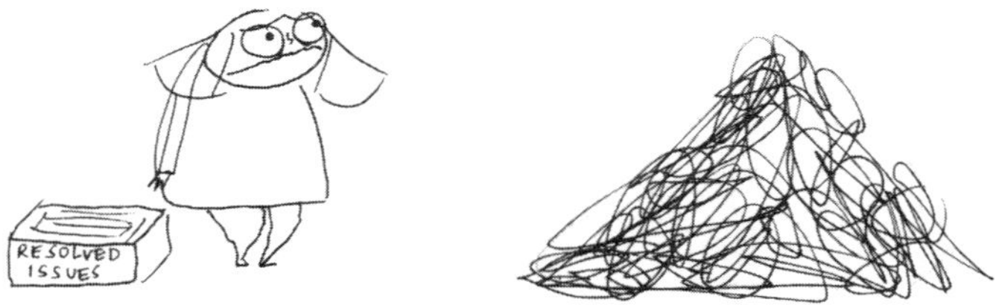
RESOLVED ISSUES

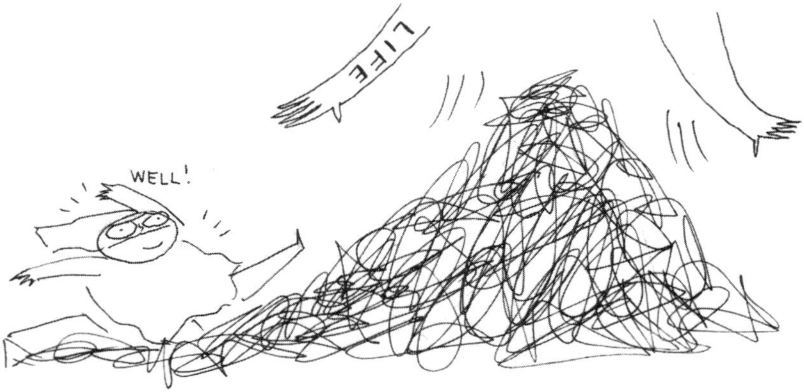
LIFE
WELL!

SOON!

SOON

I WILL DO IT ALL

VERY SOON

NOT RIGHT NOW CUZ I'M PARALYZED BY FEAR AND ANXIETY AND SHIT

BUT SOON!

YOU SAY "PULL YOURSELF TOGETHER"

GET UP! GO OUT! STOP MOANING! OTHER PEOPLE HAVE IT WORSE
YOU'RE USELESS, A FAKER, THEY'RE RIGHT, YOU'RE PATHETIC

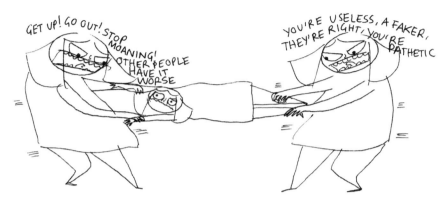

AND THIS ONLY HELPS ME PULL MYSELF APART

IF THIS WAS SOMETHING I COULD

SNAP!

MYSELF OUT OF, DON'T YOU THINK I WOULD HAVE BY NOW?

WELL LOOKIE THAT, STILL NOT WELL, WHO WOULDA THOUGHT PROFOUNDLY COMPLEX AND DIFFICULT ILLNESS WOULDN'T BE CURED BY A BIT O'THE OL' SNAPPIN'...MMM...

BIPOLAR DISORDER

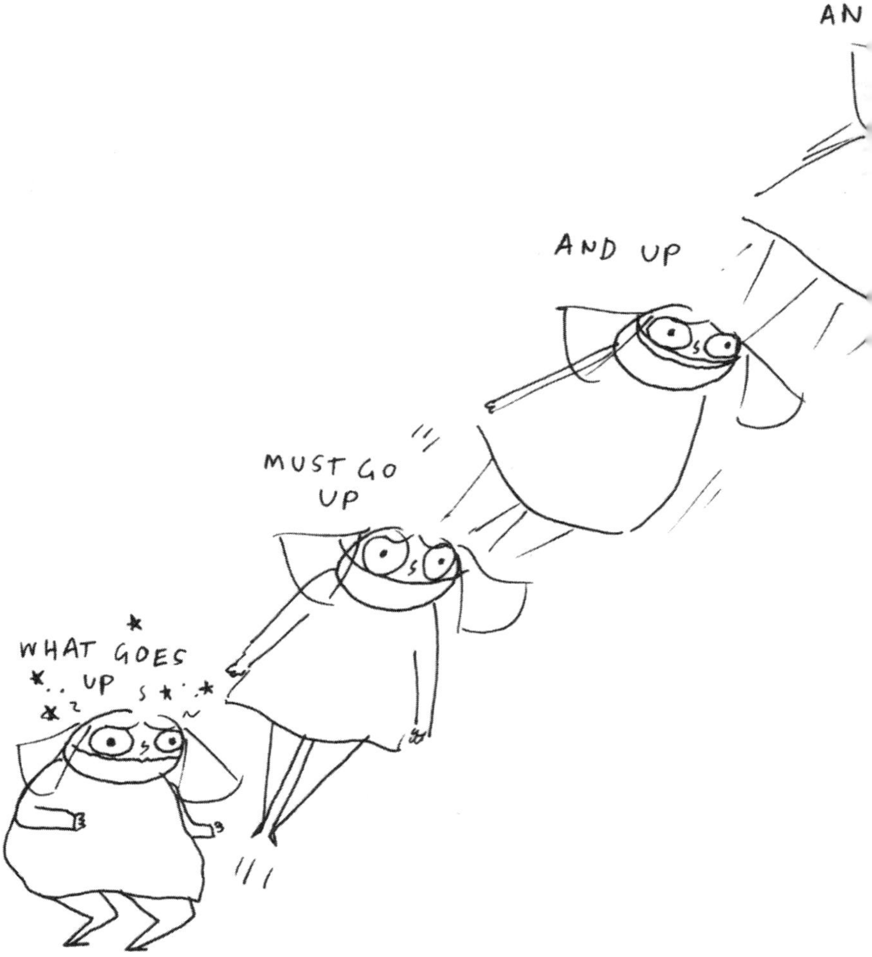
AN
AND UP
MUST GO UP
WHAT GOES UP

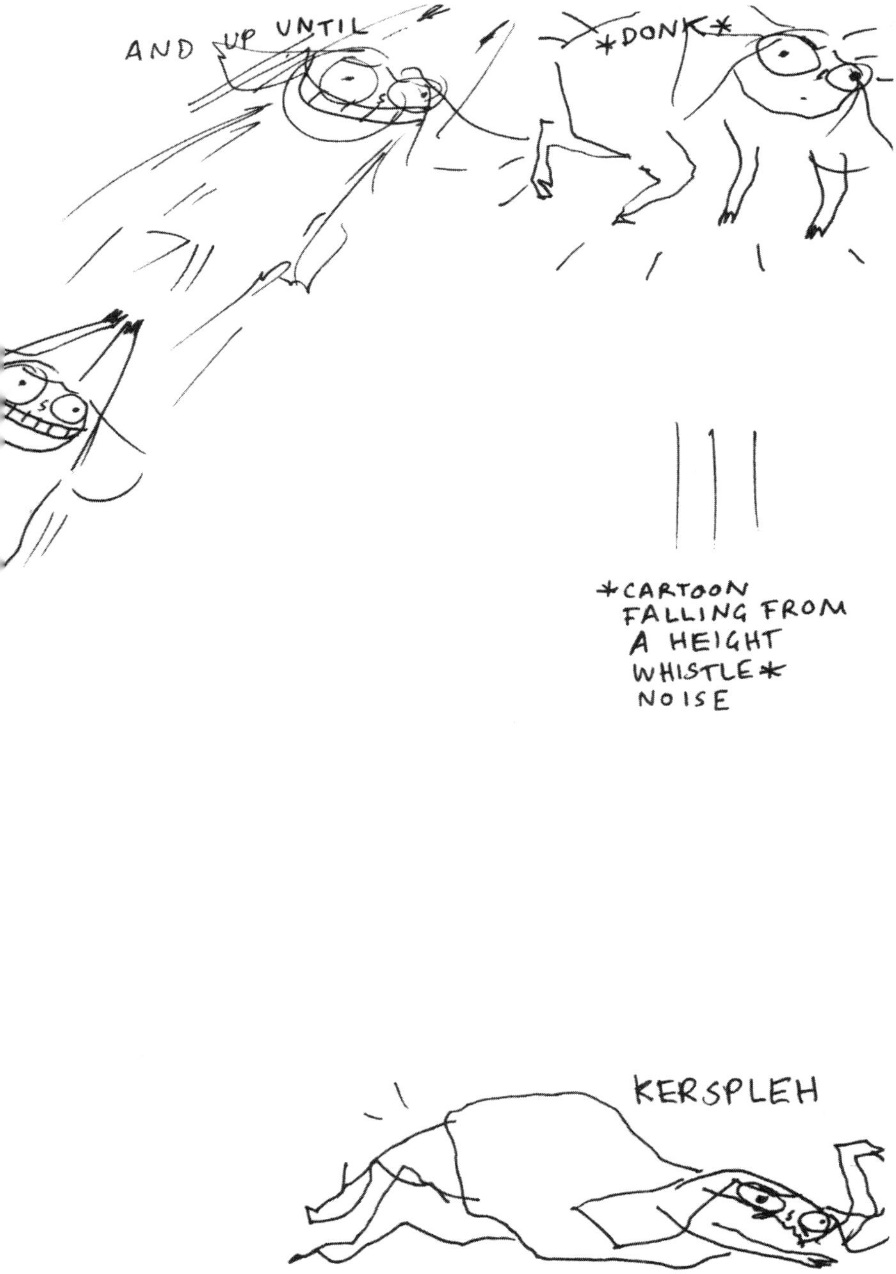
AND UP UNTIL
DONK
CARTOON FALLING FROM A HEIGHT WHISTLE NOISE
KERSPLEH

Things bipolar is

- An illness

- Massively shit a lot of the time

- One part of my life and a bit of who I am, not my entire identity

Things bipolar ain't

- **A fun, zany quirk!**—nope. I don't walk around covered in butterflies with a cheeky twinkle in my eye, and having bipolar doesn't make me or anyone else an object of curious fascination. There is too much romanticized crap about it simply being an affliction of the tortured creative. Yes, some people with bipolar happen to make art or films or write novels while playing the harp with their toes. I guess I'm one. But I also happen to have brown hair and a wok and no one would ever say to me "ahh yes the brown hair and having of the wok, that's GOT to be the reason you make art." Fuck off. It's a chronic and life-affecting illness and shouldn't be treated as a novelty.

- **An adjective you can use to describe someone who's a little flighty or something that's erratic**—nopeity nope. Not clever or funny and undermines the suffering of those who are unwell. Find another word; I hear there are lots.

- **Being happy when you wake up and then maybe a bit sad and then alright again**—nah. Everyone has ups and downs; that's part of life, and it can suck and that is valid. But the moods, or mood episodes as they're called (yes, it IS like being the star of your own terrifying TV show) associated with bipolar go way beyond the bounds of what we consider to be "normal." Bipolar doesn't exclude me from these healthy mood swings; I get all o' those, just with the addition of very extreme lows and highs in the form of depressive and manic episodes with all their associated symptoms. It is A Lot!

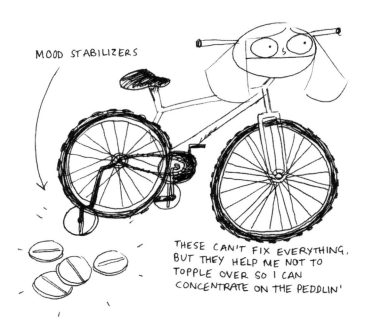

MOOD STABILIZERS

THESE CAN'T FIX EVERYTHING,
BUT THEY HELP ME NOT TO
TOPPLE OVER SO I CAN
CONCENTRATE ON THE PEDDLIN'

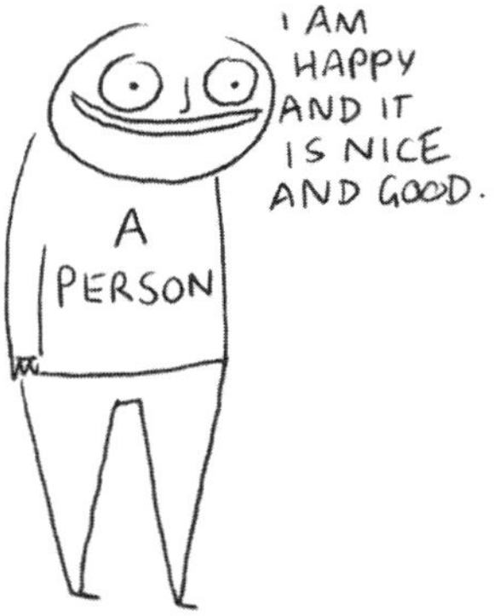
I AM HAPPY AND IT IS NICE AND GOOD.
A PERSON

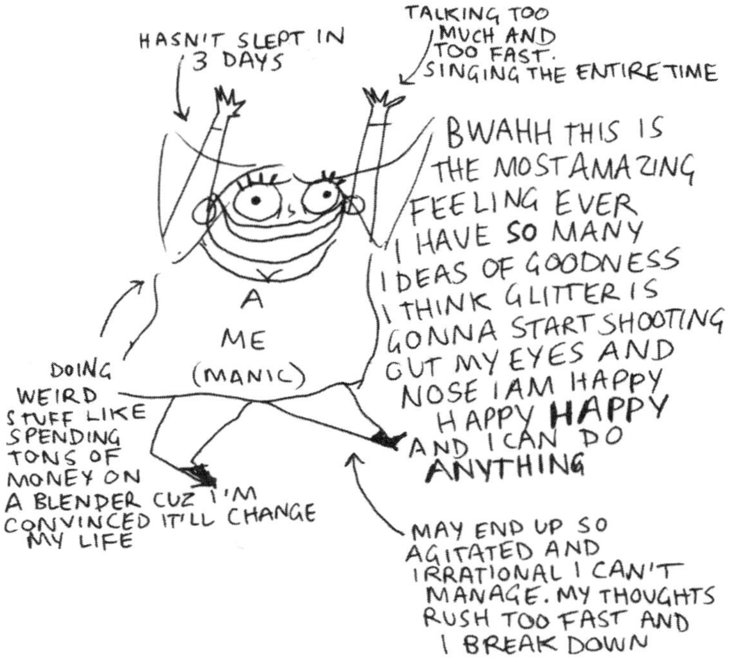
HASN'T SLEPT IN 3 DAYS
TALKING TOO MUCH AND TOO FAST. SINGING THE ENTIRE TIME
BWAHH THIS IS THE MOST AMAZING FEELING EVER I HAVE SO MANY IDEAS OF GOODNESS I THINK GLITTER IS GONNA START SHOOTING OUT MY EYES AND NOSE I AM HAPPY HAPPY HAPPY AND I CAN DO ANYTHING
A ME (MANIC)
DOING WEIRD STUFF LIKE SPENDING TONS OF MONEY ON A BLENDER CUZ I'M CONVINCED IT'LL CHANGE MY LIFE
MAY END UP SO AGITATED AND IRRATIONAL I CAN'T MANAGE. MY THOUGHTS RUSH TOO FAST AND I BREAK DOWN

PRETTY SAD RIGHT NOW. EVERYTHING IS SHIT ... MEH
A PERSON

I'M NOT REAL. I'M JUST AN ENDLESS HIGHWAY OF SAD GOING ABSOLUTELY NOWHERE. WHEN I'M NOT SAD I'M NUMB. THIS WILL NEVER CHANGE SO WHAT'S THE ARSING POINT OF CARRYING ON AT ALL...
MEH
A ME (DEPRESSED)
MAY END UP SO LOW I CAN'T MANAGE. I THINK ABOUT ENDING IT.
HAS DONE LITTLE ELSE BUT SLEEP FOR WEEKS
ISOLATING MYSELF BECAUSE I'M CONVINCED I'M TOXIC TO OTHERS

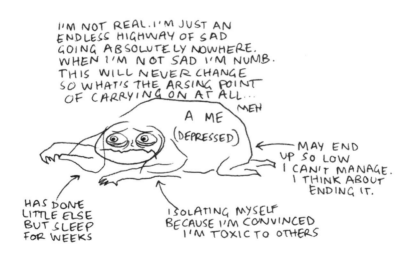

REGULAR
TIRED
LOVELY BEAUTY
OH NO OH DEAR
I'M A COMPLICATED ONE
FINDING A BALANCE

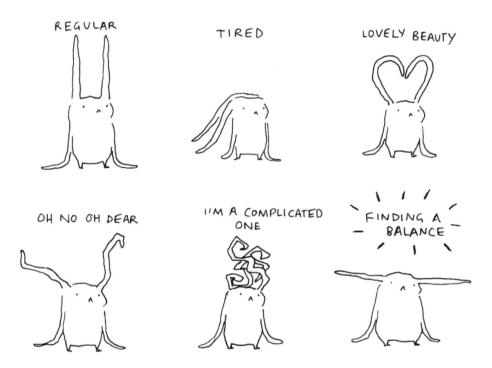

LOST:

SENSE
OF
SELF

4

WELL YOU KNOW HOW IT IS...

YOU HAVE YOUR GOOD DAYS

AND YOUR BAD DAYS

AND YOUR DAYS WHEN YOU ARE SUDDENLY A LIZARD FOR NO REASON

THAT'S JUST LIES ISN'T IT?

KNOCK KNOCKY

WHO IS THERE?

NOT SURE, HAVING SOME SORT
OF IDENTITY CRISIS AND I
THOUGHT YOU MIGHT BE ABLE
TO TELL ME?

THAT'S NOT A
HILARIOUS JOKE

YES AND IT'S
RUINING MY LIFE

EGG   SO SMOOTH

SO   VERY
MYSTERIOUS WISE

HAS A BETTER
SENSE OF SELF
THAN YOU

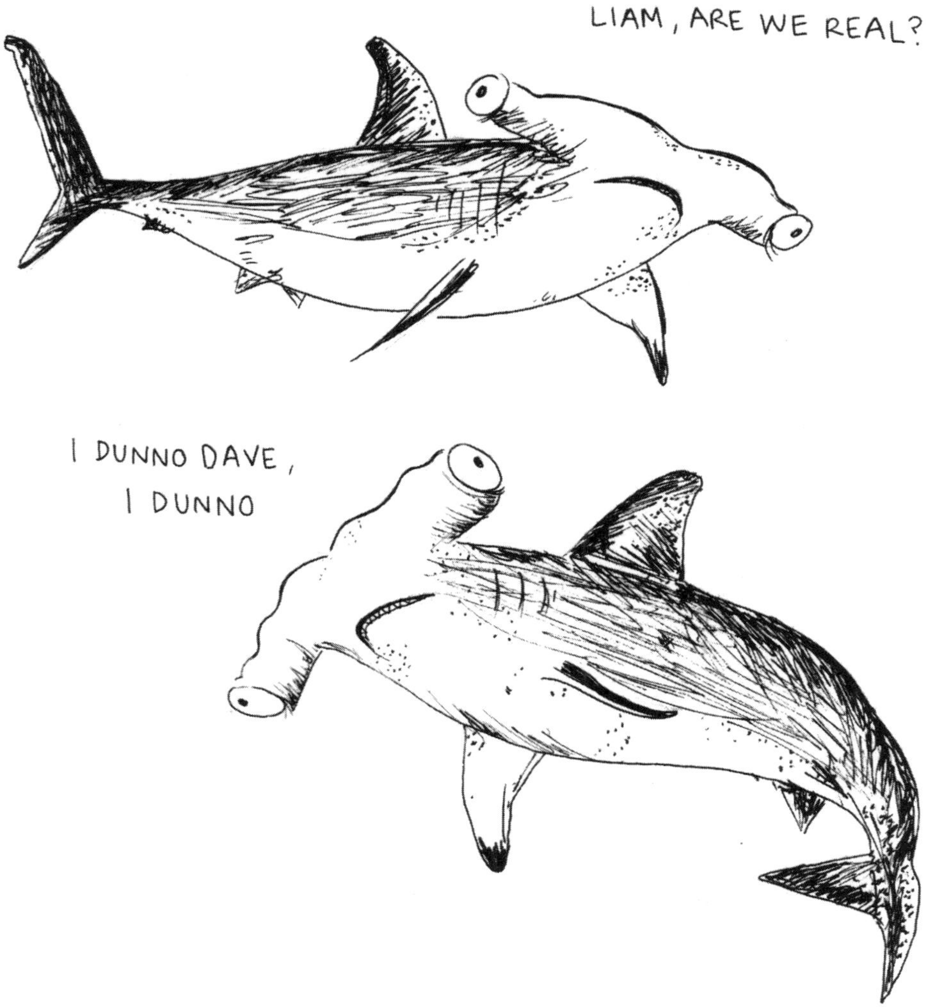
LIAM, ARE WE REAL?
I DUNNO DAVE,
I DUNNO

SO...TELL ME SOMETHING ABOUT YOURSELF

IT'S ONLY A MATTER OF TIME BEFORE PEOPLE REALIZE I'M NOT A HUMAN. I'M JUST A LOAD OF LITTLE HUMAN-LIKE BITS BADLY HELD TOGETHER WITH TAPE

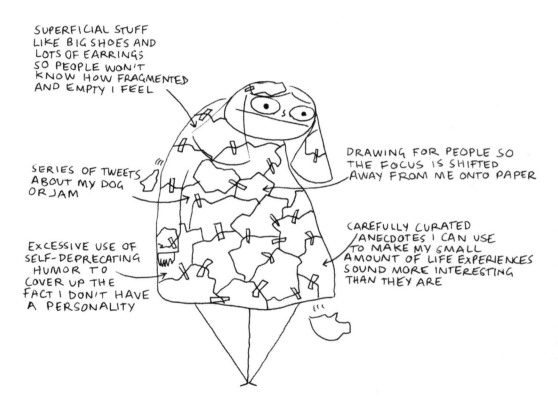

SUPERFICIAL STUFF LIKE BIG SHOES AND LOTS OF EARRINGS SO PEOPLE WON'T KNOW HOW FRAGMENTED AND EMPTY I FEEL

SERIES OF TWEETS ABOUT MY DOG OR JAM

DRAWING FOR PEOPLE SO THE FOCUS IS SHIFTED AWAY FROM ME ONTO PAPER

EXCESSIVE USE OF SELF-DEPRECATING HUMOR TO COVER UP THE FACT I DON'T HAVE A PERSONALITY

CAREFULLY CURATED ANECDOTES I CAN USE TO MAKE MY SMALL AMOUNT OF LIFE EXPERIENCES SOUND MORE INTERESTING THAN THEY ARE

OH I DON'T BLOODY KNOW WHERE I'M MEANT TO FIT
AND WHICH PEOPLE I BELONG WITH AND WHY I HAVE
THESE SIDE NUBBINS

AT LEAST THERE'S MORE THAN ONE PIECE IN A JIGSAW.
I KNOW I'M PROBABLY NOT THE ONLY ONE WADDLING
AROUND IN A STATE OF MILD CONFUSION. IT'S
VAGUELY COMFORTING...ALMOST

AHH THERE'S SO MUCH BUT
ALSO SORT OF NOTHING AND
WHAT IS GOING ON?

IS DOG

HOW DO YOU ALWAYS
KNOW JUST THE RIGHT THING
TO SAY?!!

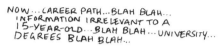
NOW...CAREER PATH...BLAH BLAH...
INFORMATION IRRELEVANT TO A
15-YEAR-OLD...BLAH BLAH...UNIVERSITY...
DEGREES BLAH BLAH...

SO WHAT IS IT
YOU WANT
TO DO?

CAREERS
OFFICERING

GET OUT

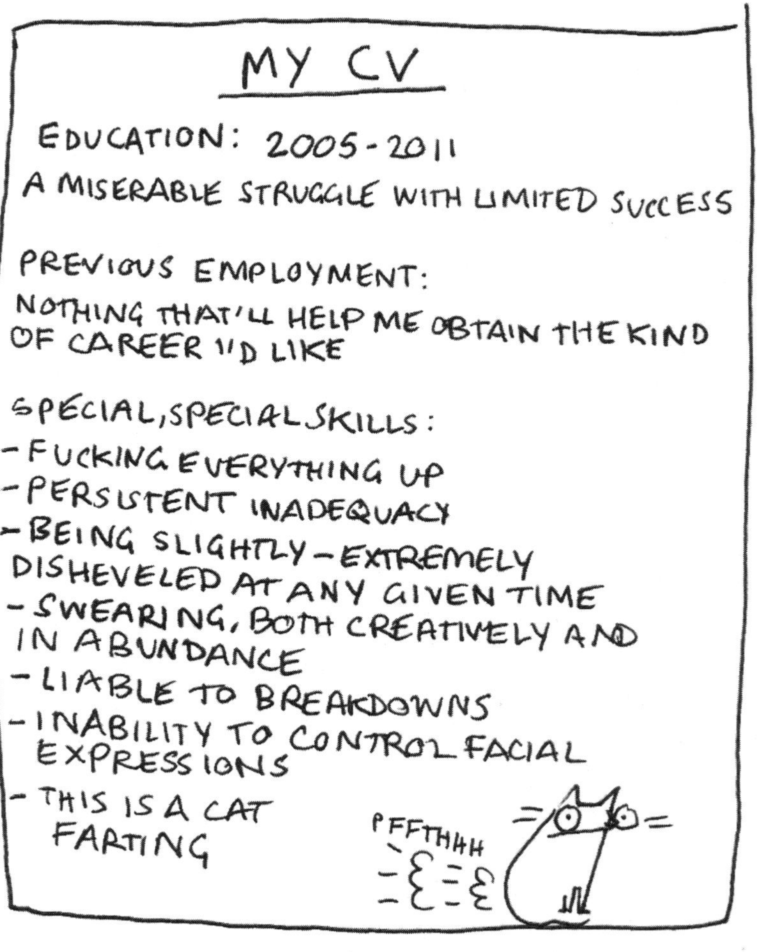
MY CV
EDUCATION: 2005-2011
A MISERABLE STRUGGLE WITH LIMITED SUCCESS
PREVIOUS EMPLOYMENT:
NOTHING THAT'LL HELP ME OBTAIN THE KIND OF CAREER I'D LIKE
SPECIAL, SPECIAL SKILLS:
- FUCKING EVERYTHING UP
- PERSISTENT INADEQUACY
- BEING SLIGHTLY - EXTREMELY DISHEVELED AT ANY GIVEN TIME
- SWEARING, BOTH CREATIVELY AND IN ABUNDANCE
- LIABLE TO BREAKDOWNS
- INABILITY TO CONTROL FACIAL EXPRESSIONS
- THIS IS A CAT FARTING
PFFTHHH

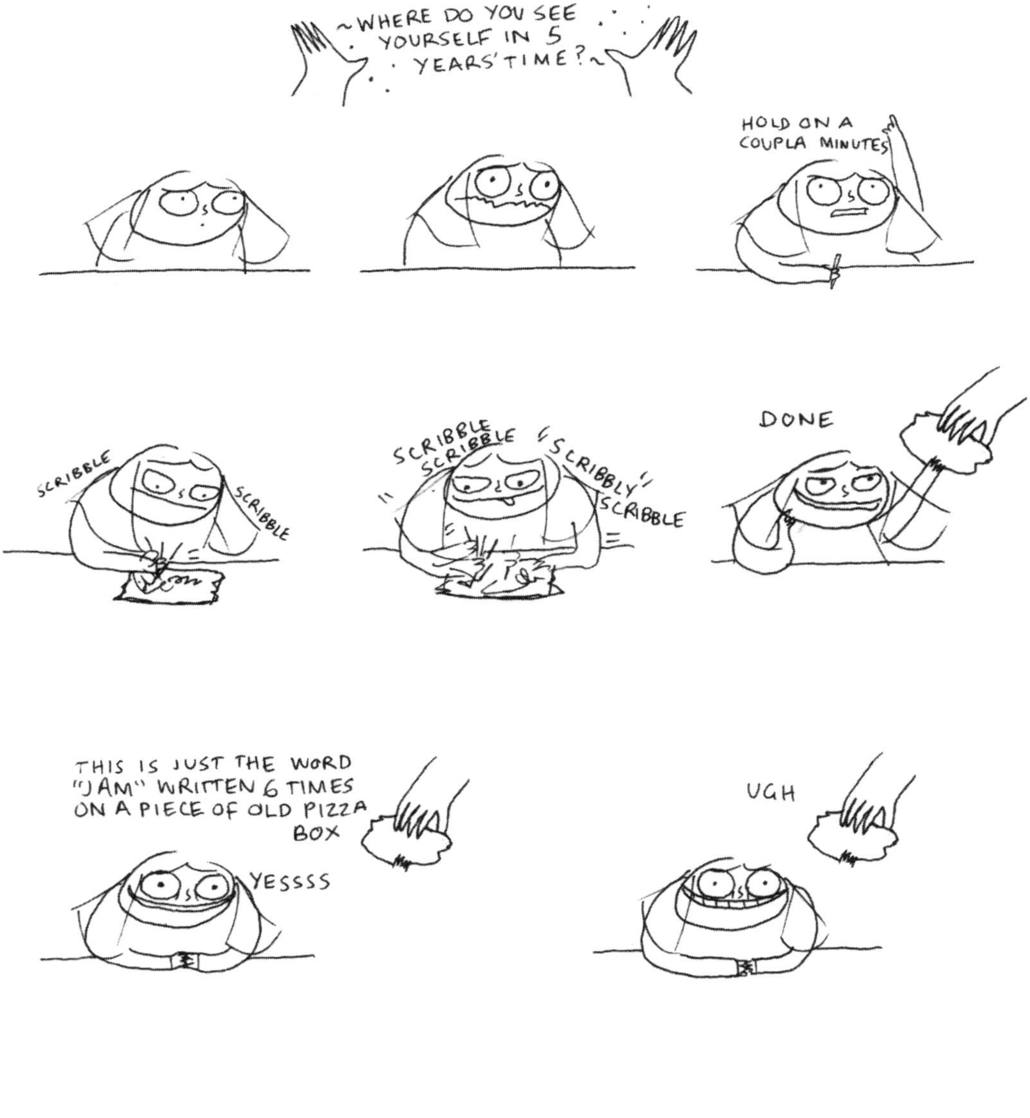
~WHERE DO YOU SEE YOURSELF IN 5 YEARS' TIME?~
HOLD ON A COUPLA MINUTES
SCRIBBLE
SCRIBBLE
SCRIBBLE SCRIBBLE
"SCRIBBLY"
SCRIBBLE
DONE
THIS IS JUST THE WORD "JAM" WRITTEN 6 TIMES ON A PIECE OF OLD PIZZA BOX
YESSSS
UGH

I'M GOING BACKPACKING ON A BIG
ADVENTURE TO DISCOVER MYSELF

IM GOING TO MEDITATE AND
CLEAR MY MIND SO I CAN GET
BACK IN TOUCH WITH MYSELF

I'M GOING TO LEARN LOADS
OF NEW THINGS AND FILL
MY HEAD WITH INTERESTING
INFORMATION IN A REALLY
PROACTIVE WAY

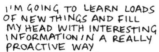

I'M GOING TO STAND INCREDIBLY STILL
AND HAVE A SMALL BREAKDOWN OVER HOW
BORING AND NOTHING I AM WITHOUT MAKING
ANY ATTEMPT TO CHANGE THINGS OR HELP
MYSELF BECAUSE HAHAHA IT'S TOO MUCH

YES, I AM SAFE HERE. YES, I AM DESPERATELY LONELY. NO YOU SHUT UP

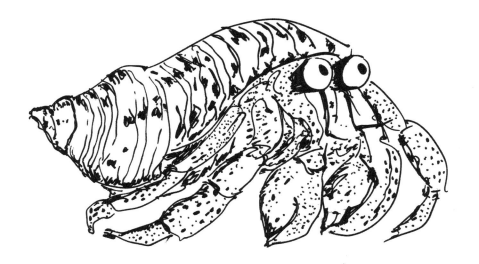

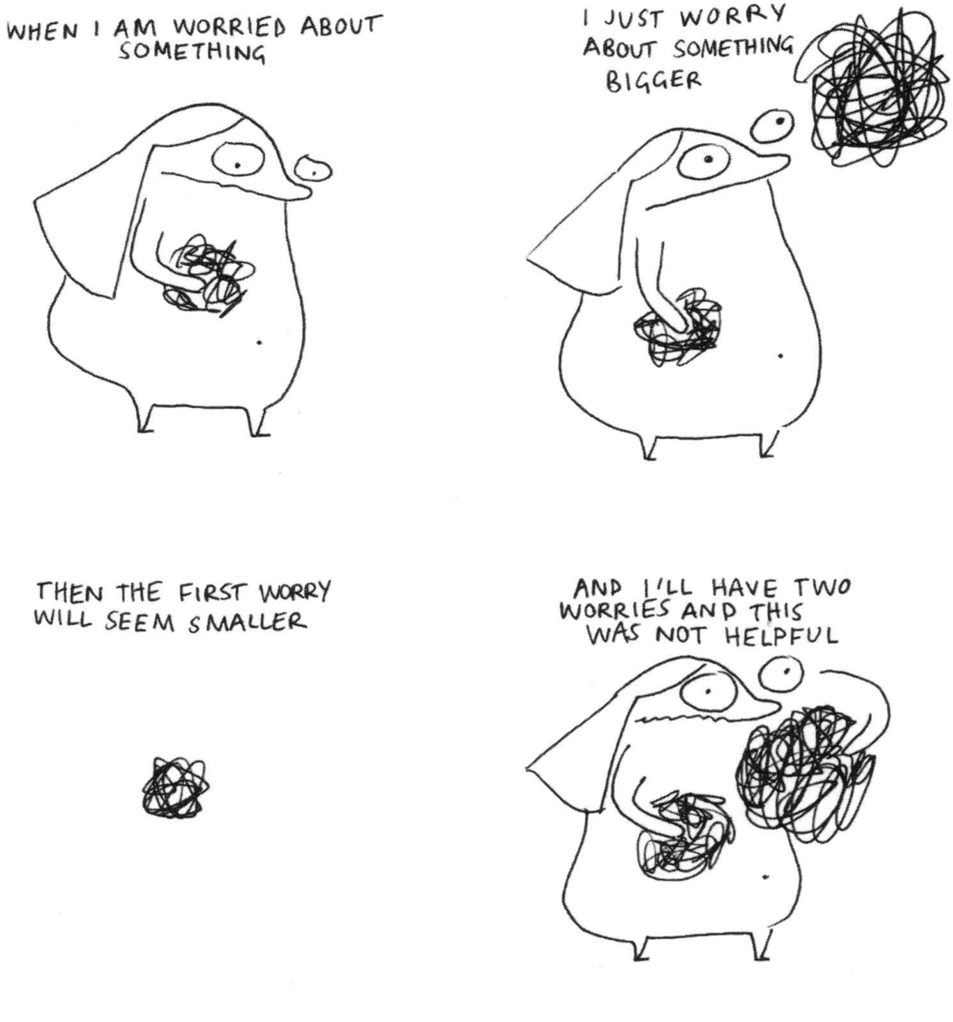
WHEN I AM WORRIED ABOUT SOMETHING
I JUST WORRY ABOUT SOMETHING BIGGER
THEN THE FIRST WORRY WILL SEEM SMALLER
AND I'LL HAVE TWO WORRIES AND THIS WAS NOT HELPFUL

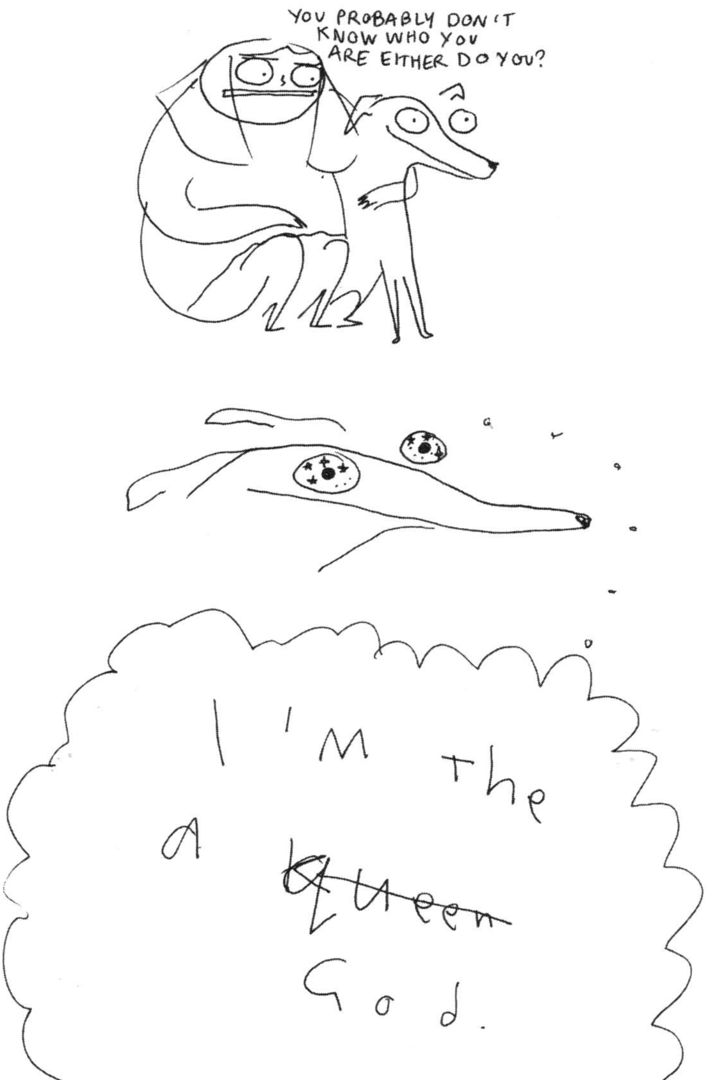
YOU PROBABLY DON'T KNOW WHO YOU ARE EITHER DO YOU?
I'm the
a ~~Queen~~
God.

WHAT THE
HELL ARE YOU
DOING?

ACTIVELY ATTEMPTING
TO RELAX
AND NOT
FEEL
BAD
ABOUT
MYSELF

HOW'S
THAT
GOING?

YES,
BEAUTIFULLY AND
GREAT
AND
GREAT

I am standing in a dimly lit room full of other humans, most of whom I have never met before. The space seems slightly too small for everyone to exist comfortably, just like the dress I'm wearing. The music is being played at a volume that all but eliminates the possibility of following a conversation, but what's odd is that when I look around I see half the people are doing very good "I am definitely hearing what you are saying, taking it in, and demonstrating my interest via the medium of nods" expressions. The other half are already drunk enough to believe them, and will continue talking about their Kickstarter campaign for a lo-fi film they are making about the time they spent backpacking in Thailand. We are all having a wonderful time and whose fucking idea was this anyway?

Sometimes I wish everyone would show up to stuff looking like they did two hours ago when they were at home, wearing a pajama top and some old sweatpants they'd been absentmindedly picking half a dried-up old cornflake off of for half an hour as they finished binge-watching another series of *House of Game of Mad Cards*. I just feel it would save a lot of time. When two people meet each other, instead of having to go through the whole "SO WHAT DO YOU DO?" faff where both parties fabricate information that'll make them appear Not Weird they could just point at each other's cornflakes and go "hah, yeah."

But people are always asking, directly or otherwise, who you are and what do you do and what are you into and what are your opinions on this thing you would be stupid to have no opinions on. It's stuff that you're expected to have answers for, certainly as an adult. Whenever I meet someone with a strong personality I balk, because working out what I am is hard. A combination of shit self-esteem and adolescence entirely subsumed by illness left me spat out feeling like an unfathomable question mark of a person in a world full of self-assured humans who appeared to know exactly what they were doing. It's been painstaking trying to slowly scrape enough bits of me back together and build new ones that I can use to anchor and contextualize myself and present to the outside world as being Mine. I've got a few, and relatively speaking I feel more of a Person than I used to, but that doesn't stop the emptiness from lingering like the clingy unwanted bastard that it is, poking holes in my certainty from time to time with its jabby little fingers and making me feel like a rather sad nubbin of Swiss cheese.

All I know is that I can't compare myself to others so acutely or live in terms of everything I'm not, because those are both pretty toxic ways to exist. As scary as it feels, I can only go from where I am today, right now, holding on to what I have so far and remembering that, just like everyone else, I am on my own trajectory, which is okay! And besides, I don't think anyone knows what the fuck's going on all of the time; some people are just better at pretending.

ARTICULATE DOG
I DON'T KNOW WHAT I'M DOING
BUT I AM A BRILLIANT ACTOR
AND I'VE GOT IT ALL WORKED OUT

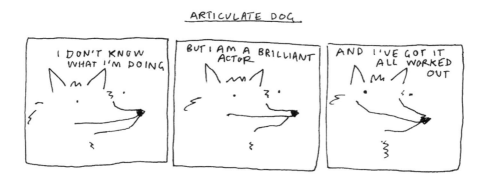

I'VE GOT A LOT

ON MY PLATE

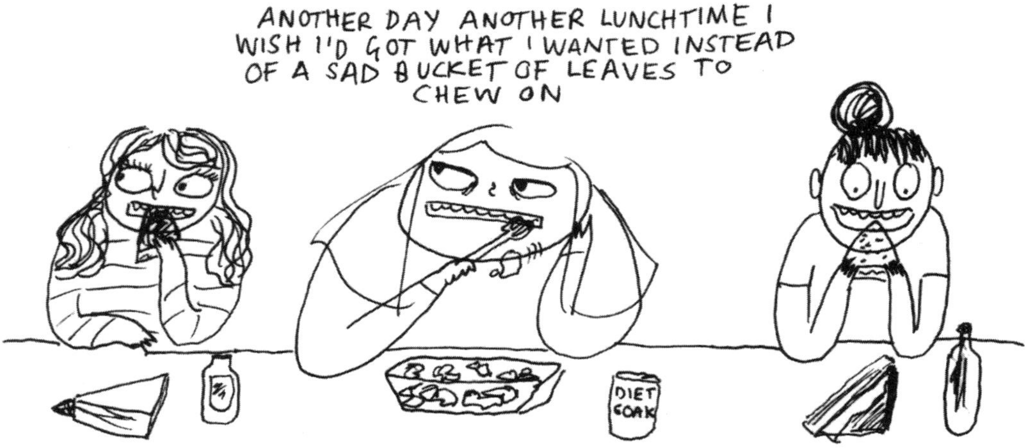
ANOTHER DAY ANOTHER LUNCHTIME I WISH I'D GOT WHAT I WANTED INSTEAD OF A SAD BUCKET OF LEAVES TO CHEW ON
DIET COAK

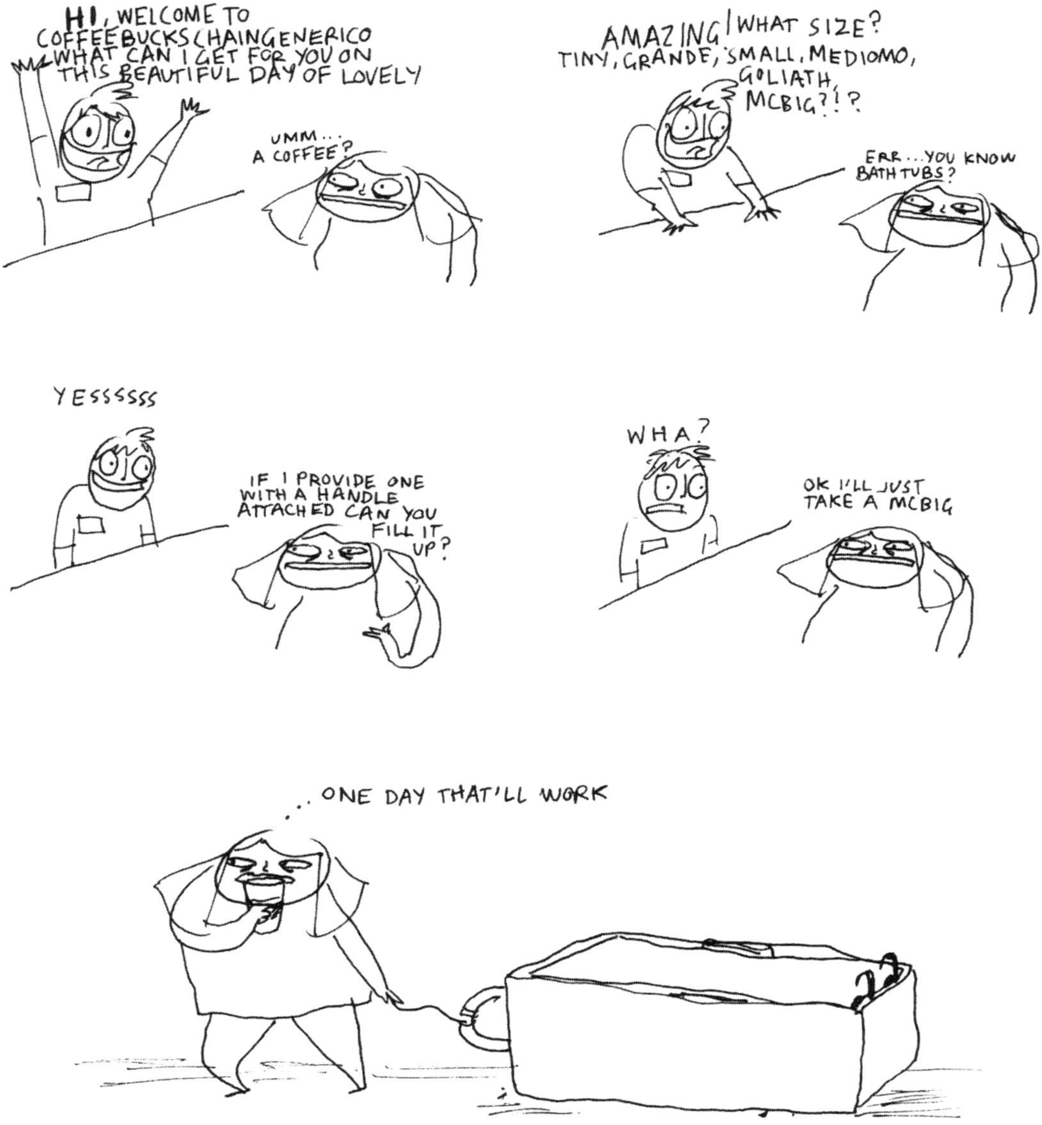
HI, WELCOME TO COFFEEBUCKSCHAINGENERICO WHAT CAN I GET FOR YOU ON THIS BEAUTIFUL DAY OF LOVELY
UMM... A COFFEE?
AMAZING! WHAT SIZE? TINY, GRANDE, SMALL, MEDIOMO, GOLIATH, MCBIG?!?
ERR... YOU KNOW BATHTUBS?
YESSSSSS
IF I PROVIDE ONE WITH A HANDLE ATTACHED CAN YOU FILL IT UP?
WHA?
OK I'LL JUST TAKE A MCBIG
... ONE DAY THAT'LL WORK

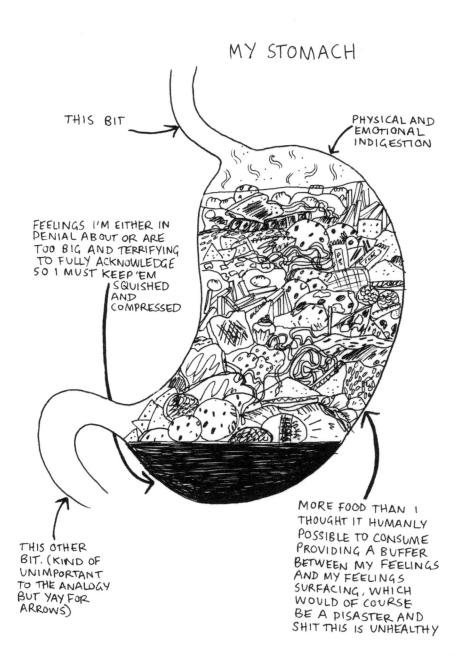

MY STOMACH

THIS BIT

PHYSICAL AND EMOTIONAL INDIGESTION

FEELINGS I'M EITHER IN DENIAL ABOUT OR ARE TOO BIG AND TERRIFYING TO FULLY ACKNOWLEDGE SO I MUST KEEP 'EM SQUISHED AND COMPRESSED

THIS OTHER BIT. (KIND OF UNIMPORTANT TO THE ANALOGY BUT YAY FOR ARROWS)

MORE FOOD THAN I THOUGHT IT HUMANLY POSSIBLE TO CONSUME PROVIDING A BUFFER BETWEEN MY FEELINGS AND MY FEELINGS SURFACING, WHICH WOULD OF COURSE BE A DISASTER AND SHIT THIS IS UNHEALTHY

(HIGHLY IRONIC)
PIE CHART ABOUT
EATING DISORDERS

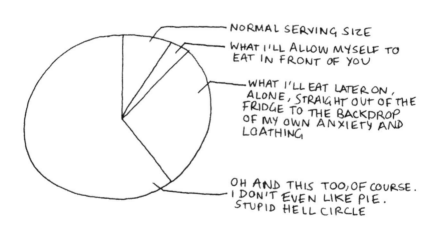

NORMAL SERVING SIZE

WHAT I'LL ALLOW MYSELF TO EAT IN FRONT OF YOU

WHAT I'LL EAT LATER ON, ALONE, STRAIGHT OUT OF THE FRIDGE TO THE BACKDROP OF MY OWN ANXIETY AND LOATHING

OH AND THIS TOO, OF COURSE. I DON'T EVEN LIKE PIE. STUPID HELL CIRCLE

MY SON, MY TREASURE, I HAVE GOT YOU THIS REALLY NICE WORM FOR TEA
I'M A FUCKING VEGAN
GET OUT OF MY HOUSE HOME

FOOD THAT IS LYING ABOUT BEING REAL FOOD
~~RYVITA~~
RECTANGULAR TILES OF COMPRESSED DUST
~~DIET CEREAL~~
OVERPRICED FLAKES MADE IN HELL, OF HELL
SPESHAL
K
BUY THIS YOU ARE FAT
~~LOW-FAT YOGURT~~
OLD MILK STRIPPED OF ALL JOY THAT IS THEN AGGRESSIVELY MARKETED AT WOMEN
NO
~~LOW-CALORIE READY MEALS~~
ABSOLUTELY NOT A MEAL. MAINLY AN OLD PEA BOBBING ABOUT IN UNIDENTIFIABLE SAUCE. SMELLS OF DEATH A BIT
healthy VEGTBLEH CURRY
~~ANYTHING THAT DESCRIBES ITSELF AS "LIGHT"~~
GET IT OUT OF MY HOUSE HOME THIS INSTANT
NOTHING 0% LIGHT
LIES
LIGHT SPREAD

HUNGER

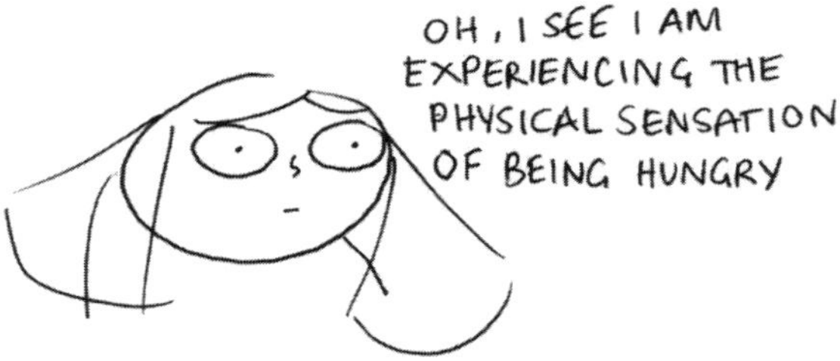
OH, I SEE I AM EXPERIENCING THE PHYSICAL SENSATION OF BEING HUNGRY

PRE-PERIOD HUNGER

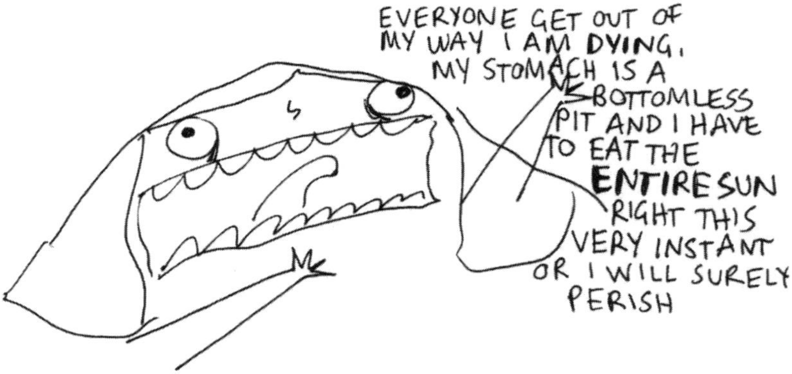
EVERYONE GET OUT OF MY WAY I AM **DYING.** MY STOMACH IS A BOTTOMLESS PIT AND I HAVE TO EAT THE **ENTIRE** SUN RIGHT THIS VERY INSTANT OR I WILL SURELY PERISH

IDEAL WITCH POWERS

FLAWLESS ESTIMATION
OF PASTA
QUANTITIES

THAT'S IT, THAT'S
ALL I WANT—TO NOT
END UP STARING AT
A SAD CLUMP OF
LEFTOVER YELLOW IN
THE PAN AND
CURSING MY INABILITY
TO DO ANYTHING
RIGHT EVERY TIME
I MAKE SPAGHETTI

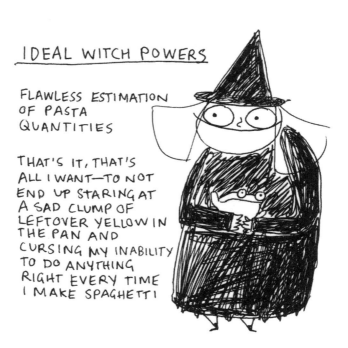

OH YEAH I **LOOVE** FOOD*

*TERMS AND CONDITIONS APPLY. ABOVE STATEMENT ~~MAY NOT~~ DEFINITELY WON'T BE A FULL AND ACCURATE REFLECTION OF HOW COMPLICATED MY RELATIONSHIP WITH FOOD IS, AND HOW YEARS OF EATING DISORDERS AND FOOD FUCKERY HAVE LEFT ME WITH A BACKLOG OF RESIDUAL ANXIETY OVER WHAT I DO AND DON'T PUT ON MY PLATE

BUT HEY, YOU TRY AND FIT THAT ALL IN ONE SENTENCE...

SHOPPING

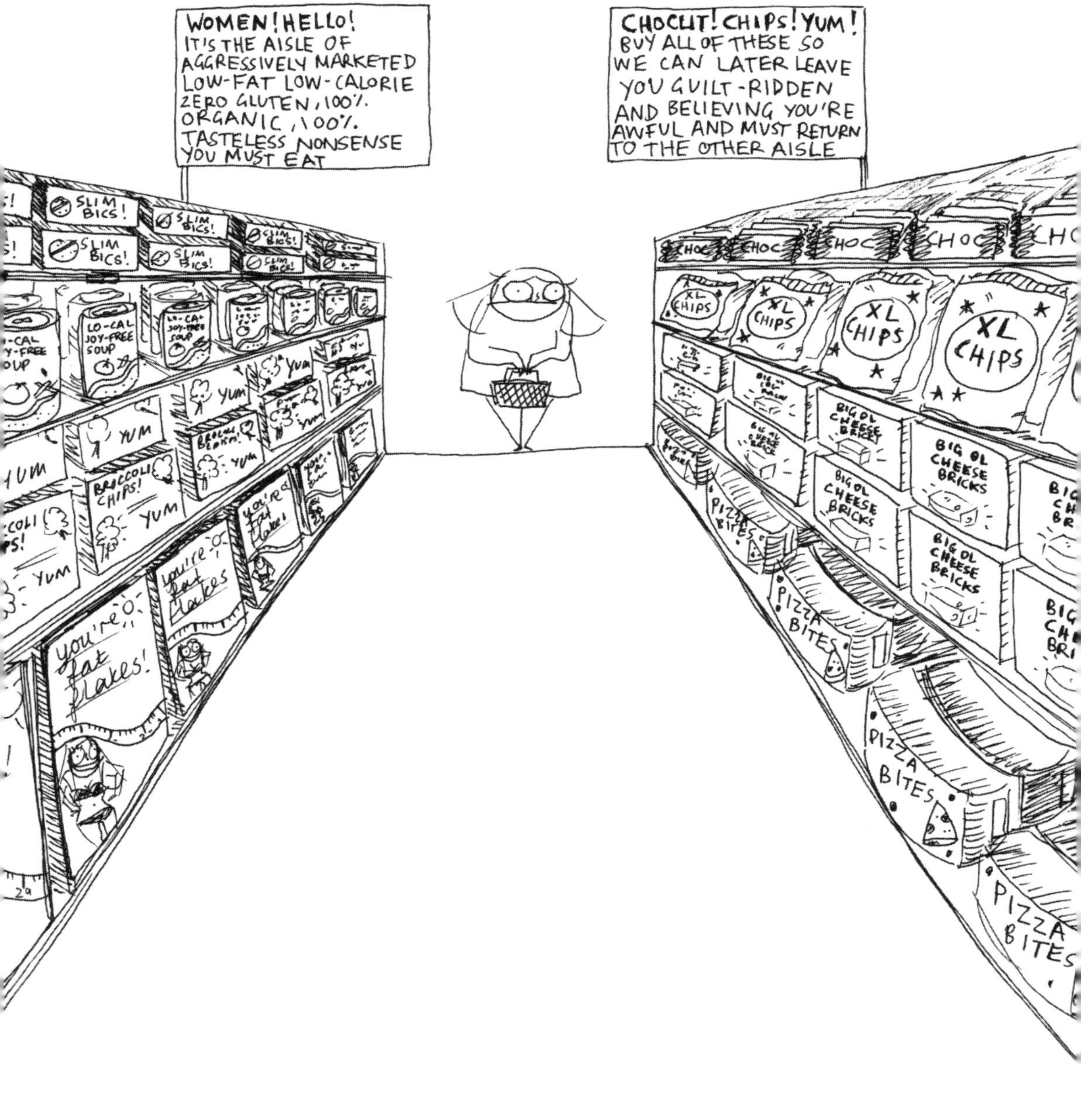
WOMEN! HELLO!
IT'S THE AISLE OF AGGRESSIVELY MARKETED LOW-FAT LOW-CALORIE ZERO GLUTEN, 100% ORGANIC, 100% TASTELESS NONSENSE YOU MUST EAT
CHOCLIT! CHIPS! YUM!
BUY ALL OF THESE SO WE CAN LATER LEAVE YOU GUILT-RIDDEN AND BELIEVING YOU'RE AWFUL AND MUST RETURN TO THE OTHER AISLE
SLIM BICS!
LO-CAL JOY-FREE SOUP
YUM
BROCCOLI CHIPS!
YOU'RE FAT FLAKES!
CHOC
XL CHIPS
BIG OL CHEESE BRICKS
PIZZA BITES

GOLDILOCKS & THE THREE BEARS (AND BULIMIA)

ONCE UPON AN UGH, A GIRL CALLED GOLDILOCKS STUMBLED ACROSS A HOUSE IN THE WOODS. SHE WANDERED INTO THE KITCHEN, AND THERE ON THE TABLE WERE THREE BOWLS OF PORRIDGE

SHE STARED AT THE PORRIDGE FOR A LONG TIME, WILLING HERSELF NOT TO EAT IT. BUT THE MORE SHE TOLD HERSELF "NO" THE MORE SHE WANTED TO EAT

IN THE END SHE SAT DOWN AND ATE THE FIRST BOWL

AND THEN THE SECOND, NOT BOTHERING WITH THE SPOON THIS TIME

BY THE TIME THE
THIRD BOWL WAS
FINISHED, GOLDILOCKS
WAS FEELING VERY
FULL, OF FOOD AND
OF GUILT

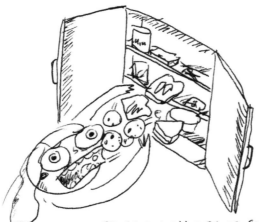

THIS CAUSED SO MUCH PANIC SHE
FLUNG OPEN THE KITCHEN CUPBOARDS
AND SHOVELED EVERYTHING THAT
WAS REMOTELY EDIBLE INTO HER MOUTH

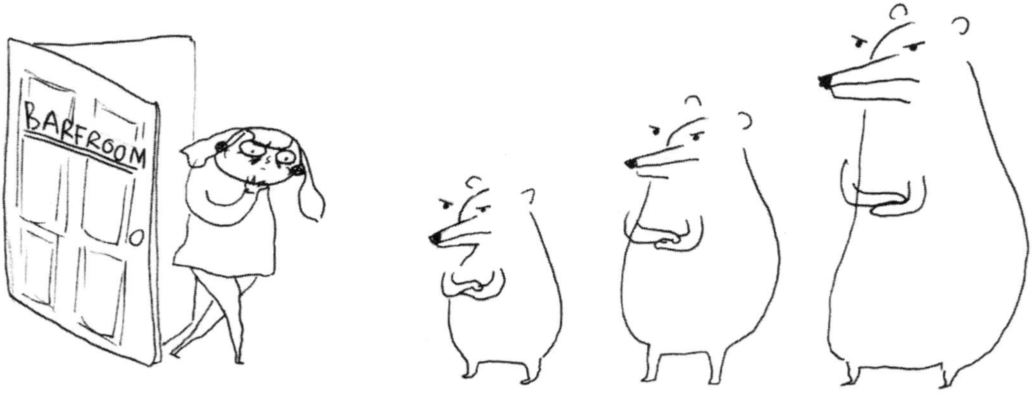
BARFROOM

WHEN THE OWNERS ARRIVED HOME AND DISCOVERED THEIR BOMB SITE OF A KITCHEN THEY LOOKED FOR THE INTRUDER AND FOUND GOLDILOCKS STUMBLING OUT OF THE BATHROOM. THEY WERE SUITABLY PISSED OFF.

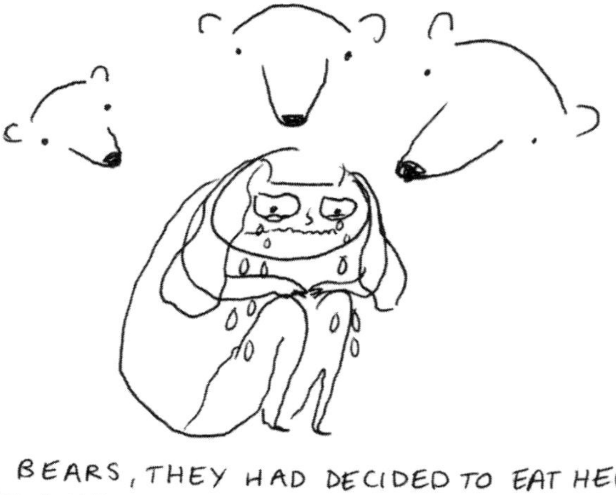

BEING BEARS, THEY HAD DECIDED TO EAT HER ON SIGHT, BUT WHEN SHE SAT DOWN ON THE FLOOR AND BEGAN TO CRY THEY PAUSED, UNABLE TO CONTEMPLATE SUCH A SAD LOOKING MEAL

LUCKILY, THE SMALLEST BEAR HAD A PSYCHOLOGY DEGREE
AND HAPPENED TO BE A REGISTERED PSYCHOTHERAPIST
WITH HIS OWN SUCCESSFUL PRACTICE. HE TOOK GOLDILOCKS
GENTLY BY THE HAND AND POINTED TO THE BED BECAUSE
HE THOUGHT A NAP MIGHT DO HER GOOD.

"THERE," HE SAID

"YOU HAVE A LITTLE REST NOW AND BE KIND
TO YOURSELF, STRANGE FURLESS BEAR"

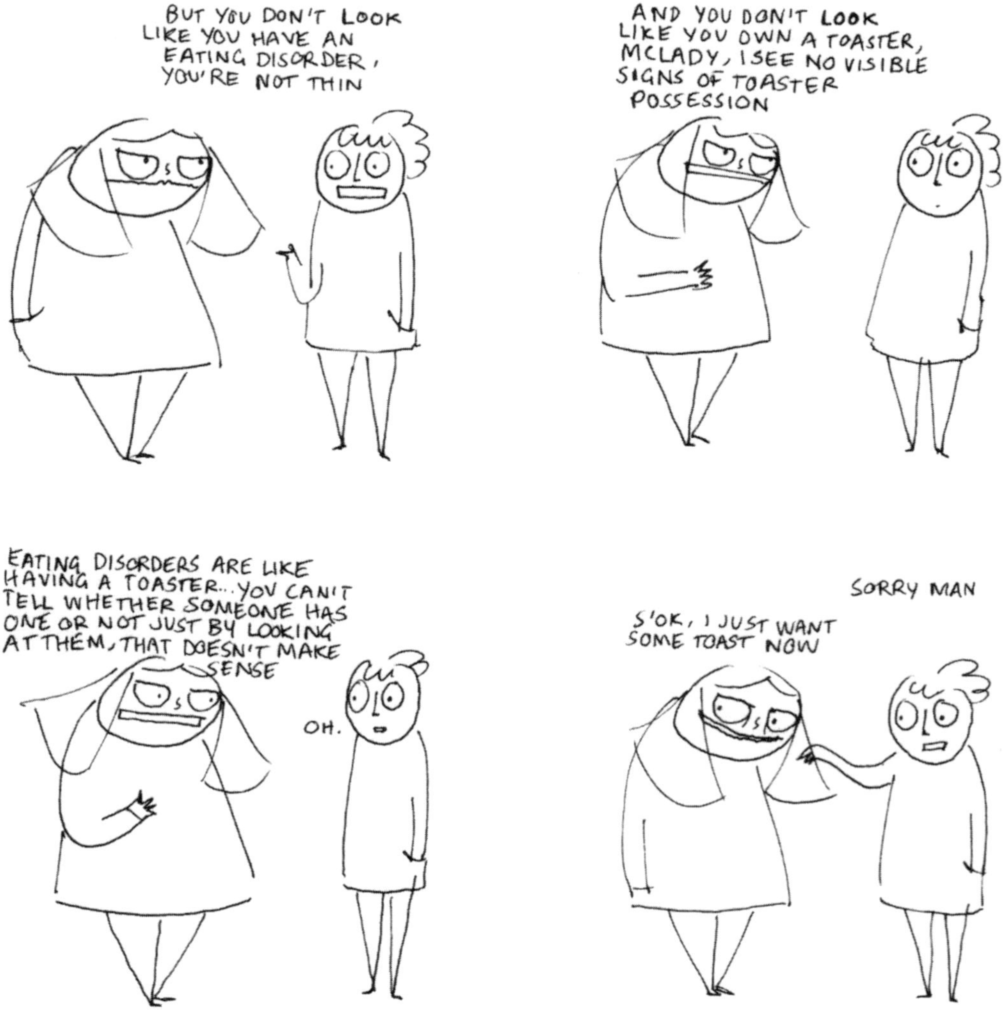
BUT YOU DON'T LOOK LIKE YOU HAVE AN EATING DISORDER, YOU'RE NOT THIN
AND YOU DON'T LOOK LIKE YOU OWN A TOASTER, MCLADY, I SEE NO VISIBLE SIGNS OF TOASTER POSSESSION
EATING DISORDERS ARE LIKE HAVING A TOASTER... YOU CAN'T TELL WHETHER SOMEONE HAS ONE OR NOT JUST BY LOOKING AT THEM, THAT DOESN'T MAKE SENSE
OH.
SORRY MAN
S'OK, I JUST WANT SOME TOAST NOW

NOT READY YET

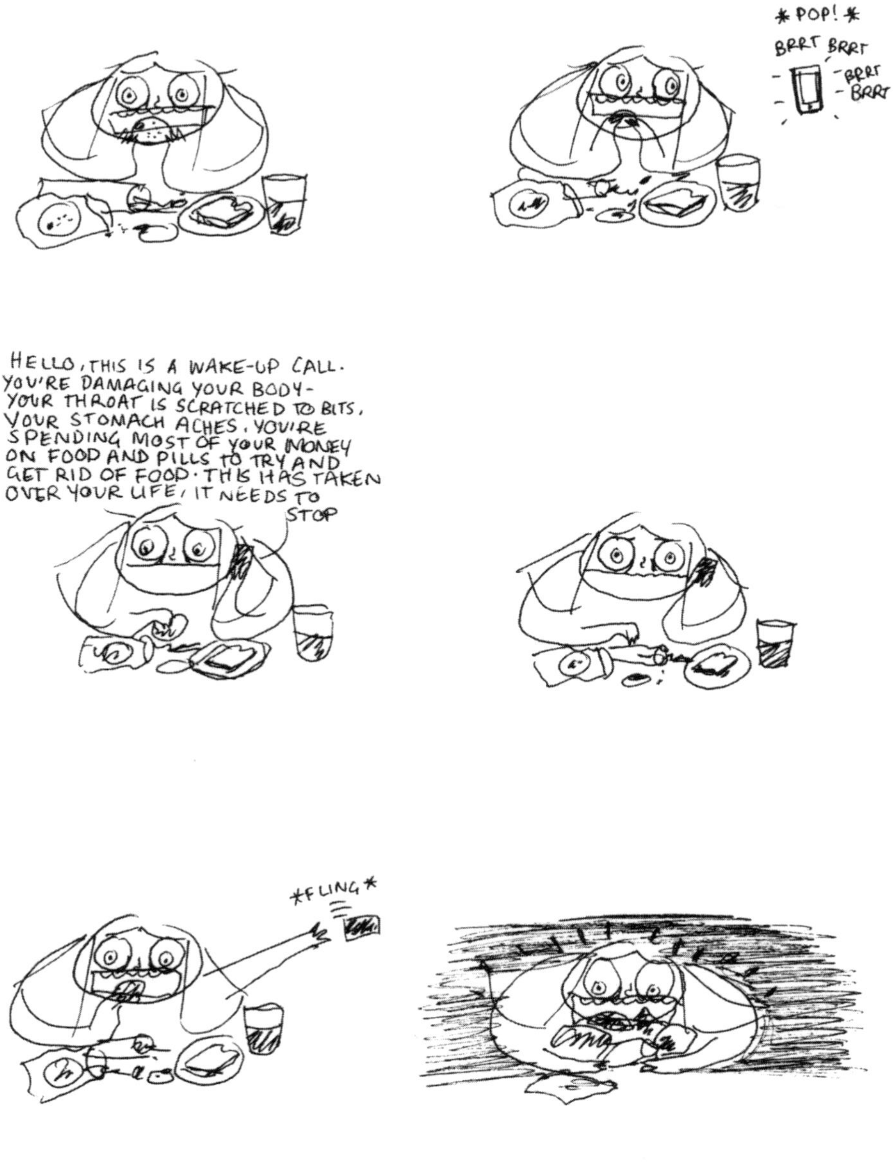
POP!
BRRT BRRT
BRRT
BRRT
HELLO, THIS IS A WAKE-UP CALL. YOU'RE DAMAGING YOUR BODY- YOUR THROAT IS SCRATCHED TO BITS, YOUR STOMACH ACHES, YOU'RE SPENDING MOST OF YOUR MONEY ON FOOD AND PILLS TO TRY AND GET RID OF FOOD. THIS HAS TAKEN OVER YOUR LIFE, IT NEEDS TO STOP
FLING

How do I begin to describe what having an eating disorder is like? I could sit here and tell you horror stories about my experiences with anorexia, bulimia, and binge eating. I could because I've been there done that and got the T-shirts in every single bloody size, but if you've ever had an eating disorder all that stuff will be very familiar anyway. And if you haven't, I don't want to cough up a load of misery porn at you written only in terms of dramatic weight loss or out of control calorie consumption. Those things are just some of the tangible manifestations of a very real and complex mental illness. I want to focus on the bit that happens above the shoulders; about what an eating disorder does to yer noggin.

So, putting aside the fact that I'm (shockingly) not a neuroscientist, let's call this the mind. (Yes, I know, I could have drawn a brain but I don't have time for that squiggly nonsense.)

Typically, the mind will be occupied by a load of stuff—thoughts and opinions, hopes and fears, important relationships, things you're interested in and things you hate, experiences you've had and a bit of space for those you haven't, with all the usual mundane bollocks floating around in between.

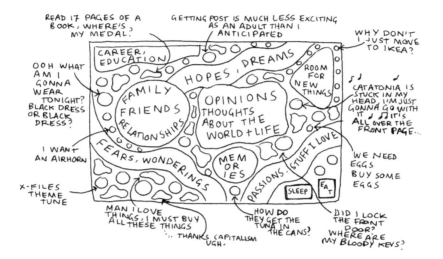

READ 17 PAGES OF A BOOK, WHERE'S MY MEDAL?

GETTING POST IS MUCH LESS EXCITING AS AN ADULT THAN I ANTICIPATED

WHY DON'T I JUST MOVE TO IKEA?

OOH WHAT AM I GONNA WEAR TONIGHT? BLACK DRESS OR BLACK DRESS?

CAREER, EDUCATION

HOPES, DREAMS

ROOM FOR NEW THINGS

FAMILY

OPINIONS

FRIENDS

THOUGHTS ABOUT THE WORLD + LIFE

RELATIONSHIPS

FEARS, WONDERINGS

MEMORIES

PASSIONS

STUFF I LOVE

SLEEP

EAT

CATATONIA IS STUCK IN MY HEAD, I'M JUST GONNA GO WITH IT ♪ ♫ IT'S ALL OVER THE FRONT PAGE...

I WANT AN AIRHORN

WE NEED EGGS BUY SOME EGGS

X-FILES THEME TUNE

MAN I LOVE THINGS, I MUST BUY ALL THESE THINGS

⁞ THANKS CAPITALISM UGH.

HOW DO THEY GET THE TUNA IN THE CANS?

DID I LOCK THE FRONT DOOR? WHERE ARE MY BLOODY KEYS?

In the bottom right hand corner I've shown a couple of the biological functions we are all pre-programmed to perform in order to stay alive. They don't take up a lot of thought-space because they should be pretty straightforward. We get tired, we need rest, we sleep. We get hungry, the brain shouts "hey, you with the face, make a sandwich or something," we eat the sandwich and we move on.

Something I think people don't often get is that eating disorders aren't really about losing weight or wanting to be thin. Yes, they are often defined by obsessive preoccupation with weight and food and very extreme, often dangerous behaviors around eating, but these are simply the physical mediums through which deep underlying psychological distress is expressed. This is why it's inaccurate to call anorexia "a diet that spiralled out of control" or think of binge eating disorder and bulimia as problems attributable to laziness and lack of willpower around food. These are mental illnesses.

I was fourteen when I first developed an eating disorder. I won't go into what the exact causes of this were (that's a whole other very complicated kettle of calorie-counted fish), but anorexia took hold very suddenly and aggressively on both my body and mind. After a while I began to struggle with binge eating and bulimia too, and I continued to fluctuate between these for years; sometimes very physically ill, sometimes less so, but always in a pretty consistently disordered mental state.

Here's a picture of what my mind looked like in the throes of illness.

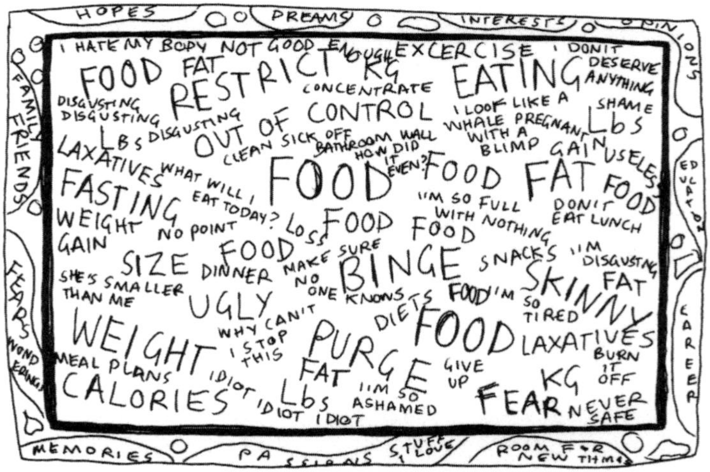
HOPES
DREAMS
INTERESTS
OPINIONS
FAMILY
FRIENDS
FEARS
CAREER
MEMORIES
PASSIONS
STUFF I LOVE
I HATE MY BODY
NOT GOOD ENOUGH
EXCERCISE
I DON'T DESERVE ANYTHING
FOOD
FAT
RESTRICT
KG
CONCENTRATE
EATING
DISGUSTING
DISGUSTING
SHAME
OUT OF CONTROL
I LOOK LIKE A WHALE
PREGNANT WITH A BLIMP
Lbs
DISGUSTING
CLEAN SICK OFF BATHROOM WALL
HOW DID IT EVEN?
GAIN
USELESS
LAXATIVES
WHAT WILL I EAT TODAY?
FOOD
FOOD
FAT
FOOD
FASTING
I'M SO FULL WITH NOTHING
DON'T EAT LUNCH
WEIGHT GAIN
NO POINT
LOSS
FOOD
FOOD
FOOD
SIZE
DINNER
MAKE SURE NO ONE KNOWS
BINGE
SNACKS
I'M DISGUSTING
SHE'S SMALLER THAN ME
SKINNY
FAT
UGLY
DIETS
FOOD
I'M SO TIRED
WEIGHT
WHY CAN'T I STOP THIS
PURGE
FOOD
LAXATIVES
MEAL PLANS
FAT
GIVE UP
BURN IT OFF
CALORIES
IDIOT
IDIOT
IDIOT
Lbs
I'M SO ASHAMED
KG
FEAR
NEVER SAFE

Gets out pointy stick like they have in lectures So yep, as you can see the small "want the sandwich make the sandwich eat the sandwich" area has grown wildly in size, pushing everything else of and about me to the very peripheries of my mind, its importance eclipsed entirely by eating and a barrage of associated eating-related anxieties and self-loathing. There is very little space or energy left to invest in anything outside of that. And for me that's one of the most agonizing realities of an eating disorder: being completely consumed by fear of what I am or am not consuming.

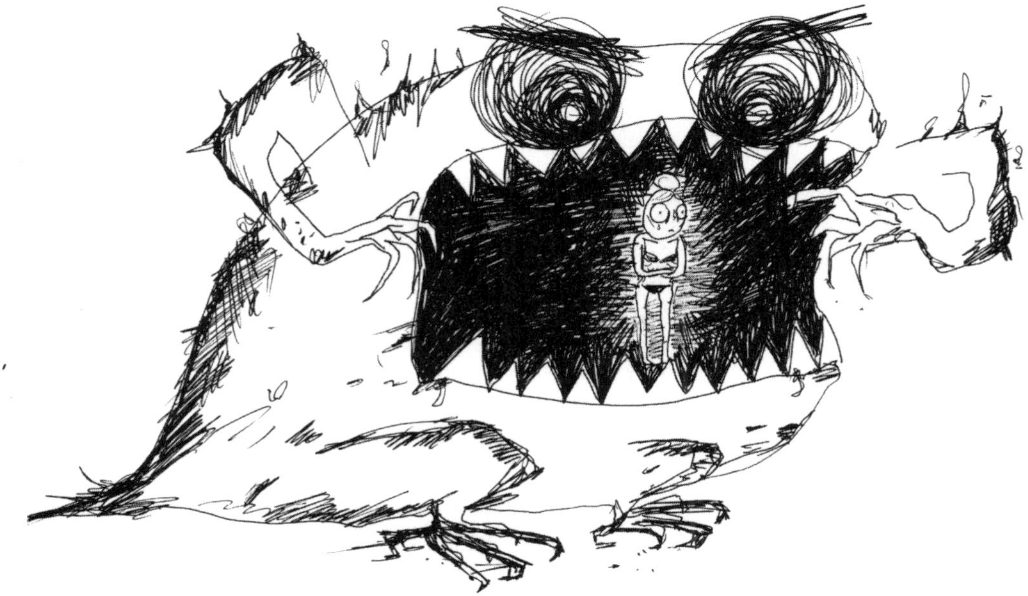
ANOREXIA, FOR AN ILLNESS SO CONCERNED WITH DEPRIVATION
YOU ARE INCONCEIVABLY GREEDY

For months, while friends my age were worrying about their finals or dealing with hangovers for the first time, I sat behind a table at home or in the hospital crying tears at a cheese sandwich like someone had asked me to eat a plate of rusty nails. And I couldn't count the number of occasions I canceled seeing friends and turned work opportunities down because I had an important couple of meetings with the contents of the fridge and the toilet. It's like the most miserable, isolating full-time job ever.

Recovery is a word I handle with care, particularly when it comes to this stuff. For me it creates an unnecessary polarization of "illness" and "wellness," when really the task of managing an eating disorder and reclaiming life back from it is a very nonlinear and messy process with lots of intermediary and convalescence stages. I always had this fantasy that one day I'd wake up and things would go back to a happy healthy glowy normal. I'd skip about drinking green tea and eating handfuls of wholesome granola and be able to talk courageously of My Journey To Health.

Rather frustratingly, the physical, behavioral, and mental progressions don't happen in synchronization, so for lengthy periods of time I might have got myself physically "well," but the behaviors and amount of space eating disordered thoughts took up in my mind were still extensive and profoundly distressing. Other times I'd develop really healthy and important insights into what was going on for me, but still be unable to utilize those in the face of entrenched and compulsive behaviors. And when I DID start making real headway, I was left with this huge nothingness in my mind where the eating disorder used to be, a daunting cavity I didn't know how the hell I would fill when the other stuff had been squashed out of existence for so long.

Basically what I'm saying is that this shit is complicated and takes ages.

It's been a series of attempts, battles, and tiny, subtle victories (even if I haven't been jumping for joy at the time)—the first day I stopped forcing myself to drink scalding hot black coffees and thought "fuck it, I'll put some normal non-ridiculous non-low-fat milk in"; the first time I ate a regular meal in front of someone again instead of an "oh that's alright I'm not very hungry" salad, and made it into bed that night without throwing any of it up; the first time I opened the kitchen cupboard fully intent on demolishing everything inside it, but managed to close the doors and go for a walk instead to come home feeling calmer. These may sound like inconsequential things, but for someone with an eating disorder they are akin to turning around and kicking the giant monster that's been chasing you for years on end squarely in the nads. These weren't epiphanies or concrete I AM NOW IN RECOVERY moments, because the next time I was in these situations I wouldn't manage, and the time after I might only manage some of it. They weren't end points; they were subtle yet significant breakthroughs. And slowly (ever so slowly) as more and more of them trickled in, more and more life stuff could trickle in too and tip the balance back toward something more regular, both physically and emotionally.

It's been eight years since I was first diagnosed and my mind is pretty far into the process of refilling itself. I have residual issues and times when I struggle, but there is so much more going on in my mind outside of all that, and the world is opening up and happening at me from all sorts of new and interesting directions in a way that my eating disorder would have never allowed me to experience. Basically I am able to prioritize my life over strange feelings toward a sandwich, and for today that feels really good. That feels like enough.

WEIGHT LOSS TIPS FOR JANUARY

GET RID OF ALL
THE WEIGHT LOSS
ADVICE, THAT SHIT
WEIGHS A TON

BULLSHIT CAPITALIZING ON INSECURITIES THE DIET INDUSTRY HAS CREATED

UNSUSTAINABLE FOOD PLANS

PALEO
LO-FAT
5:2
FADDY MCFAD

TRY THESE NEW GUILT-FREE FOODS! . . .

ALL FOODS

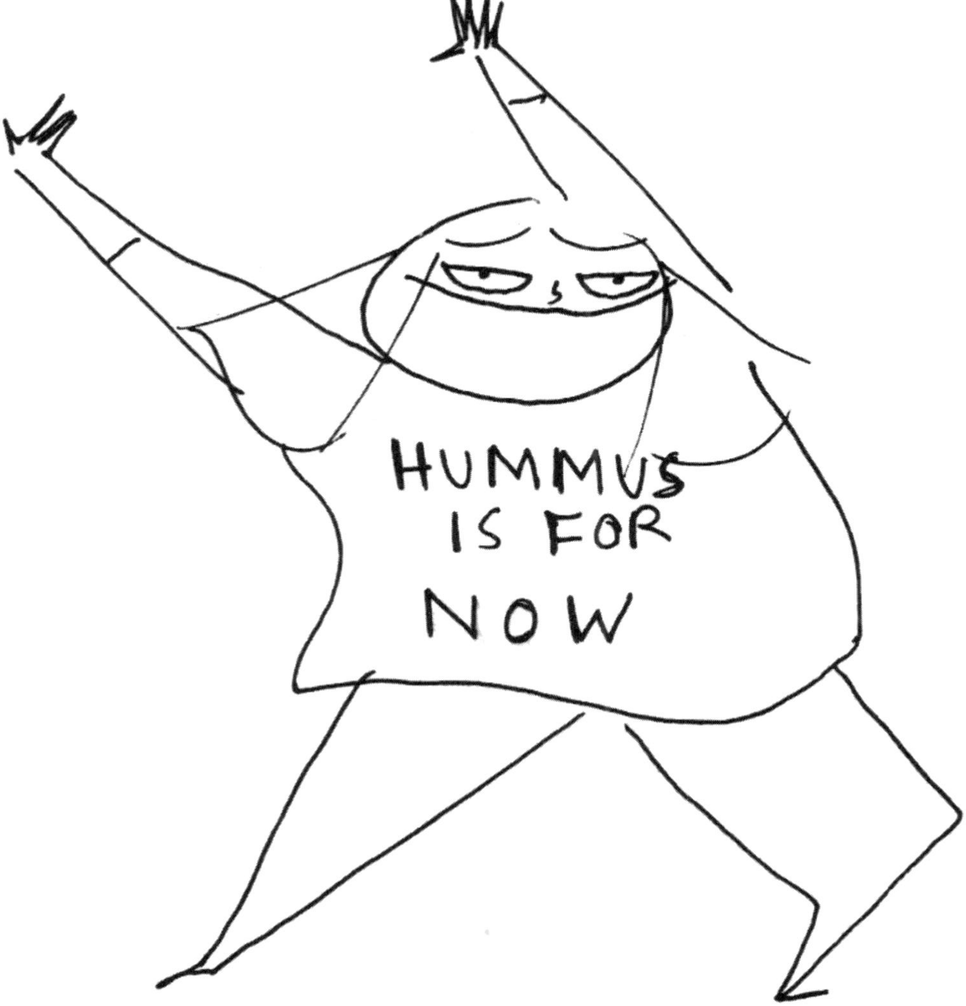
HUMMUS
IS FOR
NOW

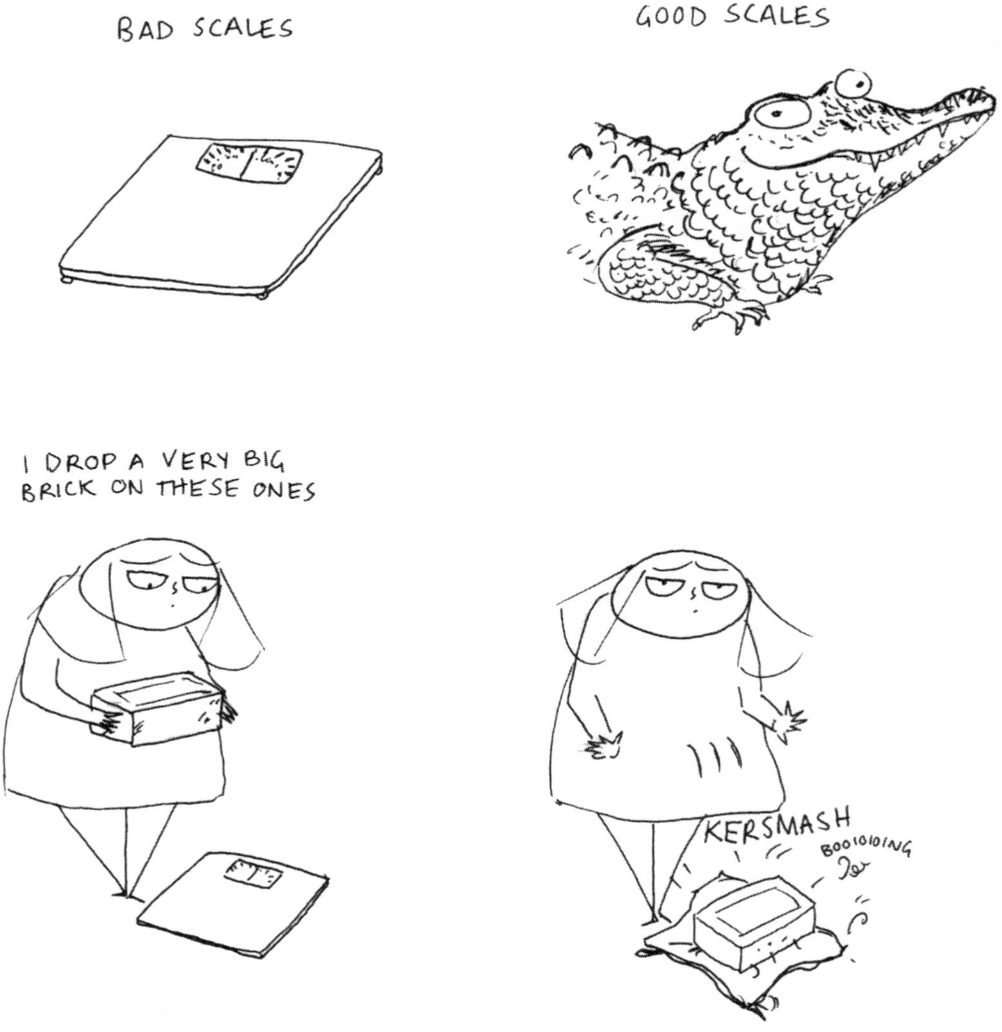
BAD SCALES
GOOD SCALES
I DROP A VERY BIG BRICK ON THESE ONES
KERSMASH
BOOIOIOING

I HAVE MORE IMPORTANT THINGS TO BE GETTING ON WITH

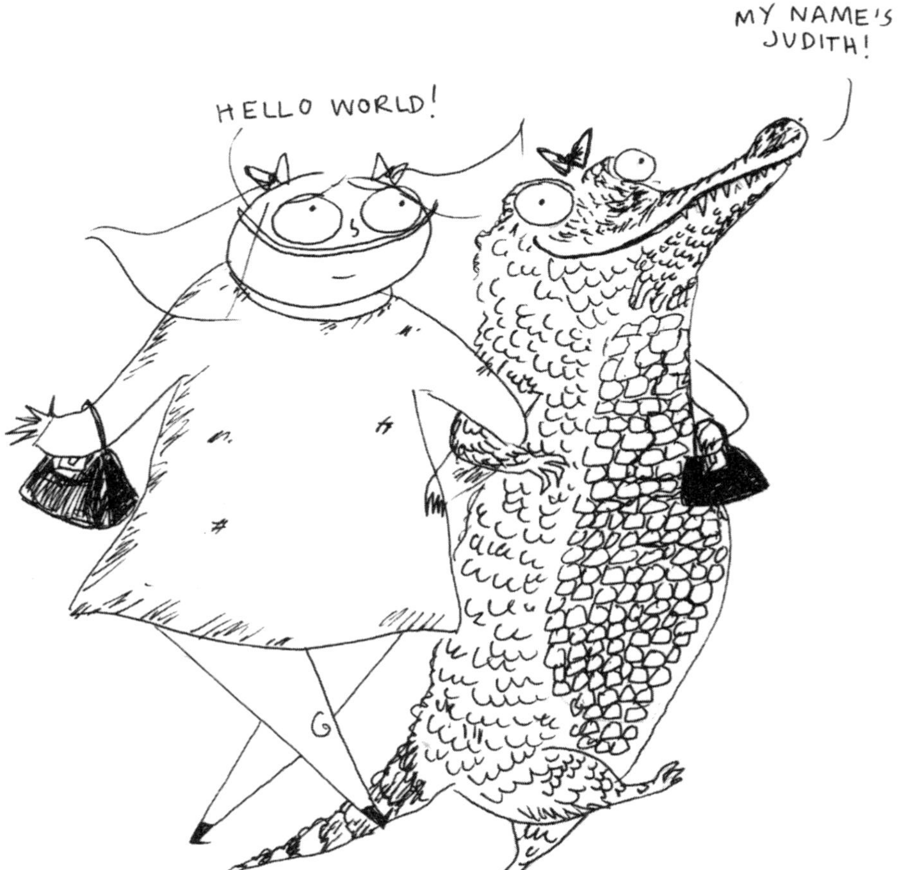
HELLO WORLD!
MY NAME'S JUDITH!

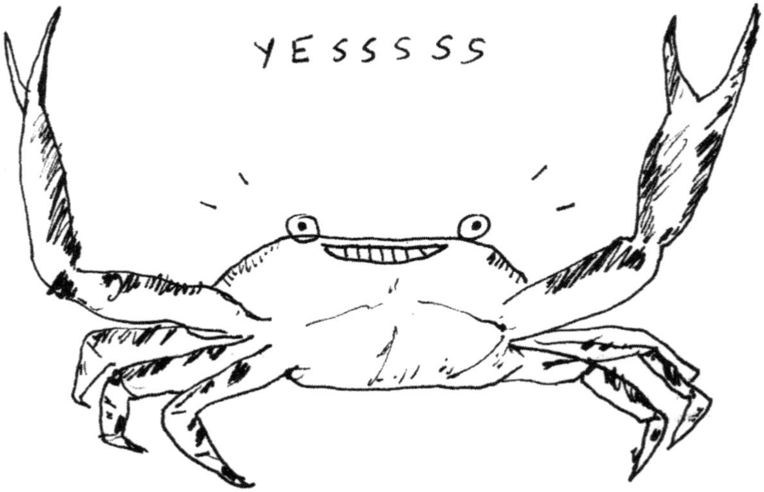
YESSSSS

AH, FACE,
WE MEET AGAIN

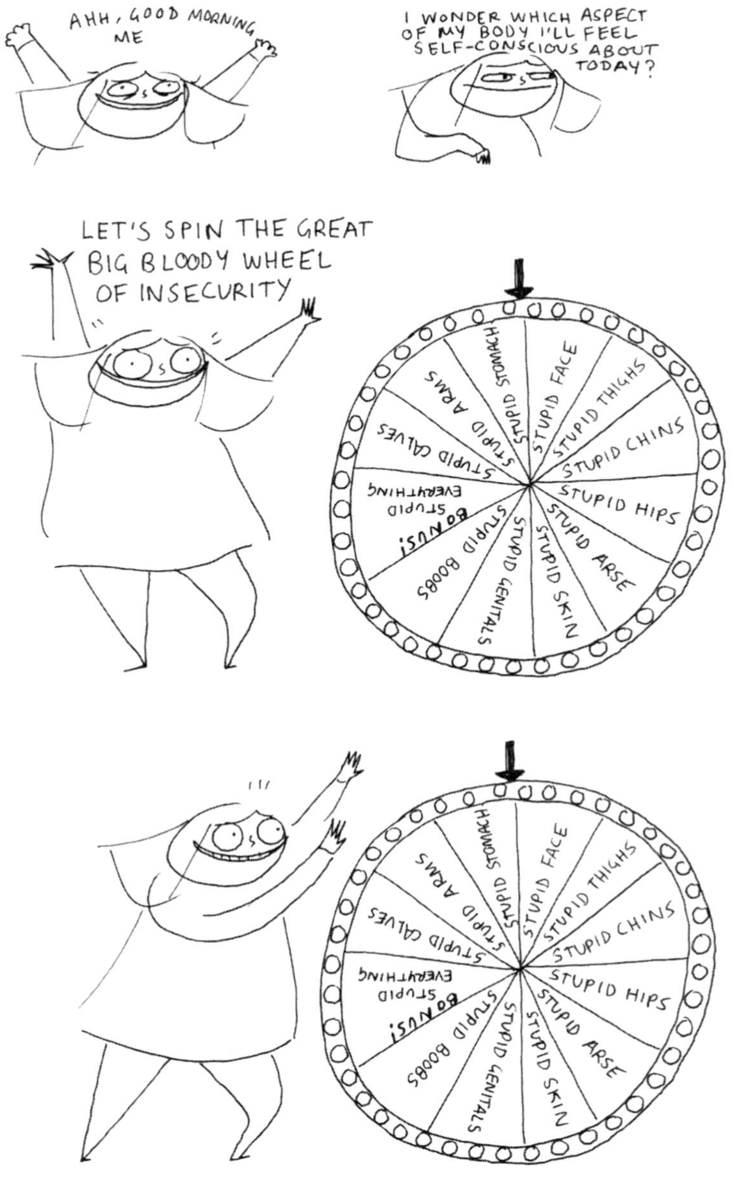
AHH, GOOD MORNING ME
I WONDER WHICH ASPECT OF MY BODY I'LL FEEL SELF-CONSCIOUS ABOUT TODAY?
LET'S SPIN THE GREAT BIG BLOODY WHEEL OF INSECURITY
STUPID STOMACH
STUPID FACE
STUPID THIGHS
STUPID CHINS
STUPID HIPS
STUPID ARSE
STUPID SKIN
STUPID GENITALS
STUPID BOOBS
BONUS! STUPID EVERYTHING
STUPID CALVES
STUPID ARMS

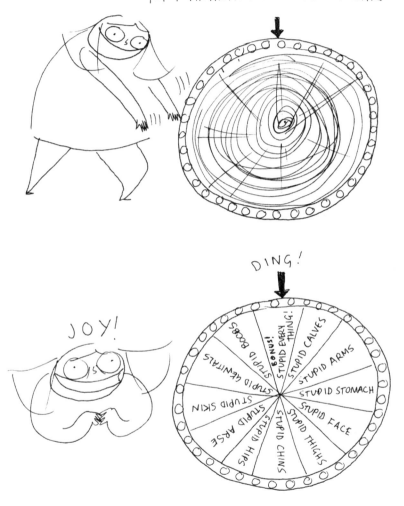

TOO SHORT

TOO LONG

TOO TIGHT

TOO SHAPELESS

TOO JAZZY

NOT JAZZY ENOUGH

PERFECT CLOTHE

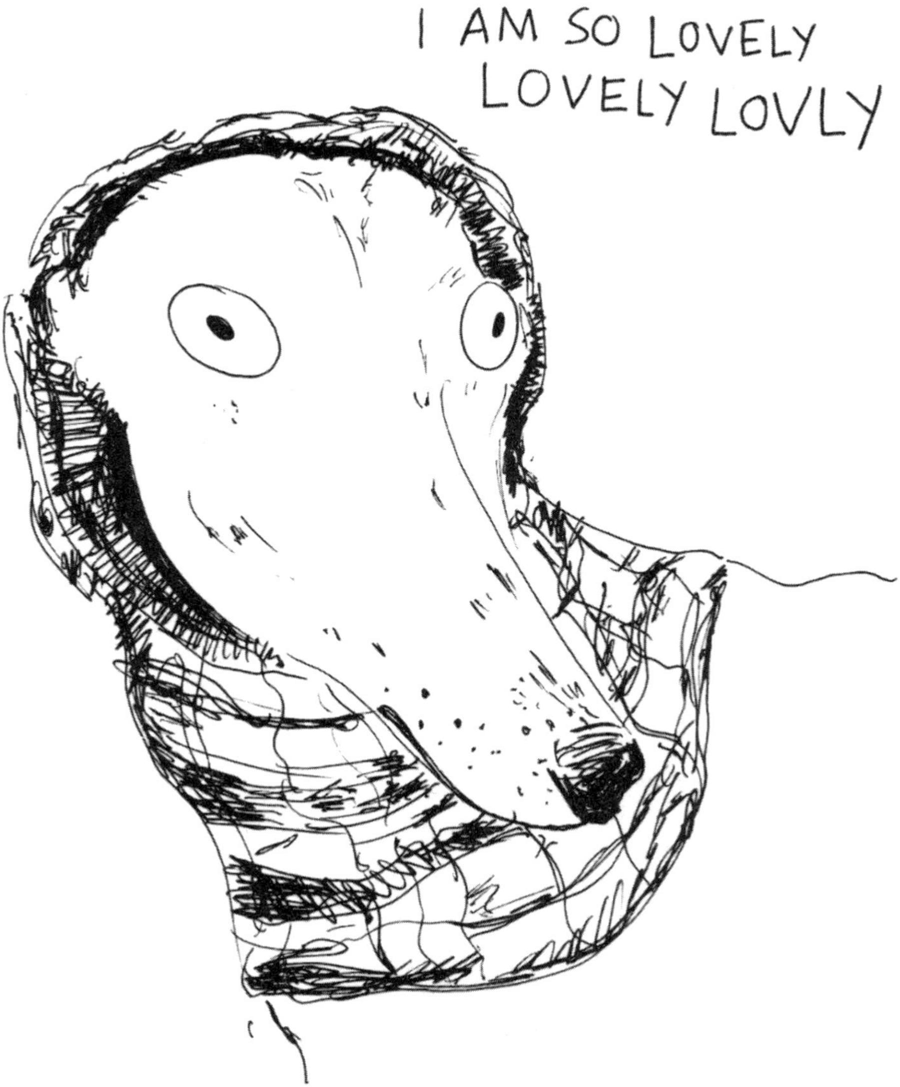
I AM SO LOVELY
LOVELY LOVLY

Those little things a girl can't leave 💗
💗 the house without !!

makeup!

a cute bag!

a spritz of her favorite perfume

tiny party crab

PEW PEW
ZZZAP
laser eyes

flamethrower

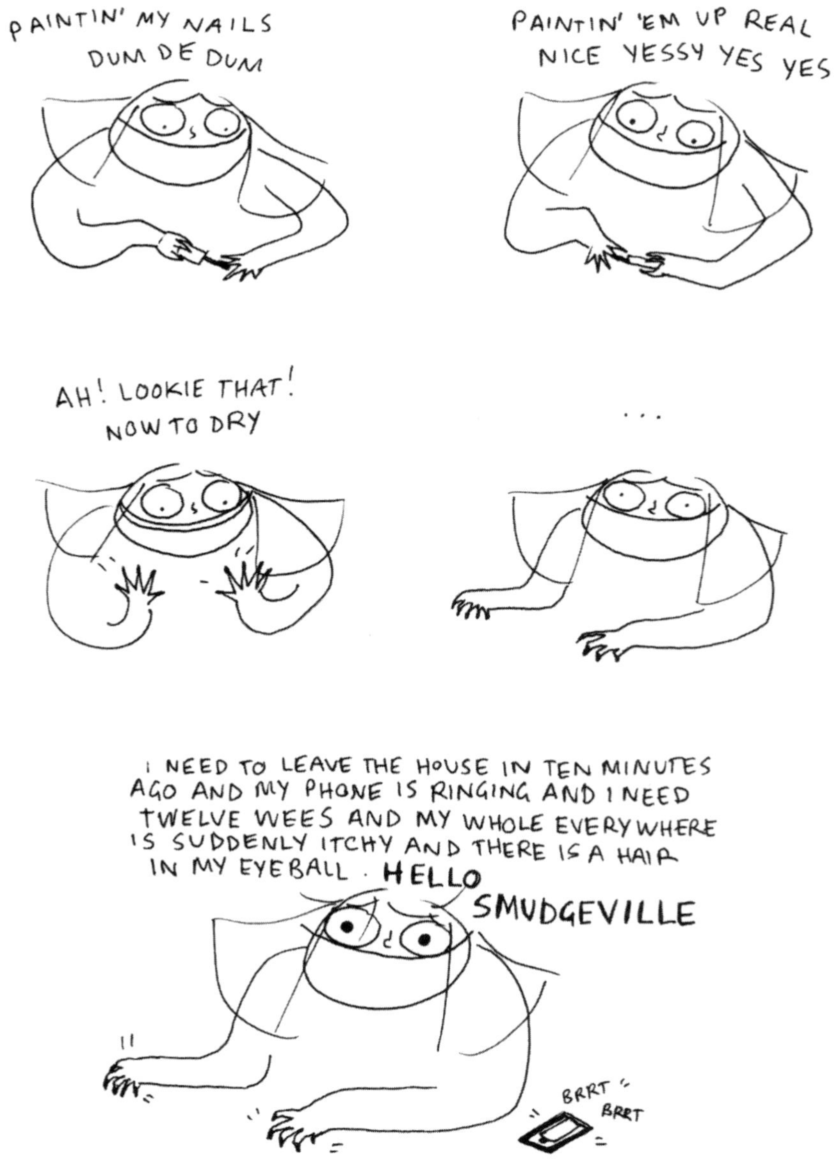
PAINTIN' MY NAILS
DUM DE DUM
PAINTIN' 'EM UP REAL NICE YESSY YES YES
AH! LOOKIE THAT! NOW TO DRY
...
I NEED TO LEAVE THE HOUSE IN TEN MINUTES AGO AND MY PHONE IS RINGING AND I NEED TWELVE WEES AND MY WHOLE EVERYWHERE IS SUDDENLY ITCHY AND THERE IS A HAIR IN MY EYEBALL. HELLO SMUDGEVILLE
BRRT
BRRT

REGGULAR

ELEGGANT

MY FAVORITE IS WHEN IT GETS
COLD ENOUGH TO WEAR MY
BIG COAT. THE POCKETS ARE
ROOMY ENOUGH FOR PENS AND
CHIPS AND A LARGE ROCK
PROBABLY, IF I WANTED. NO ONE
KNOWS WHAT I LOOK LIKE
UNDER HERE, I AM THE GIANT
INTIMIDATING SACK OF DARKNESS
I'VE ALWAYS DREAMED OF BEING

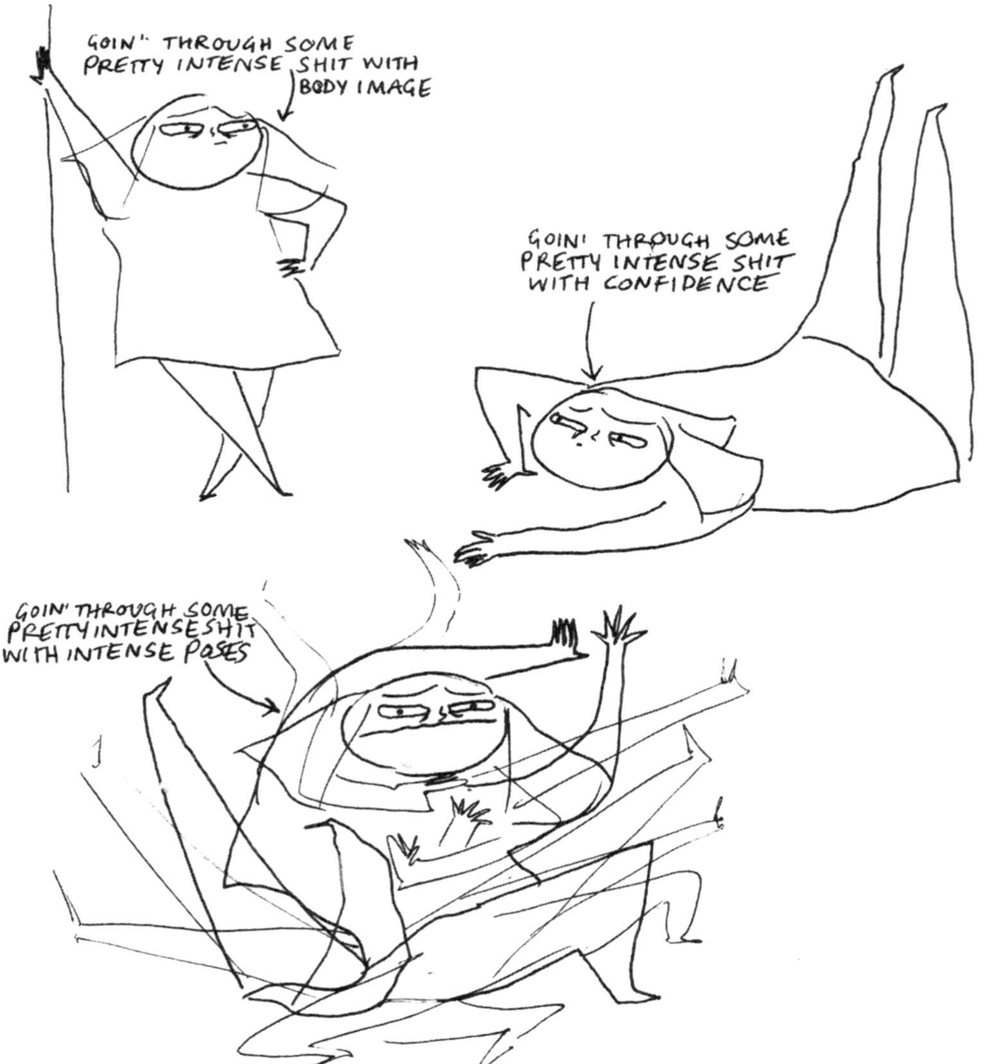
GOIN' THROUGH SOME PRETTY INTENSE SHIT WITH BODY IMAGE
GOIN' THROUGH SOME PRETTY INTENSE SHIT WITH CONFIDENCE
GOIN' THROUGH SOME PRETTY INTENSE SHIT WITH INTENSE POSES

BOOTS

GO AWAYS

PISS OFFS

FUCK THE
SHUT UPS

VERY FAR
AWAYS

INFINITIES

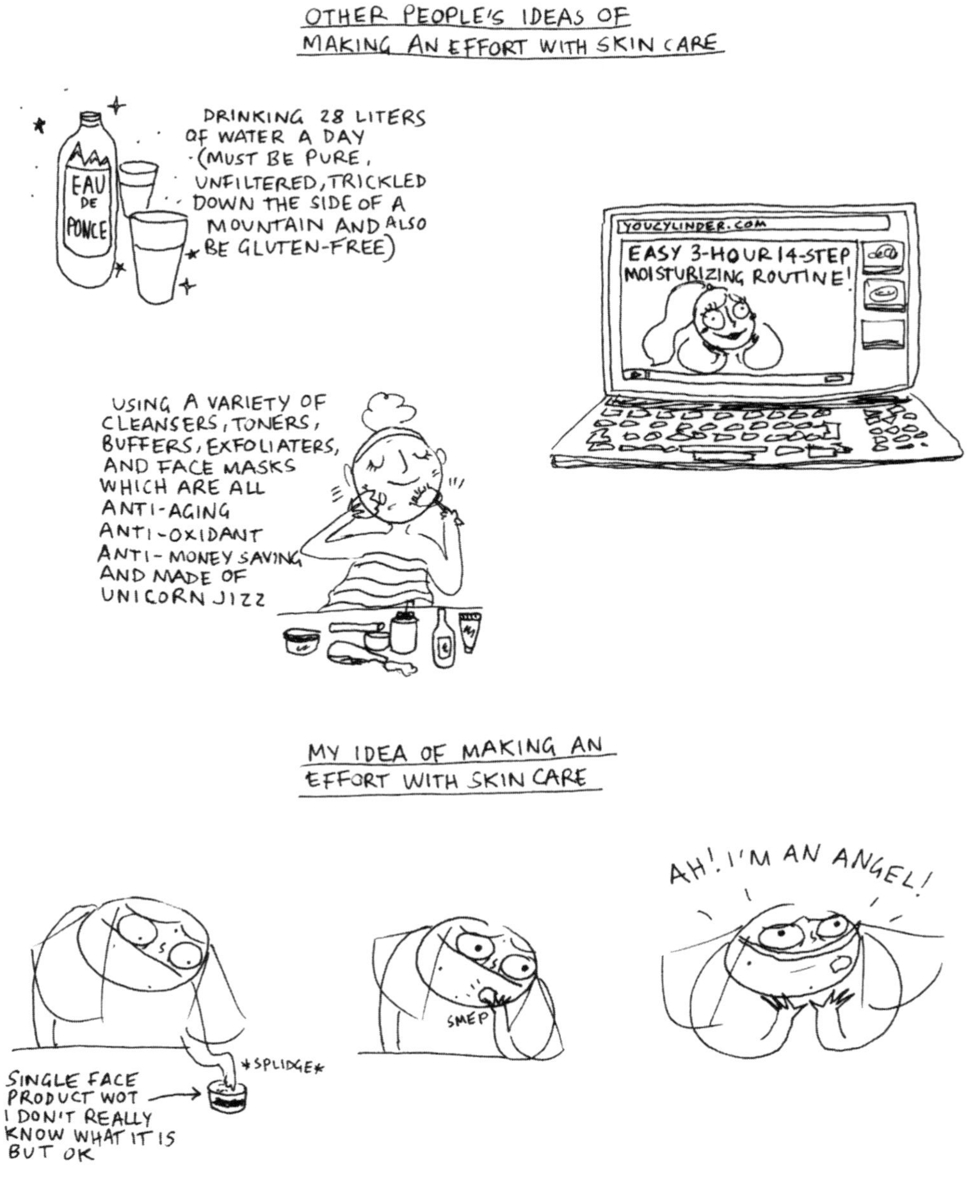
OTHER PEOPLE'S IDEAS OF MAKING AN EFFORT WITH SKIN CARE
EAU DE PONCE
DRINKING 28 LITERS OF WATER A DAY (MUST BE PURE, UNFILTERED, TRICKLED DOWN THE SIDE OF A MOUNTAIN AND ALSO BE GLUTEN-FREE)
YOUCYLINDER.COM
EASY 3-HOUR 14-STEP MOISTURIZING ROUTINE!
USING A VARIETY OF CLEANSERS, TONERS, BUFFERS, EXFOLIATERS, AND FACE MASKS WHICH ARE ALL ANTI-AGING ANTI-OXIDANT ANTI-MONEY SAVING AND MADE OF UNICORN JIZZ
MY IDEA OF MAKING AN EFFORT WITH SKIN CARE
SINGLE FACE PRODUCT WOT I DON'T REALLY KNOW WHAT IT IS BUT OK
SPLIDGE
SMEP
AH! I'M AN ANGEL!

BRA SHOPPING

AKA: THE ULTIMATE SOUL-CRUSHING ACTIVITY

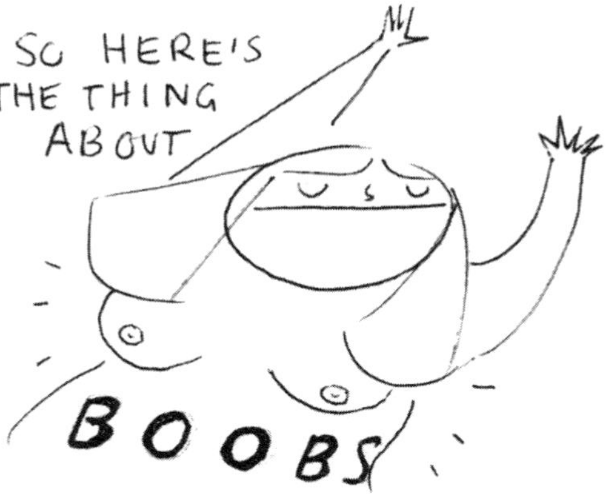
SO HERE'S THE THING ABOUT
BOOBS

THEY'RE FUCKING WEIRD

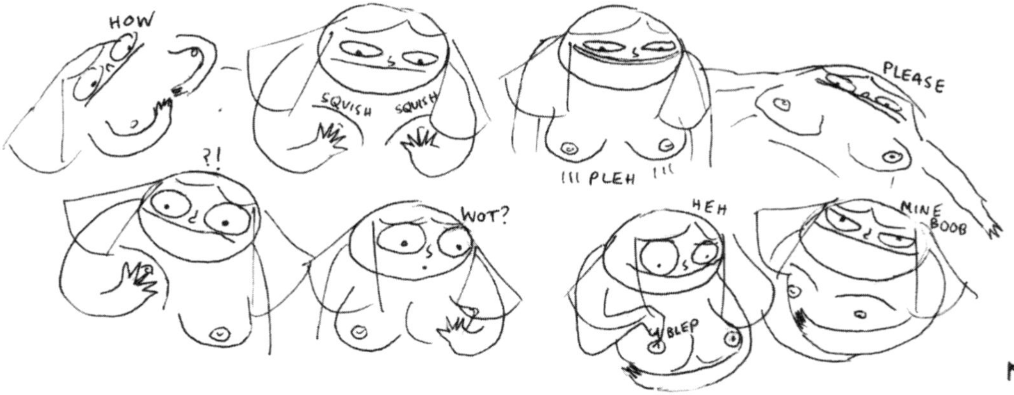
HOW
SQUISH
SQUISH
PLEASE
?!
!!! PLEH !!!
WOT?
HEH
MINE BOOB
BLEP

I MEAN THEY'RE GREAT, BUT SERIOUSLY, WHAT IS THIS ALL ABOUT

BOOBS JUST WANNA ROAM FREE

BUT FOR PRACTICAL REASONS
(IF I DONT WANT THEM TO FLY UP
AND SMACK ME IN THE FACE
ANY TIME I MOVE FASTER
THAN A CRAWL) I HAVE TO
CRAM MINE INTO AN OVER-
THE-SHOULDER BREAST PRISON

BREAST RECEPTACLES ARE SOLD IN A VARIETY
OF CRYPTIC SIZES ACCORDING TO AN ANCIENT
AND VIRTUALLY INDECIPHERABLE CODE OF
LETTERS AND NUMBERS. IT'S TIME TO START
RIFLING THROUGH HANGERS AND SWEARING
UNDER MY BREATH

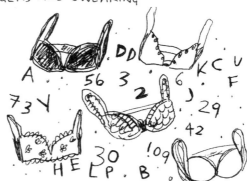

CLUTCHING A MOUND OF BRA, I WADDLE TOWARD
THE CHANGING ROOMS. FINDING THEM IS EASY;
I JUST MOVE IN THE DIRECTION OF THE SMELL
OF SWEAT AND ANGER AND THEN FOLLOW THE SIGHS

ONCE I'VE FOUGHT MY WAY INTO
MY OWN CURTAINED HELL-BOX,
THAT'S WHEN THE FUN STARTS...

360° MIRRORS SO I CAN FIND NEW ANGLES TO HATE MYSELF FROM THAT I NEVER EVEN KNEW EXISTED

HORRIBLE STRIP LIGHTING THAT ACCENTUATES EVERY LUMP, RIPPLE, SQUARE FOOT OF CELLULITE, SCAR, AND SPOT I POSSESS. MY BODY LOOKS LIKE SOME SORT OF LONG GEOGRAPHICAL RELIEF MAP COVERED IN HAIR

HOT, STUFFY, AND AN AIR OF DESPERATION. ANY MUSIC IS DROWNED OUT BY THE SOUND OF PEOPLE TRYING TO STUFF THEIR SWEATY BITS INTO SPANDEX

I AM VERY GENTLY BUT DECIDEDLY SCREAMING INSIDE

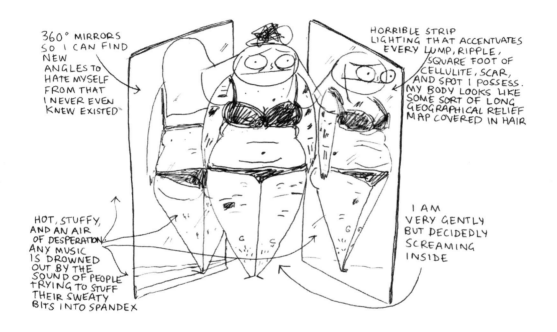

AND THIS IS ALL BEFORE I'VE EVEN TRIED THE BLOODY BRAS ON

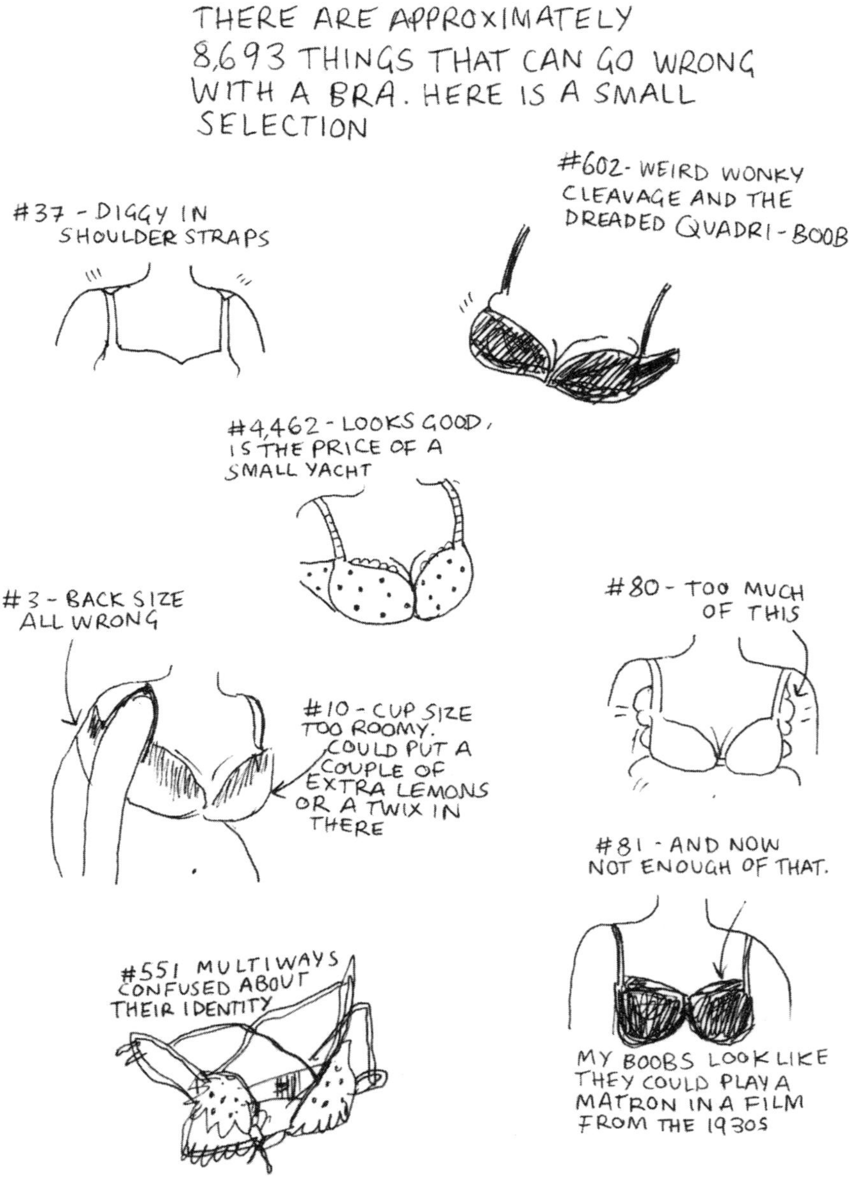

THERE ARE APPROXIMATELY
8,693 THINGS THAT CAN GO WRONG
WITH A BRA. HERE IS A SMALL
SELECTION

#602- WEIRD WONKY
CLEAVAGE AND THE
DREADED QUADRI-BOOB

#37 - DIGGY IN
SHOULDER STRAPS

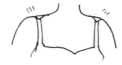

#4,462 - LOOKS GOOD,
IS THE PRICE OF A
SMALL YACHT

#3 - BACK SIZE
ALL WRONG

#80 - TOO MUCH
OF THIS

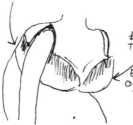

#10 - CUP SIZE
TOO ROOMY.
COULD PUT A
COUPLE OF
EXTRA LEMONS
OR A TWIX IN
THERE

#81 - AND NOW
NOT ENOUGH OF THAT.

#551 MULTIWAYS
CONFUSED ABOUT
THEIR IDENTITY

MY BOOBS LOOK LIKE
THEY COULD PLAY A
MATRON IN A FILM
FROM THE 1930s

AFTER 20 MINUTES OF HEAVING MYSELF
IN AND OUT OF THE BASTARDS I MUST SIT
DOWN ON THE FLOOR IN A DESPAIR
BALL AND HAVE HAVE A LITTLE CRY

SOUL CRUSHING IS COMPLETE!

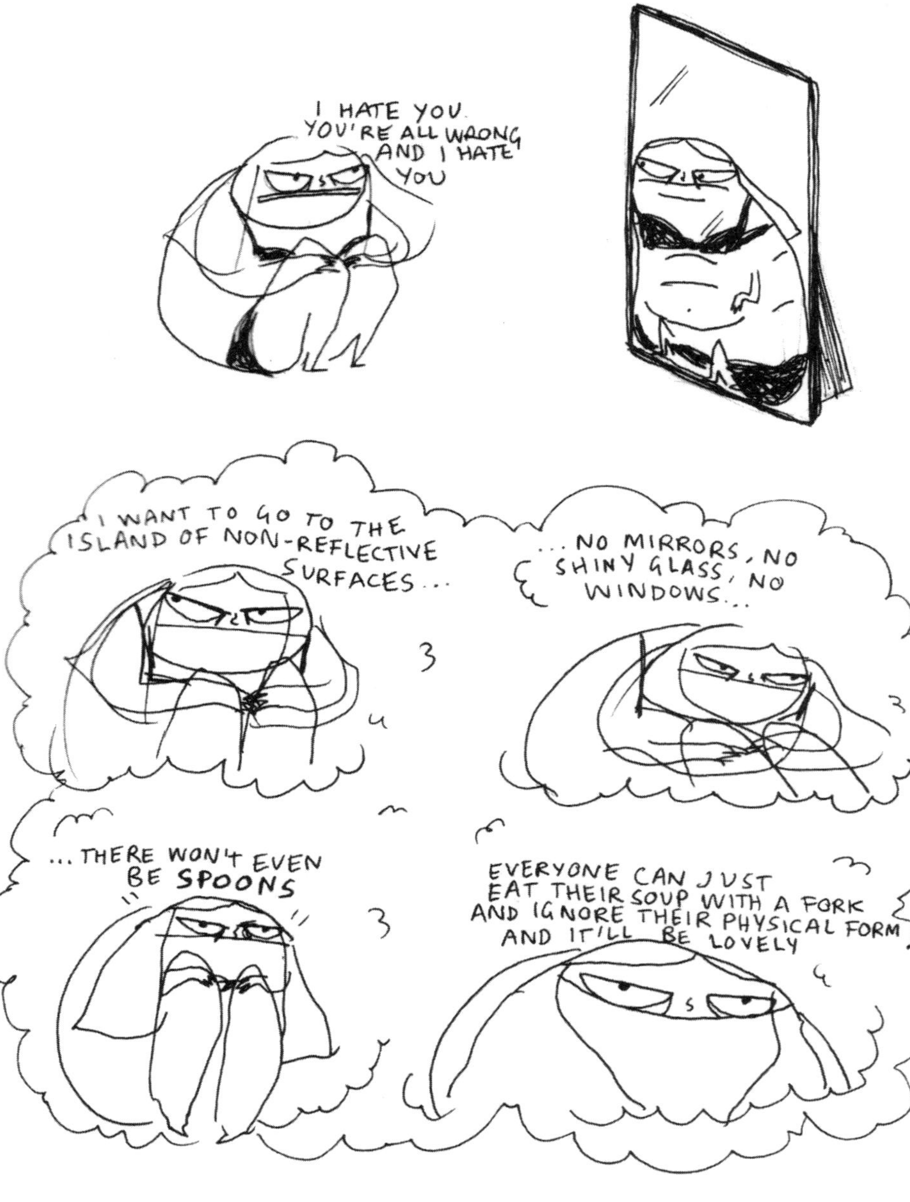
I HATE YOU. YOU'RE ALL WRONG AND I HATE YOU
I WANT TO GO TO THE ISLAND OF NON-REFLECTIVE SURFACES...
...NO MIRRORS, NO SHINY GLASS, NO WINDOWS...
...THERE WON'T EVEN BE SPOONS
EVERYONE CAN JUST EAT THEIR SOUP WITH A FORK AND IGNORE THEIR PHYSICAL FORM AND IT'LL BE LOVELY

I 'm stuck in a loveless affair with hating the way I look. My body should just be the place I live and walk around in and occasionally give things to like water and jam and antidepressants, but instead it's been transformed over the years into this huge, pervasive source of insecurity and fear. Don't get me wrong—I love spending hours at a time in front of the mirror making a comprehensive and damning mental list of everything that is wrong with my appearance, and having to try on no fewer than eight different outfits before I find the one that makes me look the least like a potato; it's a delightful use of my time.

But even without chronically dysmorphic views and the domino effect an eating disorder has had on my self-image, it's pretty bloody hard to work out HOW we are meant to feel about ourselves. Of course no gender is exempt from the torrent of unhealthy and damaging ideals hurled at us left, right, and center by the diet and beauty industries; they're very inclusive in their nastiness like that, but my experience of all this as a woman goes something like this: On the one hand we are insidiously and persistently shamed for being too fat and the wrong shape; two things which have been (wrongly) equated by society with laziness and unworthiness. Sadly I think I knew what a muffin top was before I knew what the term misogyny meant, so that says it all really. And then on the other hand we have these slightly newer ideals of loving yourself and feeling comfortable with how you look, and that the only right way to exist is by having a spectacularly harmonious and healthy relationship with one's body. We are simultaneously told to diet and indulge. We can't be fat but we can be "curvy" or "voluptuous" (shudder) IF, that is, we still fall within the bounds of what is deemed "beautiful." You can feel good about the way you look, but not before posting an Instagram photo of

TRYING TO FIND THE CORRECT BLACK CLOTHE
WHEN EVERY SINGLE CLOTHE I OWN IS ONE COLOR

yourself sprinkling healthful protein dust onto a snot green smoothie with the caption, "Just about to go for a seventeen-mile yoga jog!" Navigating how to feel about my body feels akin to walking on a very narrow tightrope in high wind with fifty-foot drops on either side. It's impossible to get right.

People derive their sense of self-worth from all sorts of places—that thing you did and that experience you had and that friend who tells you you're not terrible. What happened to me from quite a young age, and certainly as I got older is that my brain decided to use my body as the focal point from which all my value as a person had to be measured. Everything became very black and white, very polarized. When I perceived myself as looking "okay" (I could show you the imaginary 100-page document stipulating exactly what I meant by "okay" but it wouldn't be very interesting) then I was a good person. I could permit myself a shred of confidence, at least enough to get dressed and go outside to exist around other humans. I had control. However, when I looked at myself and saw something "incorrect" and not okay about my appearance, then I was a bad person. And bad person is a very understated way of saying "A TERRIBLE BASTARD TRAINWRECK OF A PERSON. NOT EVEN 'A' TERRIBLE. THE **MOST** TERRIBLE. EVER. OF ALL TIME." I wouldn't be able to get up. Plans would be canceled. I'd feel out of control. It wasn't just that I felt bad; I became the bad.

Having every single decision I made or action I took dependent on how I perceived myself on that particular day (which, by the way, was entirely unpredictable) was exhausting and pretty miserable. Extricating my sense of self-worth from my physical appearance is a long-term project. Here are some things I've concluded about it though.

People don't give a crap what I look like; they've got their own stuff going on—No one is as hyper-aware and critical of my body as I am. That person on the bus is probably thinking about whether it'd look too keen to text someone back yet, or how they are going to get a lecture when they show up to the meeting they're late for covered in toast crumbs. They might have had "Orinoco Flow" by Enya stuck in their head since they woke up, or they might even be preoccupied with their own corporeal insecurities. I wouldn't know. But I do know that unless I rip all my clothes off and start running up and down the bus, people probably aren't going to register me for more than a few seconds. And they certainly won't be grossed out by the size of my thighs or shape of my face. That wouldn't make sense. I try to remember this when I'm getting the ol' paranoia brain.

I will see a lot more if I look a lot less—Being obsessed over my body and dedicating inordinate amounts of time and mental energy trying to make sure I look "okay," sometimes through very unhealthy means, made my world very small. And very sad. There came a point when I became so fed up with chasing an ideal I could never really attain that I had to force myself away from the mirror and away from all the body checking and Go And Look At Something Else, something other than me, just for a bit. Of course this way of thinking is not a switch I can suddenly flick. I'll still cancel plans from time to time when I can't stand my face, and sit on the floor of changing rooms crying because jeans are the devil's business, but what's different is that I get on with the rest now. The more stuff I'm able to do independent of the insecurities, the more confident I become that my experience of life does not have to be contingent on my body; it's a positive feedback loop of sorts.

So body, here's the thing: I don't really love you, but I'm going to let you be.

WHEN YOUR BODY CHANGES
(BECAUSE BODIES CHANGE)

DON'T KEEP OLD CLOTHES THAT DON'T FIT

TO USE AS OBJECTS TO MAKE YOURSELF FEEL BAD

YOU REALLY DON'T NEED TO STAND IN FRONT OF A MIRROR NAKED

YOU ARE FLUID, YOU ARE BENDY, YOU ARE YOURS!

LOOK AT MY FUCKING BAG. IT'S A **STATEMENT PIECE**. NOT SURE WHAT THAT MEANS BUT LOOK AT IT

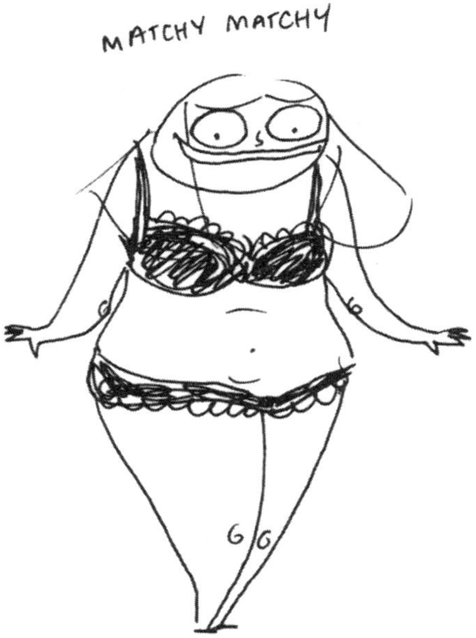
MATCHY MATCHY

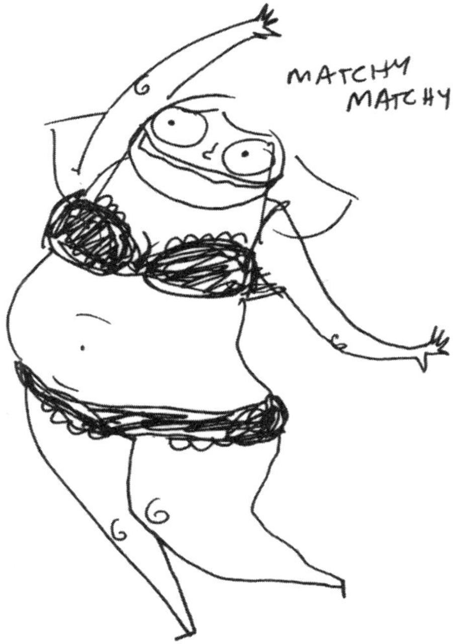
MATCHY
MATCHY

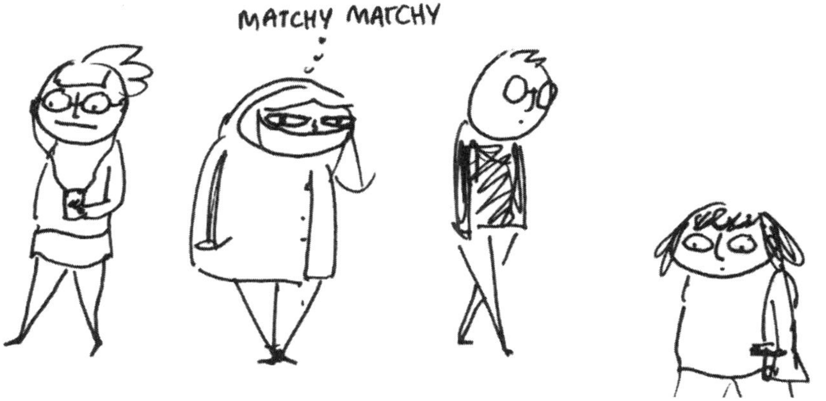
MATCHY MATCHY

I LIKE HAVING HAIRY LEGS

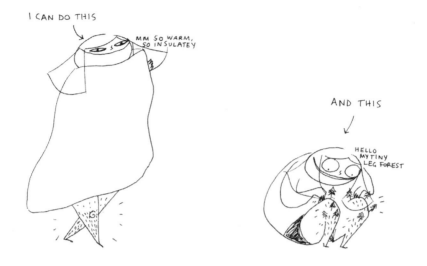

I CAN DO THIS

MM SO WARM,
SO INSULATEY

AND THIS

HELLO
MY TINY
LEG FOREST

AND NOT BECAUSE I FEEL IT'S NECESSARY TO GO SHEARING,
YANKING, AND DISSOLVING MY HAIR AWAY. IT'S NOT.
BUT SOMETIMES I DO LIKE HAVING THE LEGS OF SMOOTHNESS,
YOU KNOW SO I CAN BE ALL STREAMLINED

LIKE THIS

SWOOSH

AND CAN ALSO USE MY CALF AS A RAMP FOR HOT WHEELS

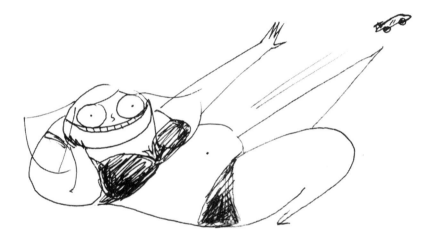

WHY ARE YOU TAKING SELFIES? THAT'S A BIT ATTENTION SEEK
HEY, WANNA PLAY FETCH?
CUZ I THINK
THERE'S A STICK
UP YOUR ASS

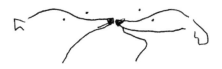

HERE I AM DOING THE THING WITH MY SWEATER,
YOU KNOW, THE THING YOUR MOTHER TOLD YOU
NOT TO DO WHEN YOU WERE A CHILDREN.
BUT NOW I AM A GROWN-UP AND SOLELY
RESPONSIBLE FOR THE SWEATERS I CAN DO IT
ALL I LIKE.

MMM,
STRETCHY
STRETCHY

I'M AN ADULT

I'M A GROAN-UP

I CAN DO IT I CAN DO IT
BANG
BANG
ICANDOITICANDOIT ICANDOITICANDOIT
BANG BANG
BANG BANG
I CANDO IT I CAN DO IT I CAN I CAN
BANG BANG BANG
BANG BANG
FUCK FUCK FUCK FUCK FUCK
BANG BANG BANG

Everyone procrastinates; it's impossible not to. These days there's the endless snappagram twitblr facespleh scrollathons that must take place every eleven minutes or less (I sound old, I'm not old, I'm totally down with the kids). But it's got to be something that's always happened since the beginning of time. All those fossils they've discovered of whateversauruses in rocks, it's not a coincidence that they're lying there with mouths wide open and limbs splayed out all panicky. I'm certain it's cuz just before the meteorite hit they'd opened an envelope with their little dinosaur paws and seen it was a telephone bill so now they were lying face down on the Jurassic ground screeching "I CAAAAAAN'T DOOOOO IIIIIIT . . . fuck it I'll just keep organizing my rocks and scrolling through leaves."

With me, avoidance of the task is more often than not associated with anxiety. Not always—sometimes I am just a bit tired or fed up (which, by the way, is allowed). But there's procrastination and then there's a fear of fucking up so monumental that it prevents me from getting anything done in the first place. And I'm not talking about particularly challenging things—basic forms, work-related emails, simple phone calls. My brain knows that objectively these tasks aren't huge, and won't even take that long, but whenever I'm presented with them my brain also decides it would be a fun idea to convert them into these great big monster worries, eighteen feet wide and twice as tall with jabby elbows and teeth as big as really big teeth. And so I do the only logical thing, which is lie face down on my bedroom floor screeching "I CAAAAAN'T DOOOOO IIIIIIT . . . fuck it better fire up the scrollin' thumbs it's time to enter the void."

It's not even yer standard single-layer anxiety, oh no, the effect of not being able to do anything results in another layer of fear centered around

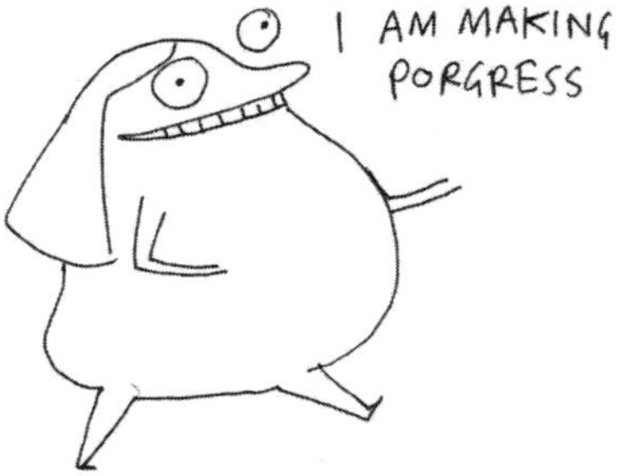
I AM MAKING PORGRESS

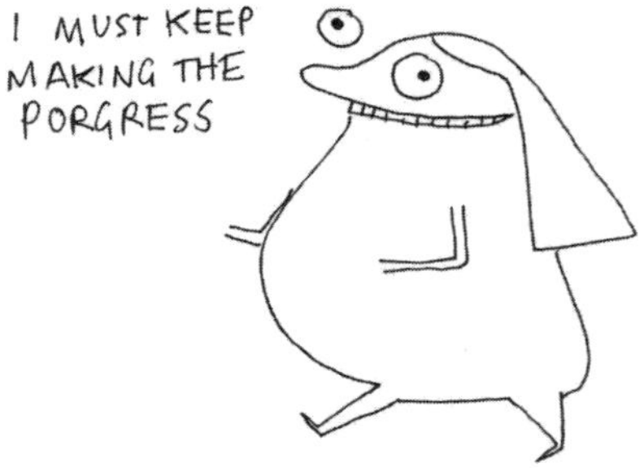
I MUST KEEP MAKING THE PORGRESS

the thought, "brilliant, first I can't do the thing, now everyone KNOWS I haven't done the thing and will think me a lazy useless bastard," which consequently leads to layer the third, perhaps the thickest and sludgiest of layers, which says "Well maybe I AM a lazy useless bastard. EVERYONE ELSE is breezing through life and here I am, unable to do this tiny thing. Time to go and live in a cave." This layer of reproachfulness and self-loathing is really what cements the underlying anxiety in place and makes it almost impossible for me to complete the original task.

I forget that I'm a capable human who just happens to have a very thinky brain, and see myself instead as this awful, ineffectual lump of idiot. It's a very horrible and isolating place to find myself. And like all these things, it's an uphill battle developing insight into what's going on and then trusting that insight enough to harness it positively.

Good news is that I'm making the porgress. I can do it now, I can on occasion tell the very harsh and punitive voice that really it needs to fuck off so I can work through the anxiety (or try to), but it's taken a long time to believe and reinforce the idea that my procrastination and avoidance is not often borne out of laziness or being a useless bastard; it's the result of overwhelming fear and very low self-esteem. And those things can't be ignored or denied; they exist and need to be given space before you can learn to override them. And once those layers start being separated and rationalized, it becomes a lot easier for me to maybe put my phone down, close the five wikipedia tabs about the history of zinc I have open on my laptop, and just Get The Stuff Done.

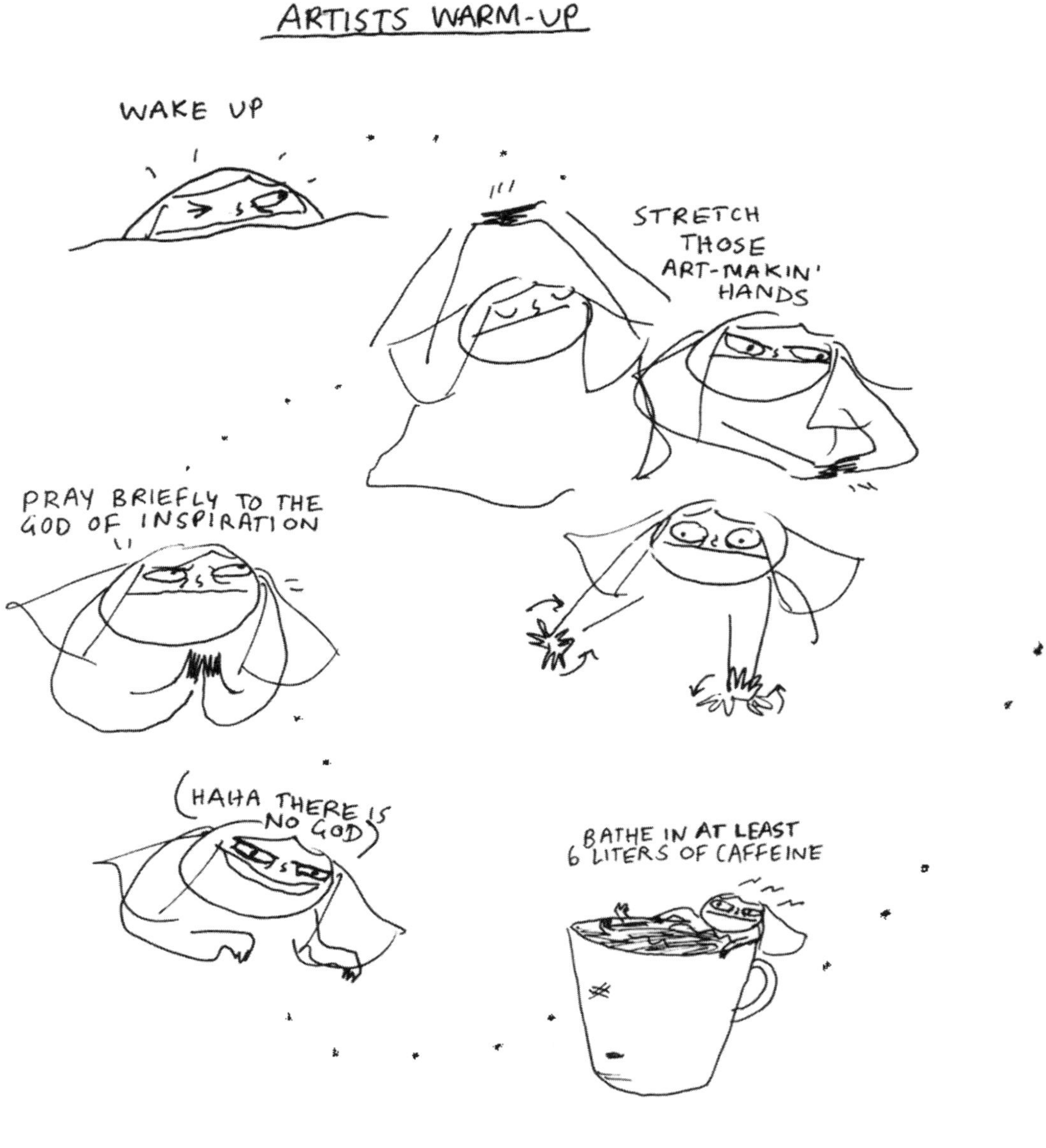
ARTISTS WARM-UP
WAKE UP
STRETCH THOSE ART-MAKIN' HANDS
PRAY BRIEFLY TO THE GOD OF INSPIRATION
(HAHA THERE IS NO GOD)
BATHE IN AT LEAST 6 LITERS OF CAFFEINE

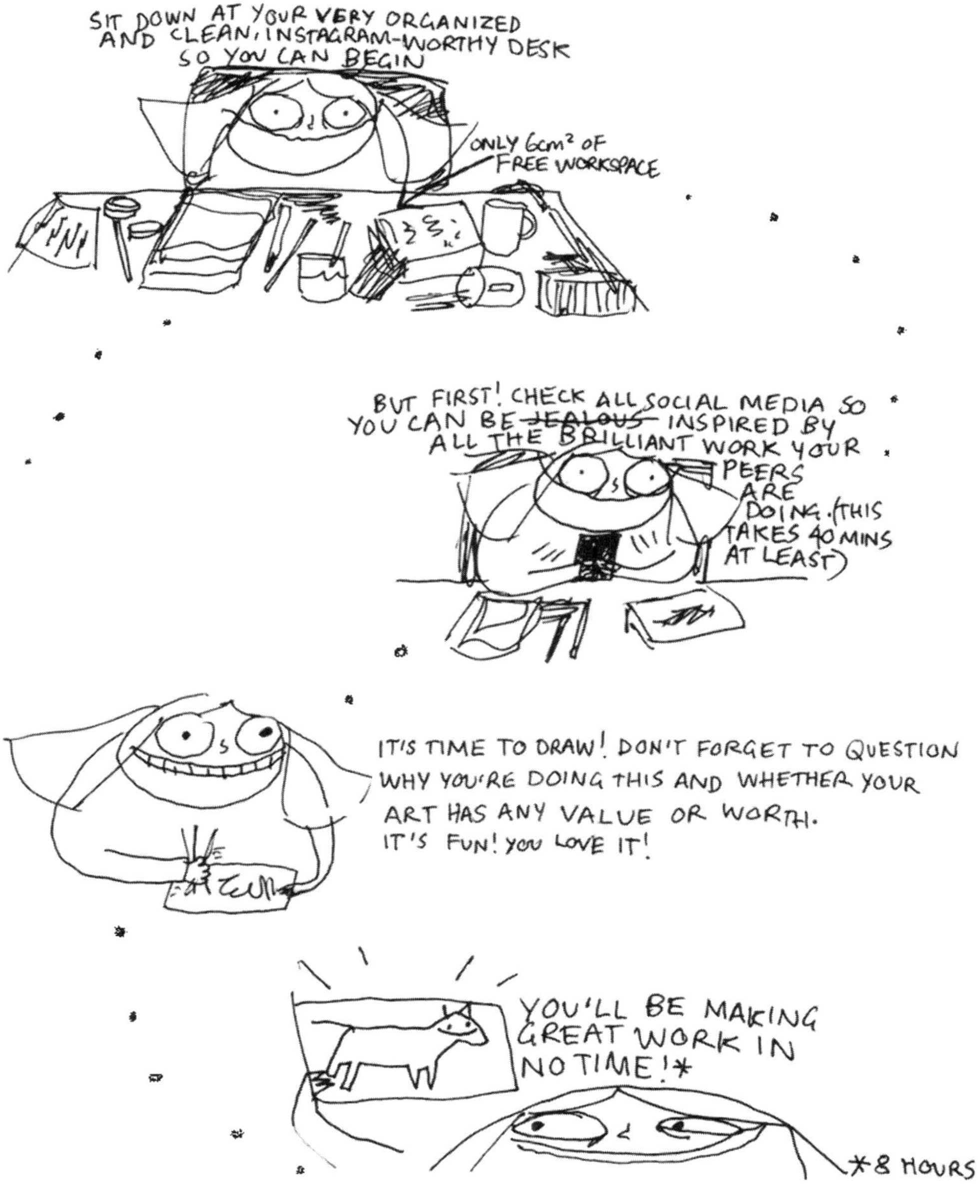
SIT DOWN AT YOUR VERY ORGANIZED AND CLEAN, INSTAGRAM-WORTHY DESK SO YOU CAN BEGIN
ONLY 6cm² OF FREE WORKSPACE
BUT FIRST! CHECK ALL SOCIAL MEDIA SO YOU CAN BE ~~JEALOUS~~ INSPIRED BY ALL THE BRILLIANT WORK YOUR PEERS ARE DOING. (THIS TAKES 40 MINS AT LEAST)
IT'S TIME TO DRAW! DON'T FORGET TO QUESTION WHY YOU'RE DOING THIS AND WHETHER YOUR ART HAS ANY VALUE OR WORTH.
IT'S FUN! YOU LOVE IT!
YOU'LL BE MAKING GREAT WORK IN NO TIME!*
*8 HOURS

THE TIDAL WAVE OF COFFEE, UNANSWERED EMAILS

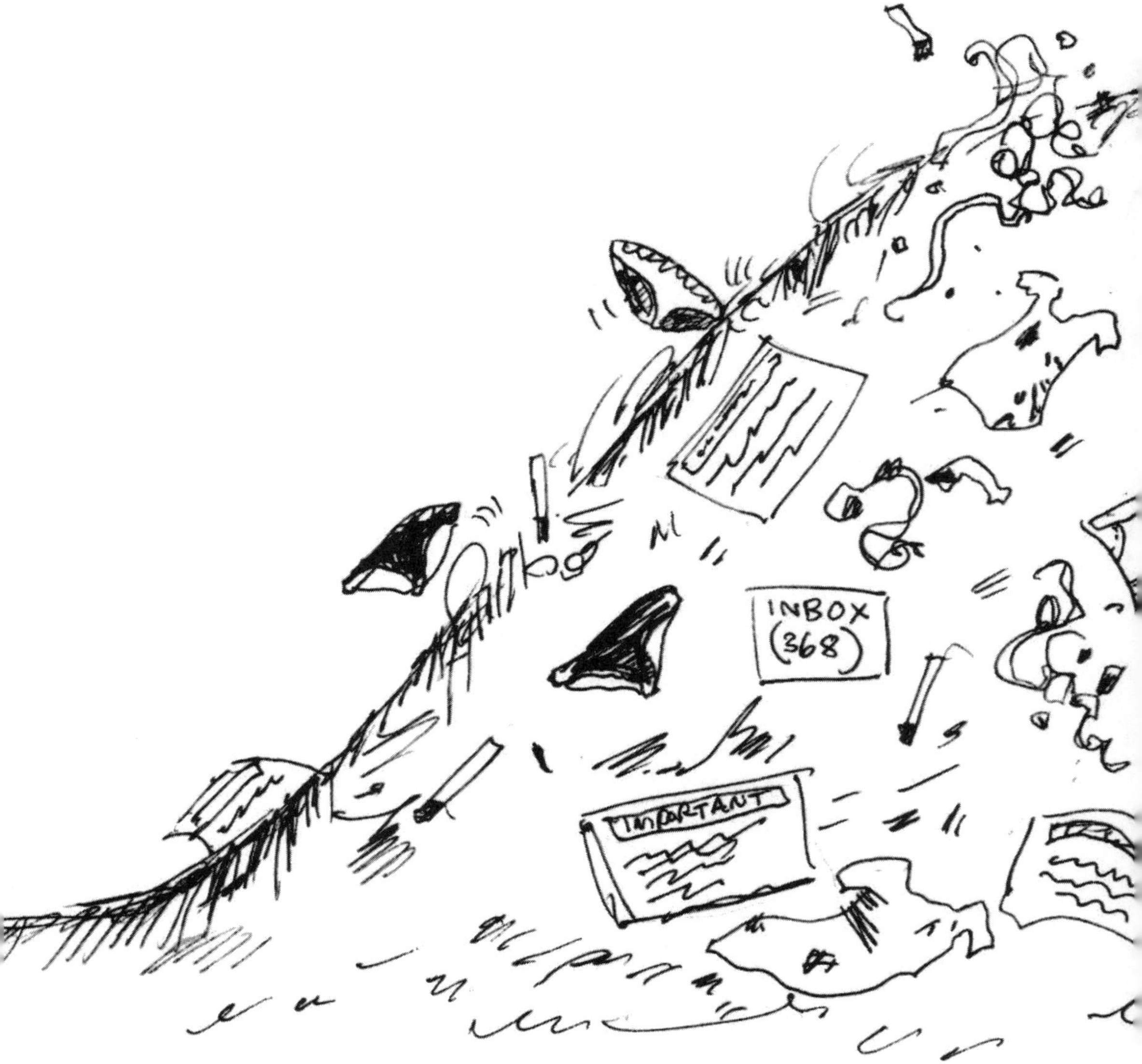
INBOX (368)
IMPORTANT

RTY LAUNDRY, CIGARETTES, AND RAMEN

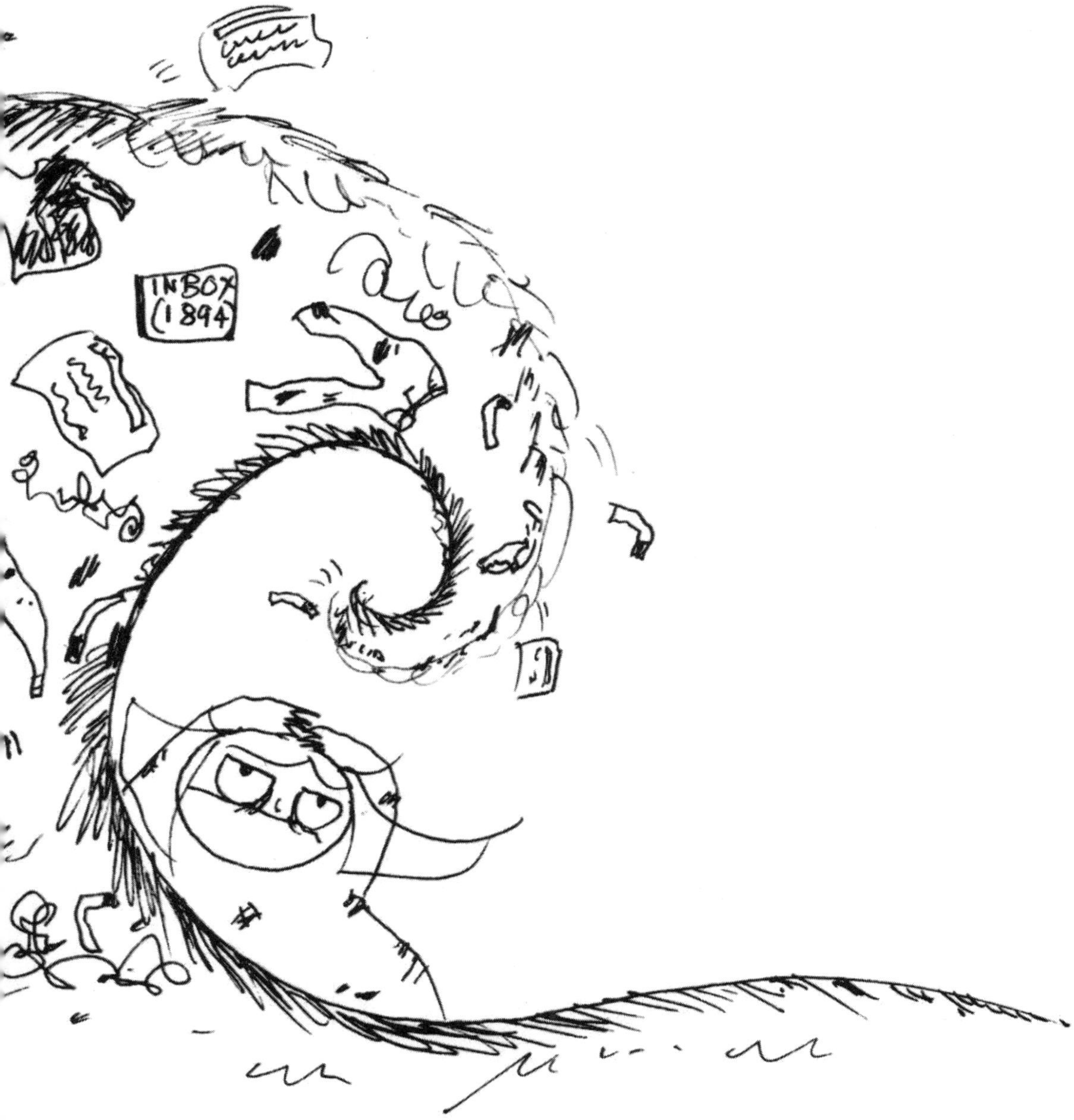
INBOX (1894)

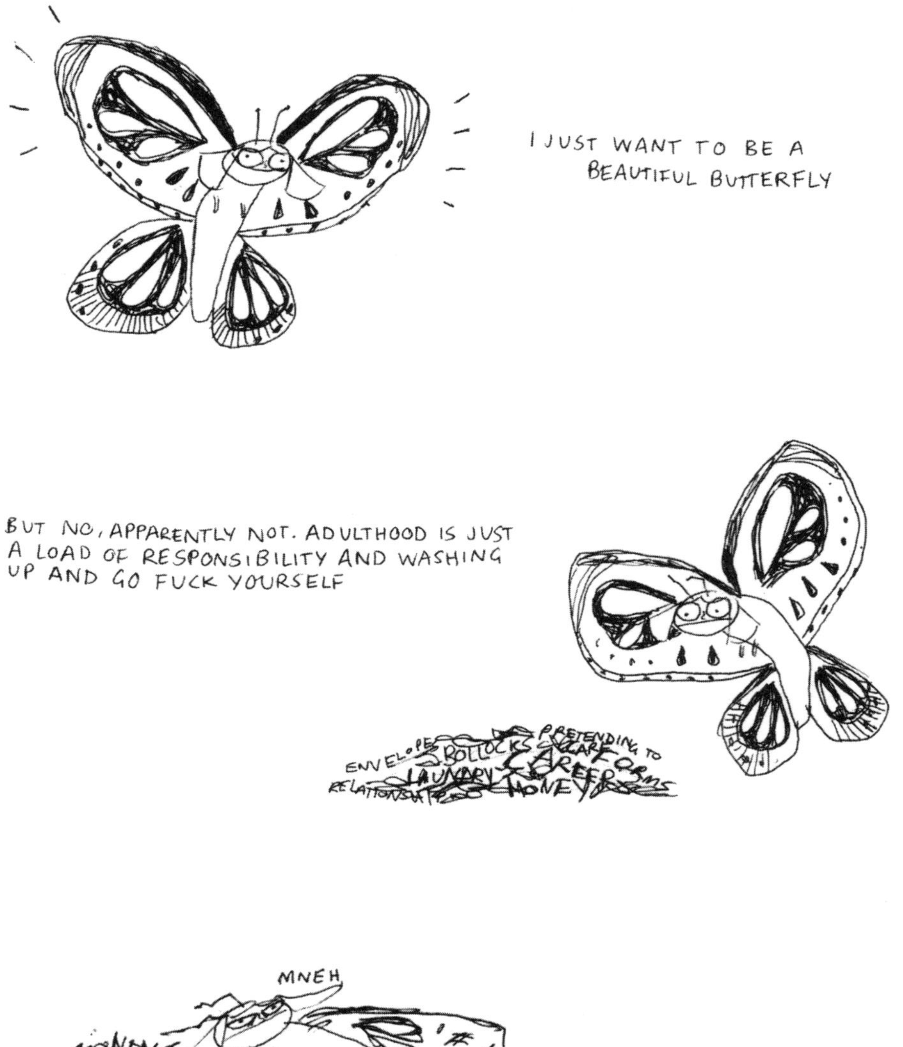
I JUST WANT TO BE A BEAUTIFUL BUTTERFLY
BUT NO, APPARENTLY NOT. ADULTHOOD IS JUST A LOAD OF RESPONSIBILITY AND WASHING UP AND GO FUCK YOURSELF
ENVELOPE
BOLLOCKS
PRETENDING TO
CAREER
FORMS
LAUNDRY
MONEY
MNEH
BOLLOCKS
HANGOVER

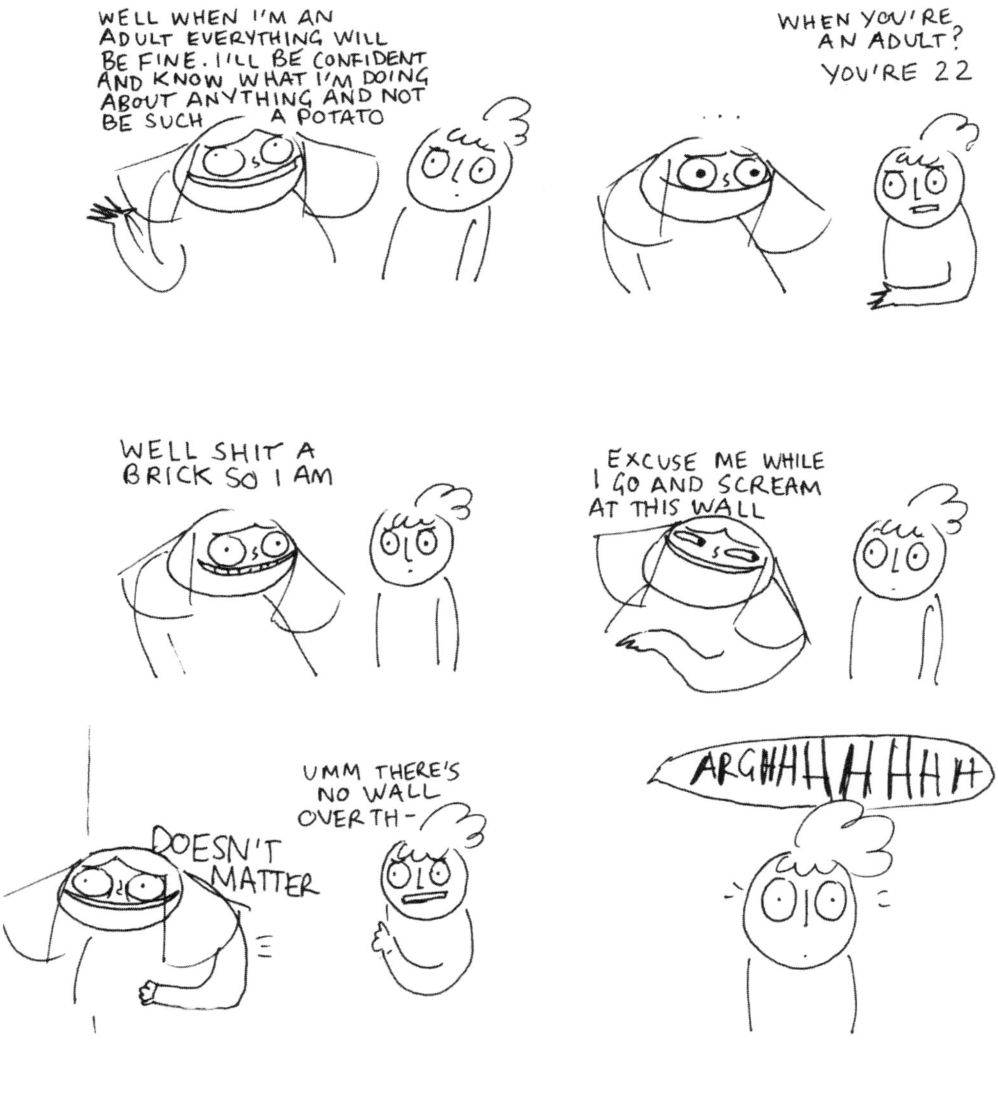
WELL WHEN I'M AN ADULT EVERYTHING WILL BE FINE. I'LL BE CONFIDENT AND KNOW WHAT I'M DOING ABOUT ANYTHING AND NOT BE SUCH A POTATO
WHEN YOU'RE AN ADULT? YOU'RE 22
...
WELL SHIT A BRICK SO I AM
EXCUSE ME WHILE I GO AND SCREAM AT THIS WALL
UMM THERE'S NO WALL OVER TH-
DOESN'T MATTER
ARGHHHHHHHH

SO DO YOU
WORK OUT?

YESSSSS

SO FAR I'VE
WORKED OUT BREATHING,

HOW TO EAT AN
OFFENSIVE AMOUNT
OF CHEESE,

AND THIS...

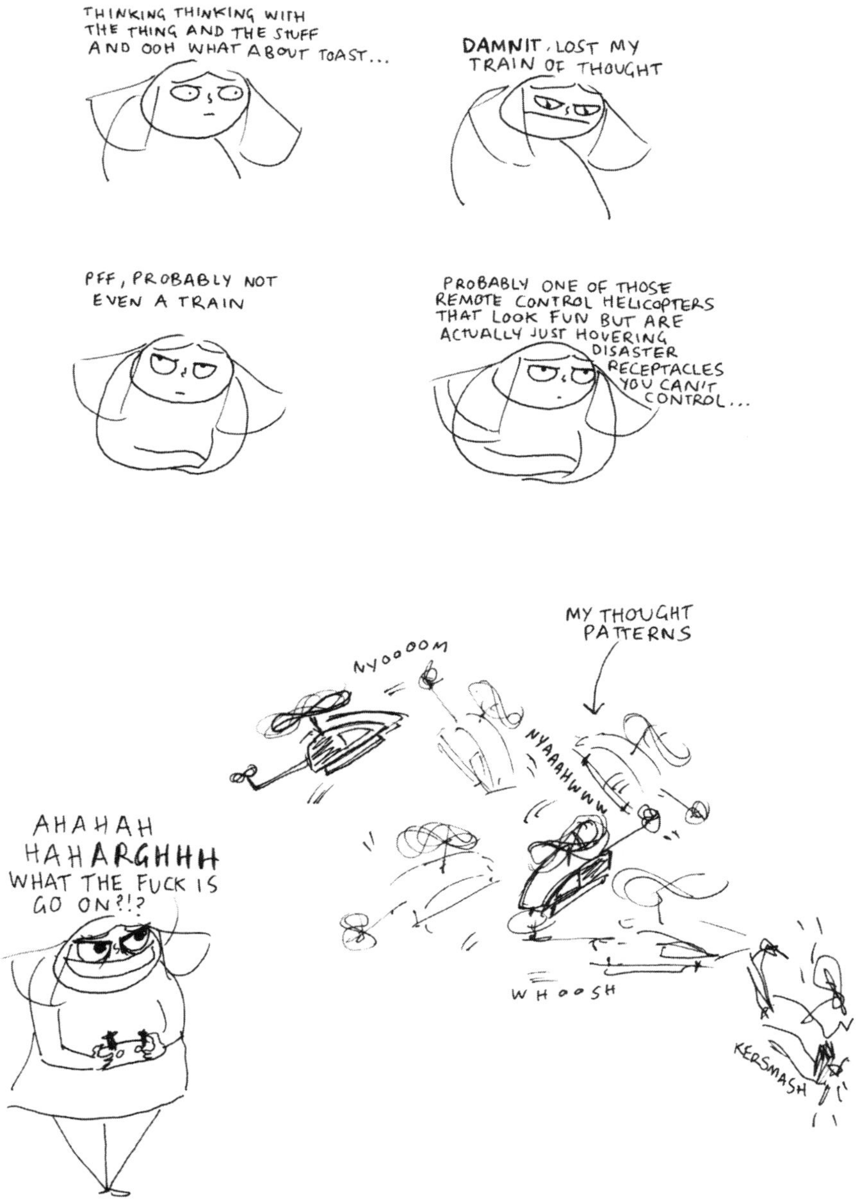
THINKING THINKING WITH THE THING AND THE STUFF AND OOH WHAT ABOUT TOAST...
DAMNIT, LOST MY TRAIN OF THOUGHT
PFF, PROBABLY NOT EVEN A TRAIN
PROBABLY ONE OF THOSE REMOTE CONTROL HELICOPTERS THAT LOOK FUN BUT ARE ACTUALLY JUST HOVERING DISASTER RECEPTACLES YOU CAN'T CONTROL...
MY THOUGHT PATTERNS
NYOOOOM
NYAAAHWWW
WHOOSH
KERSMASH
AHAHAH HAHARGHHH WHAT THE FUCK IS GO ON?!?

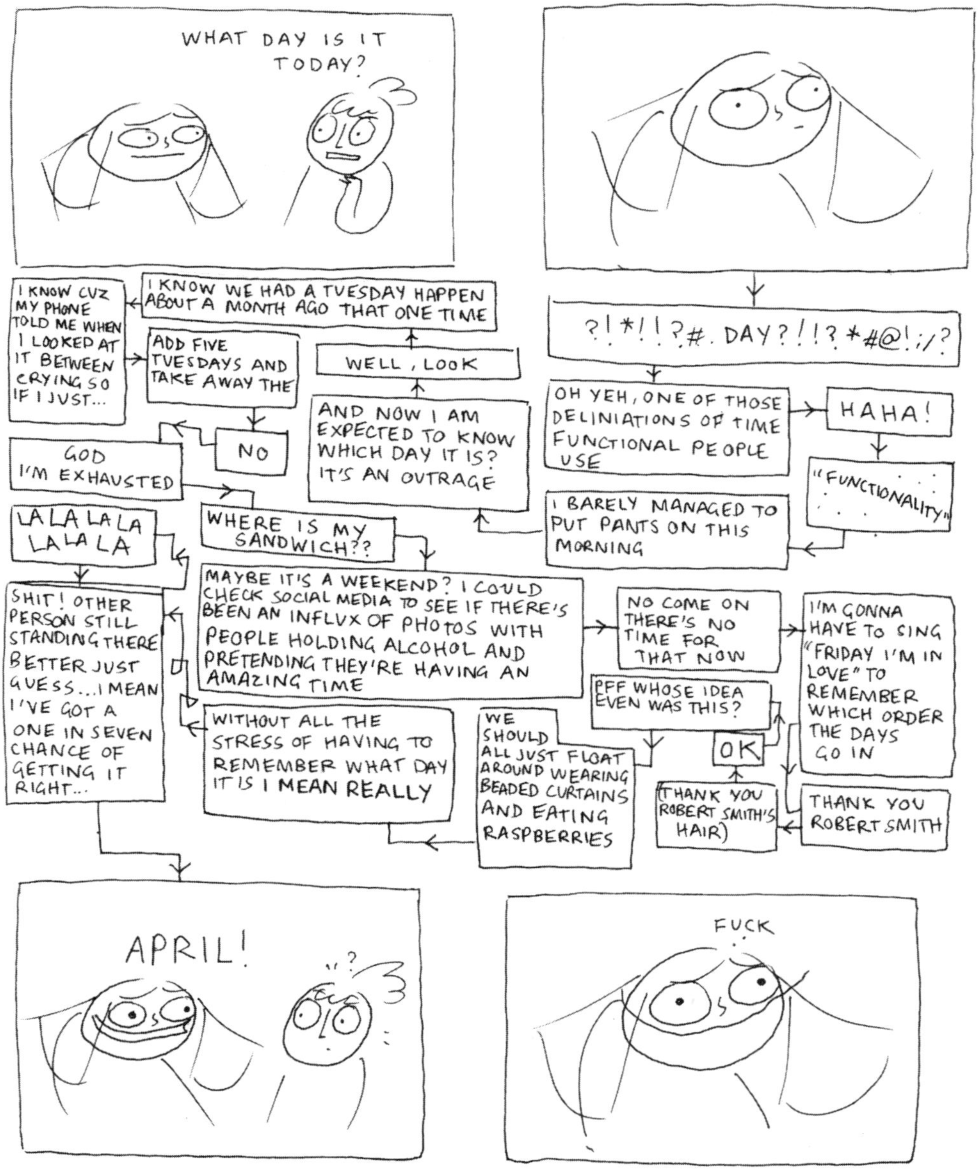
WHAT DAY IS IT TODAY?
?!*!!?#. DAY?!!?*#@!;/?
OH YEH, ONE OF THOSE DELINIATIONS OF TIME FUNCTIONAL PEOPLE USE
HAHA!
"FUNCTIONALITY"
I BARELY MANAGED TO PUT PANTS ON THIS MORNING
AND NOW I AM EXPECTED TO KNOW WHICH DAY IT IS? IT'S AN OUTRAGE
WELL, LOOK
I KNOW WE HAD A TUESDAY HAPPEN ABOUT A MONTH AGO THAT ONE TIME
I KNOW CUZ MY PHONE TOLD ME WHEN I LOOKED AT IT BETWEEN CRYING SO IF I JUST...
ADD FIVE TUESDAYS AND TAKE AWAY THE
NO
GOD I'M EXHAUSTED
WHERE IS MY SANDWICH??
MAYBE IT'S A WEEKEND? I COULD CHECK SOCIAL MEDIA TO SEE IF THERE'S BEEN AN INFLUX OF PHOTOS WITH PEOPLE HOLDING ALCOHOL AND PRETENDING THEY'RE HAVING AN AMAZING TIME
NO COME ON THERE'S NO TIME FOR THAT NOW
I'M GONNA HAVE TO SING "FRIDAY I'M IN LOVE" TO REMEMBER WHICH ORDER THE DAYS GO IN
THANK YOU ROBERT SMITH
(THANK YOU ROBERT SMITH'S HAIR)
OK
PFF WHOSE IDEA EVEN WAS THIS?
WE SHOULD ALL JUST FLOAT AROUND WEARING BEADED CURTAINS AND EATING RASPBERRIES
WITHOUT ALL THE STRESS OF HAVING TO REMEMBER WHAT DAY IT IS I MEAN REALLY
LA LA LA LA LA LA LA
SHIT! OTHER PERSON STILL STANDING THERE BETTER JUST GUESS... I MEAN I'VE GOT A ONE IN SEVEN CHANCE OF GETTING IT RIGHT...
APRIL!
?
FUCK

NAPS ARE EITHER PERFECT...

COMFIEST, COZIEST, WARMEST LITTLE DOZEY BUN

I LOOK ADORABLE

WAKING UP FEELING CALM AND REFRESHED

I AM THE ANGEL OF SNOOZE

.,, OR AN UNPRECEDENTED DIABOLICAL DISASTER

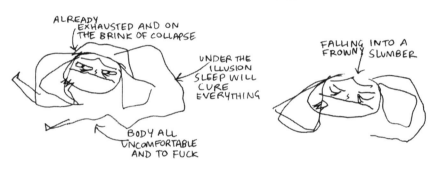

ALREADY EXHAUSTED AND ON THE BRINK OF COLLAPSE

UNDER THE ILLUSION SLEEP WILL CURE EVERYTHING

BODY ALL UNCOMFORTABLE AND TO FUCK

FALLING INTO A FROWNY SLUMBER

CRAZY HAIR

WAKING UP 3 HOURS LATER NOT KNOWING WHERE OR WHAT I AM AND I'M LATE FOR THE THING AND MY NECK IS SORE AND MY LEG WON'T WAKE UP

WHAT IS **HAPPENING**

TOO HOT AND COLD AND TIRED AND HUNGRY BUT SICK ALL AT ONCE

THERE IS NO IN-BETWEEN

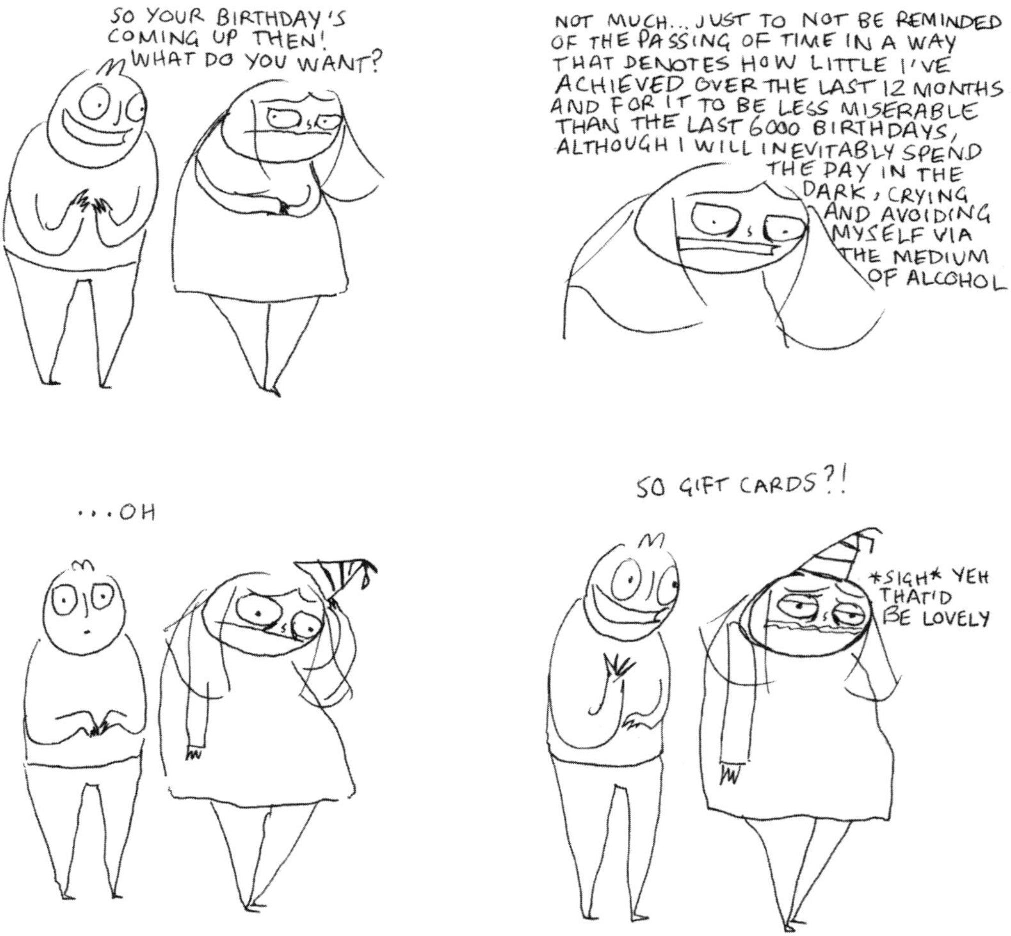
SO YOUR BIRTHDAY'S COMING UP THEN! WHAT DO YOU WANT?
NOT MUCH... JUST TO NOT BE REMINDED OF THE PASSING OF TIME IN A WAY THAT DENOTES HOW LITTLE I'VE ACHIEVED OVER THE LAST 12 MONTHS AND FOR IT TO BE LESS MISERABLE THAN THE LAST 6000 BIRTHDAYS, ALTHOUGH I WILL INEVITABLY SPEND THE DAY IN THE DARK, CRYING AND AVOIDING MYSELF VIA THE MEDIUM OF ALCOHOL
...OH
SO GIFT CARDS?!
SIGH YEH THAT'D BE LOVELY

INSTANT COFFEE

YESSS COME TO MAMA

SWIPE

DELAYED COFFEE

PLEASE... SO... TIRED...

JUST... BE CLOSER... PLEASE

PLEH

WOW

"WHAT'LL YOU HAVE?"

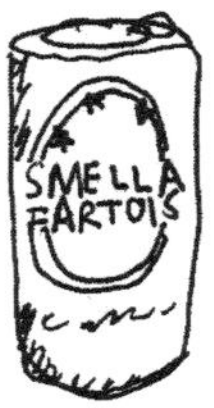
SMELLA FARTOIS

LOW-KEY
"NO REALLY
I'M FINE"
SAD

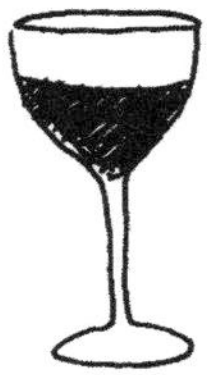

SAD AS A SAD
THING BUT GONNA
BE SOPHISTICATED
ABOUT IT

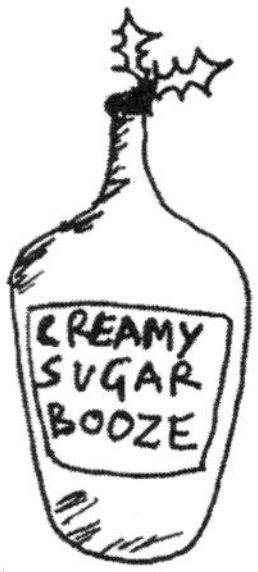
CREAMY
SUGAR
BOOZE

FUCK HOLIDAYS
GIVE ME MORE
EVERYTHING THAT
IS BAD FOR ME SAD

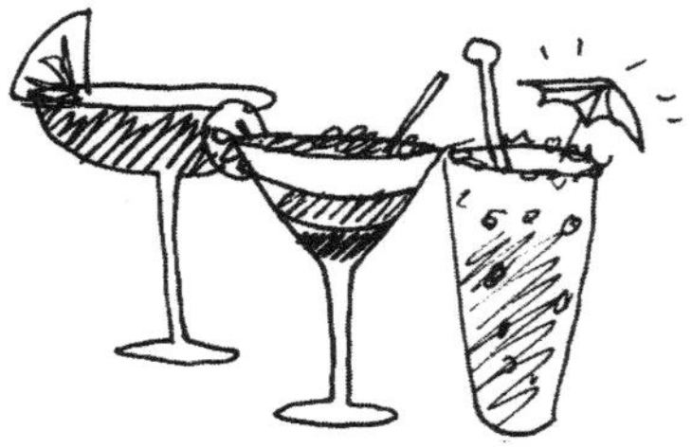

HAHA I AM SAD BUT NOT
PAYING FOR ANY OF THIS
SHIT SO I'LL HAVE TWELVETY
OF WHATEVER THESE ARE.
WEHAY WATCH ME CATCH
MY TEARS IN THIS TINY
NOVELTY UMBRELLA!

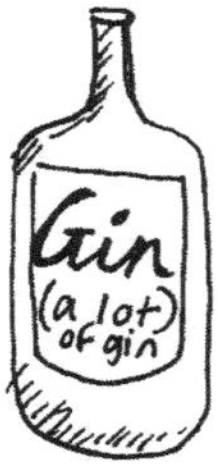
Gin
(a lot)
of gin

I AM VERY SAD AND
WOULD PREFER NOT
TO FEEL MY OWN FACE
RIGHT NOW. THANKS

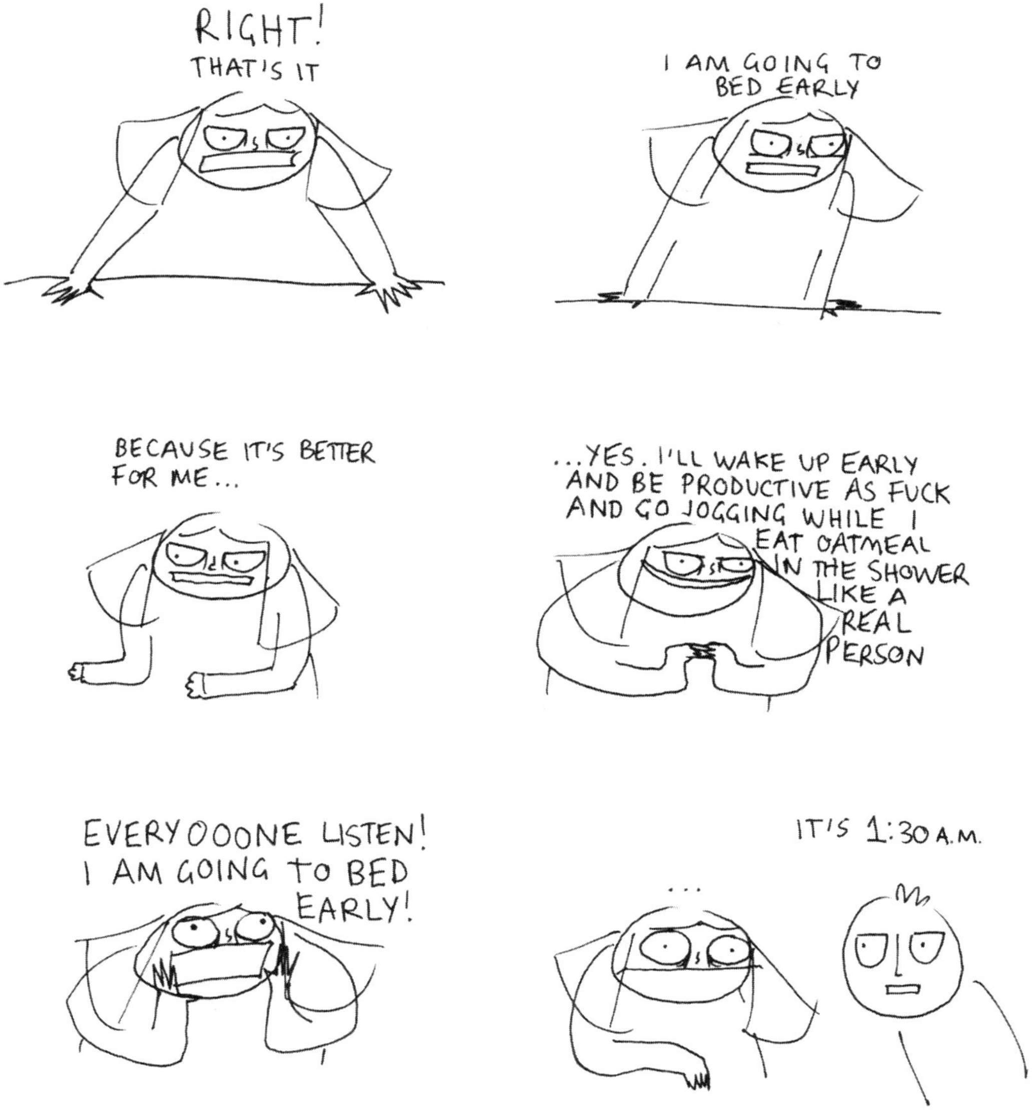
RIGHT!
THAT'S IT
I AM GOING TO BED EARLY
BECAUSE IT'S BETTER FOR ME...
...YES. I'LL WAKE UP EARLY AND BE PRODUCTIVE AS FUCK AND GO JOGGING WHILE I EAT OATMEAL IN THE SHOWER LIKE A REAL PERSON
EVERYOOONE LISTEN! I AM GOING TO BED EARLY!
IT'S 1:30 A.M.
...

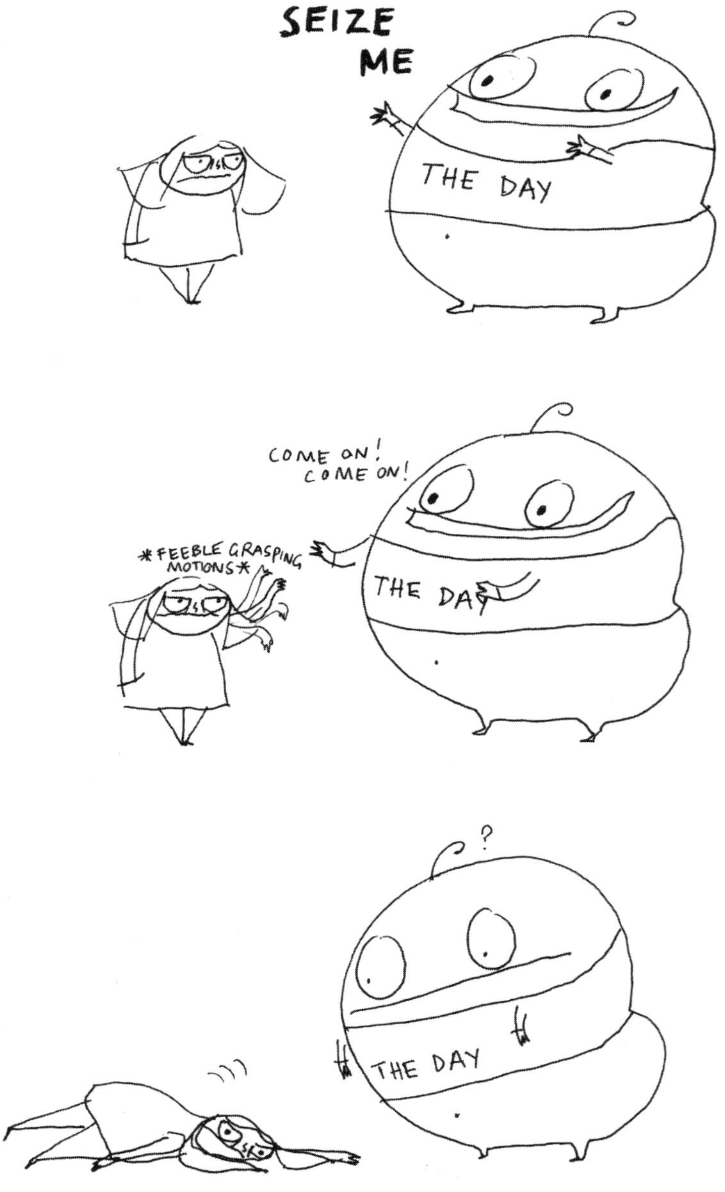
SEIZE ME
THE DAY
COME ON! COME ON!
FEEBLE GRASPING MOTIONS
THE DAY
?
THE DAY

COLLECTION OF THINGS I'VE SEEN WHILE MY EYES ARE
GLUED TO THE FLOOR WITH SHYNESS ADHESIVE

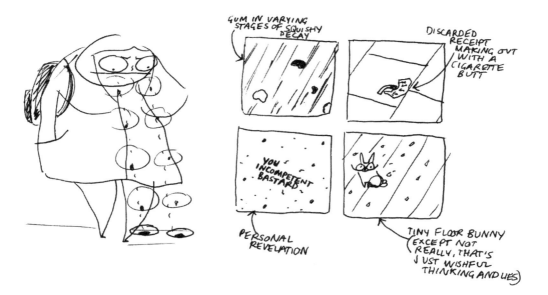

GUM IN VARYING
STAGES OF SQUISHY
DECAY

DISCARDED
RECEIPT
MAKING OUT
WITH A
CIGARETTE
BUTT

YOU
INCOMPETENT
BASTARD

PERSONAL
REVELATION

TINY FLOOR BUNNY
(EXCEPT NOT
REALLY, THAT'S
JUST WISHFUL
THINKING AND LIES)

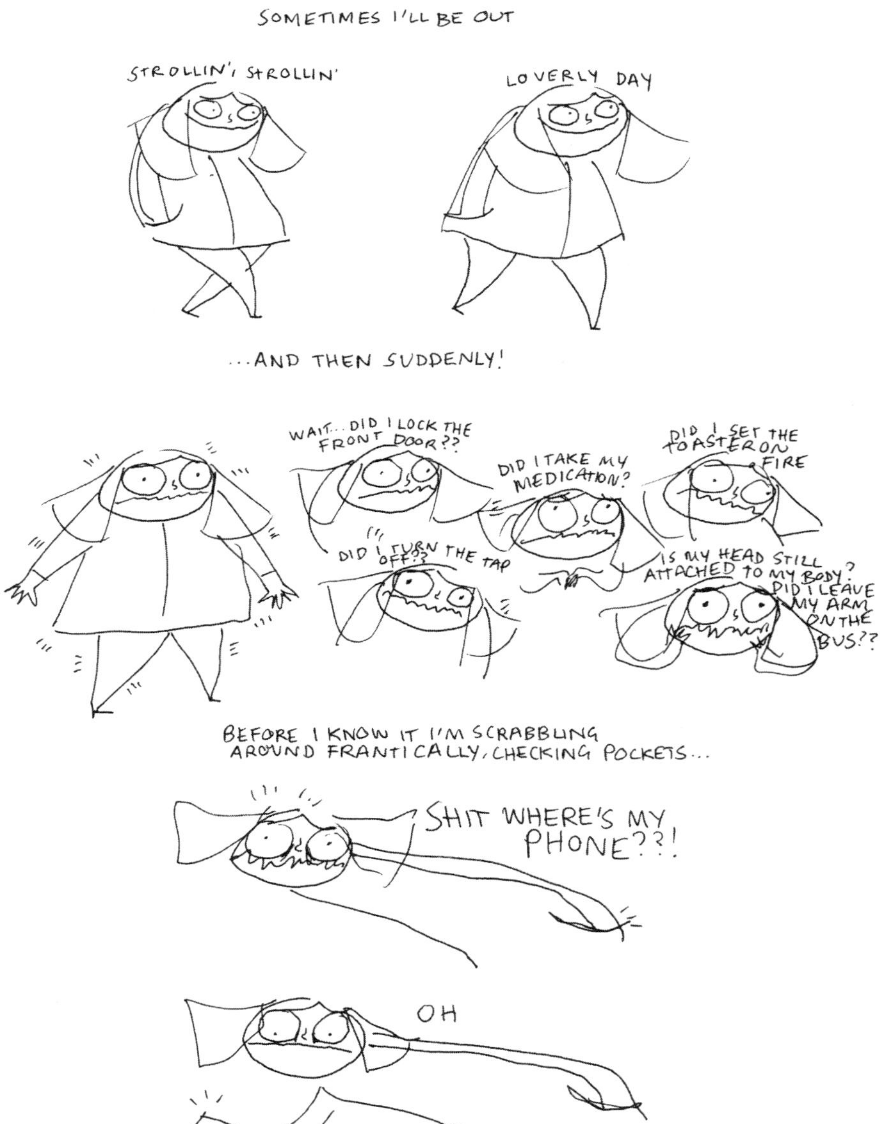
SOMETIMES I'LL BE OUT
STROLLIN', STROLLIN'
LOVERLY DAY
...AND THEN SUDDENLY!
WAIT... DID I LOCK THE FRONT DOOR??
DID I TAKE MY MEDICATION?
DID I SET THE TOASTER ON FIRE
DID I TURN THE TAP OFF??
IS MY HEAD STILL ATTACHED TO MY BODY?
DID I LEAVE MY ARM ON THE BUS??
BEFORE I KNOW IT I'M SCRABBLING AROUND FRANTICALLY, CHECKING POCKETS...
SHIT WHERE'S MY PHONE??!
OH

I'M A WALKING BAG O' PANIC

RULES

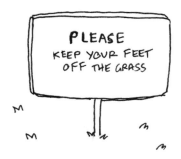

PLEASE
KEEP YOUR FEET
OFF THE GRASS

PLEASE DO NOT
SCREAM AT THE GRASS
FOR BEING A BETTER
PERSON THAN YOU

IF YOU ARE A COUPLE
NEWLY IN LOVE PLEASE
TAKE YOUR OBNOXIOUS
COUPLINESS ELSEWHERE
YOU ARE RUINING IT FOR
THE LONELY PEOPLE

PLEASE SHOW YOUR
RESPECT FOR NATURE
BY ROLLING AROUND
IN THE LEAVES SHOUTING
"PARK LIFE" AT REGULAR
INTERVALS

NO ONE WANTS TO
HEAR ABOUT HOW THAT
CLOUD LOOKS LIKE A
HEDGE TRIMMER, MOIRA

PLEASE
GIVE SUNNY PATCH
PRIORITY TO DOGS.
THEY DESERVE IT

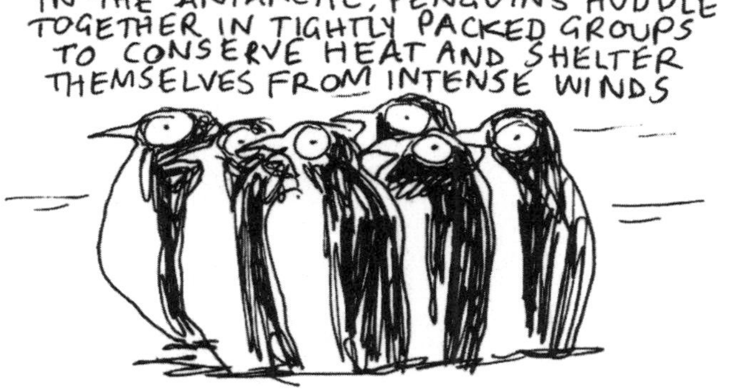
IN THE ANTARCTIC, PENGUINS HUDDLE TOGETHER IN TIGHTLY PACKED GROUPS TO CONSERVE HEAT AND SHELTER THEMSELVES FROM INTENSE WINDS

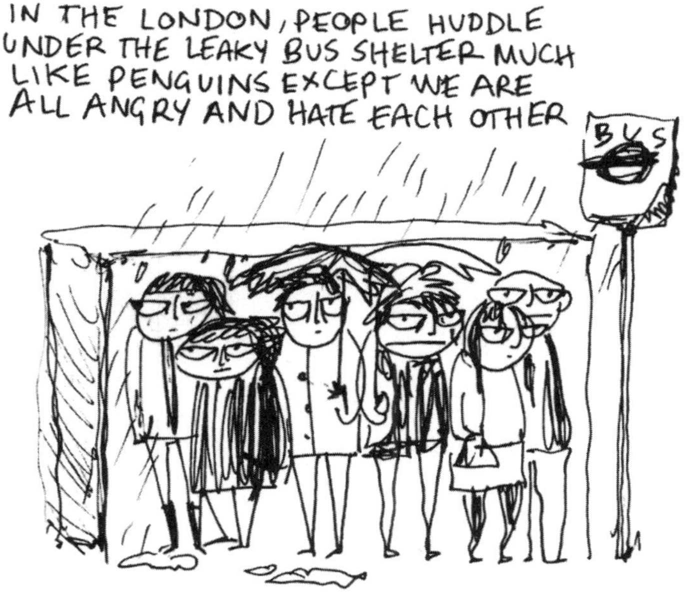
IN THE LONDON, PEOPLE HUDDLE UNDER THE LEAKY BUS SHELTER MUCH LIKE PENGUINS EXCEPT WE ARE ALL ANGRY AND HATE EACH OTHER
BUS

IT'S FINE IF EVERYTHING
YOU ARE MAKING IS CRAP

JUST KEEP MAKING
IT

GATHER IT IN AN IMPRESSIVE PILE

SURVEY YOUR OWN CRAP KINGDOM

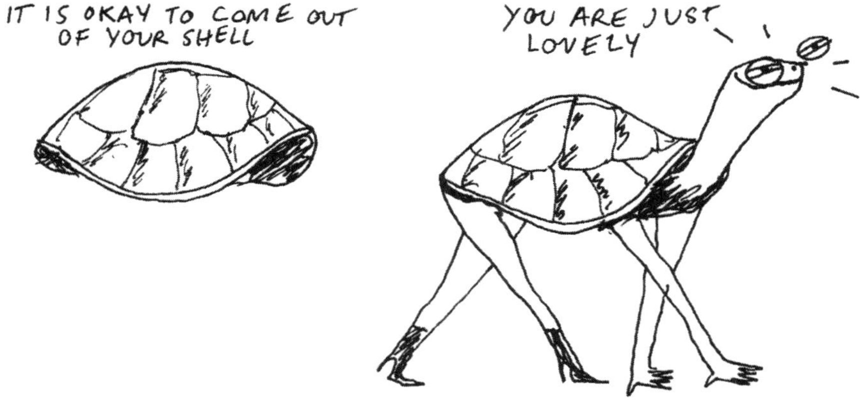
IT IS OKAY TO COME OUT OF YOUR SHELL
YOU ARE JUST LOVELY

WAYS TO FEEL IN CONTROL WHEN YOUR LIFE IS DOING BIG CHANGES

YOU WILL HAVE MANY ESSENTIAL, COMPLICATED THINGS TO SORT OUT. IT IS IMPORTANT YOU DO THEM. NOW.

17 MISSED CALLS
∞ EMAILS

mmmmm fuvvuck

UNCERTAIN FUCKERY

ADULT SHIT I DON'T UNDERSTAND

DOCUMENTS

...SO INSTEAD!

NEGLECT RESPONSIBILITY AND FOCUS ON ARRANGING TINY ORNAMENTS ON A SHELF FOR HALF AN HOUR AND SIMILARLY UNPRODUCTIVE POINTLESS TASKS. THAT WAY NOTHING GETS DONE AND YOU HAVE CONTROL OVER MICRO-AREAS OF YOUR LIFE

THEN DRINK SO MUCH CAFFEINE YOU CAN'T FEEL YOUR OWN EYES. IT'S GOING TO BE FINE

HEY SO IF YOU COULD MEET
ANYONE, ANYONE IN THE WORLD,
WHO WOULD IT
BE

PROBABLY MY OWN EXPECTATIONS,
FOR ONCE IN MY IDIOT LIFE

WAIT, WHAT?!?

CHER, I SAID CHER,
IT'S FINE

RELAX   OKAY   THAT'S TOO MUCH
                                                      RELAX

WE'RE
ALL
ABSOLUTELY
FINE

IT'S LOVELY SEEING PEOPLE BUT I CANNOT WAIT FOR THEM TO LEAVE SO I CAN BE MYSELF AGAIN AND EAT CRACKERS ALONE IN THE DARK

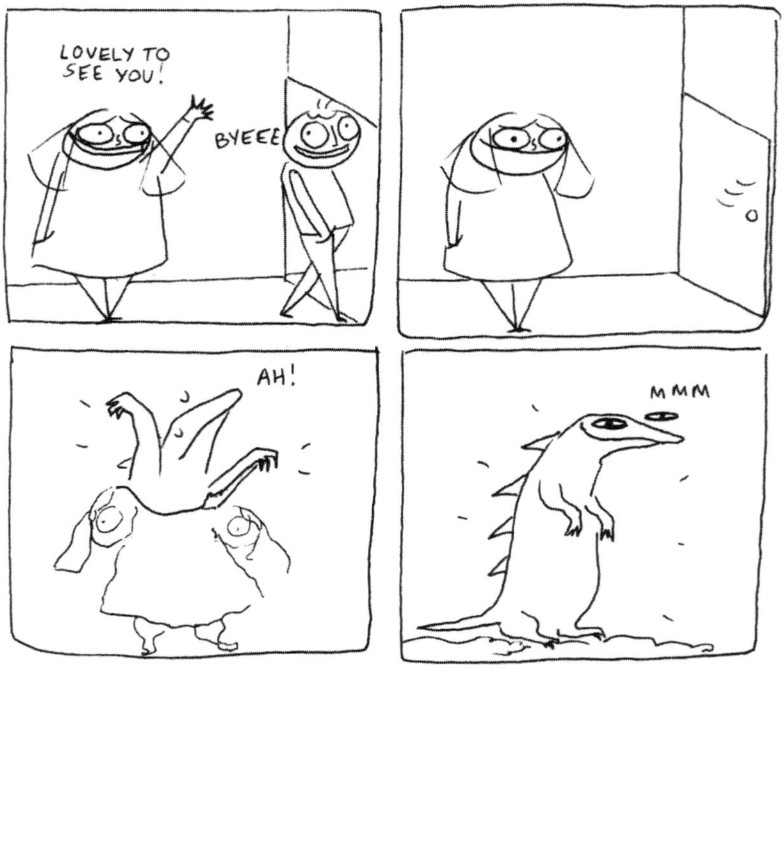
LOVELY TO SEE YOU!
BYEEE
AH!
MMM

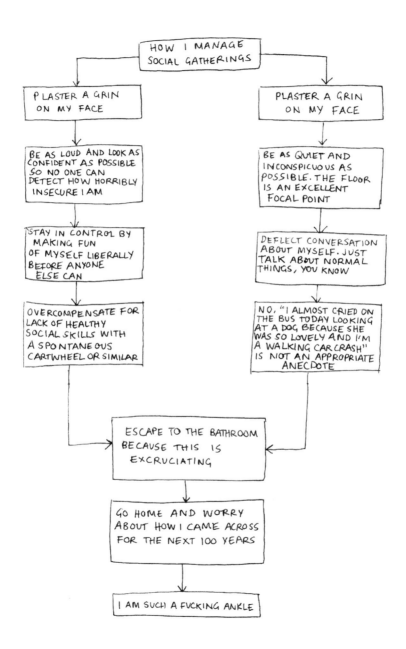

HOW I MANAGE SOCIAL GATHERINGS

PLASTER A GRIN ON MY FACE

BE AS LOUD AND LOOK AS CONFIDENT AS POSSIBLE SO NO ONE CAN DETECT HOW HORRIBLY INSECURE I AM

STAY IN CONTROL BY MAKING FUN OF MYSELF LIBERALLY BEFORE ANYONE ELSE CAN

OVERCOMPENSATE FOR LACK OF HEALTHY SOCIAL SKILLS WITH A SPONTANEOUS CARTWHEEL OR SIMILAR

PLASTER A GRIN ON MY FACE

BE AS QUIET AND INCONSPICUOUS AS POSSIBLE. THE FLOOR IS AN EXCELLENT FOCAL POINT

DEFLECT CONVERSATION ABOUT MYSELF. JUST TALK ABOUT NORMAL THINGS, YOU KNOW

NO, "I ALMOST CRIED ON THE BUS TODAY LOOKING AT A DOG BECAUSE SHE WAS SO LOVELY AND I'M A WALKING CAR CRASH" IS NOT AN APPROPRIATE ANECDOTE

ESCAPE TO THE BATHROOM BECAUSE THIS IS EXCRUCIATING

GO HOME AND WORRY ABOUT HOW I CAME ACROSS FOR THE NEXT 100 YEARS

I AM SUCH A FUCKING ANKLE

THIS IS HOW IT FEELS WHEN SOMEONE CLAIMS TO KNOW **EXACTLY** WHAT YOU'RE GOING THROUGH INSTEAD OF JUST LISTENING TO WHAT YOU'RE SAYING

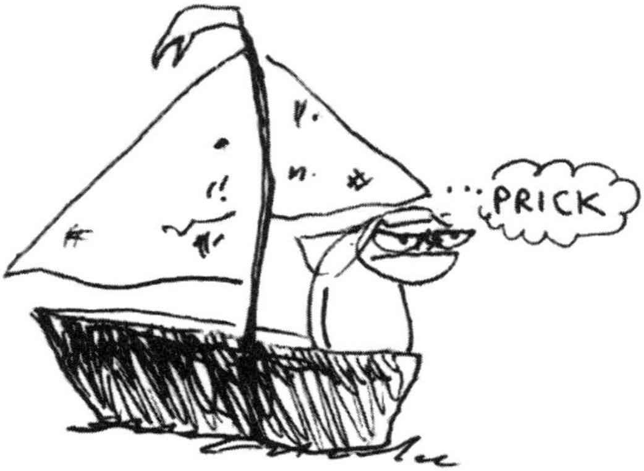
...PRICK

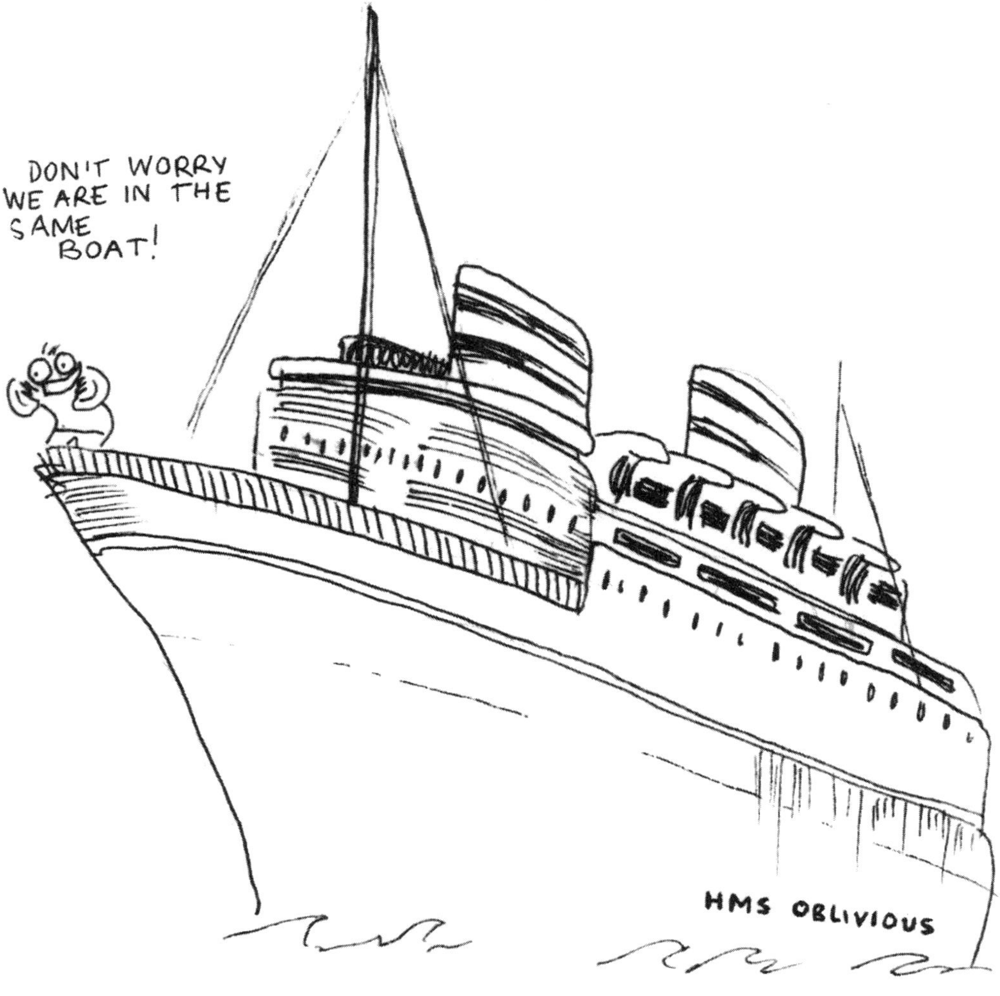
DON'T WORRY WE ARE IN THE SAME BOAT!
HMS OBLIVIOUS

DATE

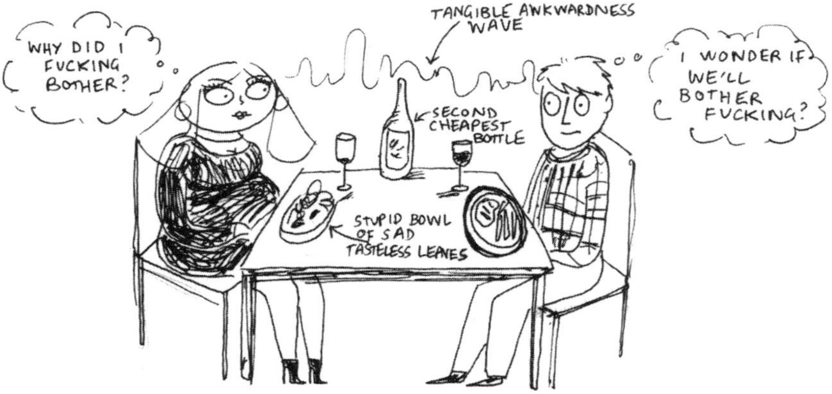
WHY DID I FUCKING BOTHER?
TANGIBLE AWKWARDNESS WAVE
I WONDER IF WE'LL BOTHER FUCKING?
SECOND CHEAPEST BOTTLE
STUPID BOWL OF SAD TASTELESS LEAVES

I'M EATING FOOD I DON'T LIKE
WITH A MAN I DON'T GET
IN A DRESS THAT'S TOO SMALL
I LIKE MY SHOES
BUT I COULD HAVE LIKED MY SHOES AT HOME
ALONE
IN FRONT OF THE TV

WITH CHIPS

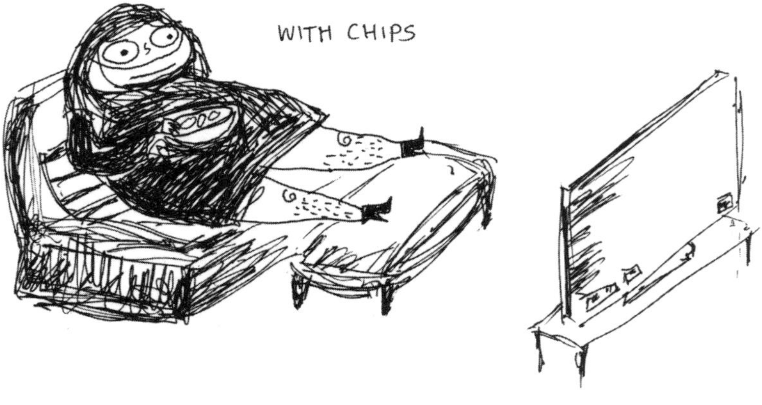

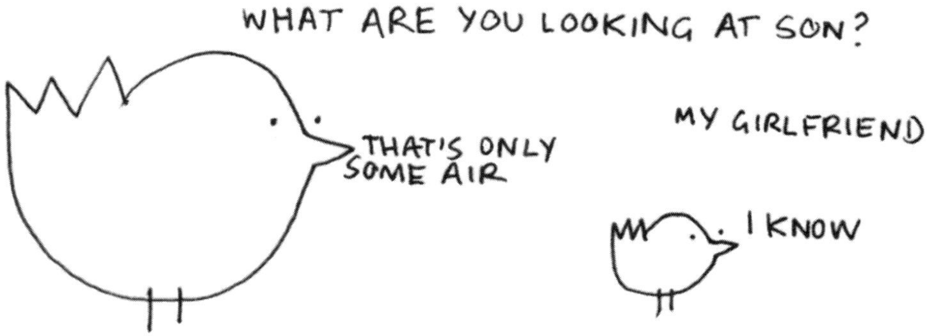
WHAT ARE YOU LOOKING AT SON?
MY GIRLFRIEND
THAT'S ONLY SOME AIR
I KNOW

ACCIDENTALLY BEGINS TALKING ABOUT SELF

LISTENING NICELY AND RESPONDING AT APPROPRIATE INTERVALS

SUDDENLY BECOMING AWARE I'VE JUST VERBALLY DIARRHEAD MY WHOLE LIFE ONTO THIS POOR PERSON FOR 25 MINUTES

YOU OK?

THE ME SHOW THE ME SHOW I MADE IT ALL ABOUT ME SHOW ARGHH

I AM SO SORRY, HOW ARE YOU? HOW IS YOUR CAT AND HOW YOU, ARE, HELLO!? VERY NICE

BRRT BRRT

HELLOO?

SHIT SHIT
SHIT

OH HEEY,
HOW ARE
YOU?

MY HEAD IS
AN ACTUAL
TOILET

AH, NOT TOO
BAD THANKS,
GOING
ALONG

SHITTING
SHITTING
SHIT

YES IT'S BEEN
TOO LONG!
LET ME JUST
CHECK
WHEN I'M
FREE

...OOH I'M PRETTY BUSY,
WEEKEND MIGHT WORK?

MON - PANIC ATTACK	THURS - PANIC ATTACK: THE SEQUEL
TUES - BODY HORROR DAY	FRI - EXISTENTIAL CRISIS
WEDS - CRYING FESTIVAL	SAT/SUN - MEH DUNNO

I'M A FOOL,
A DAMNDED
FOOL

GREAT! SATURDAY
IT IS. SEE
YA THEN!

SATURDAY

I'M A TINY
VERY LARGE
DISASTER

HOW TO GET FRIENDS

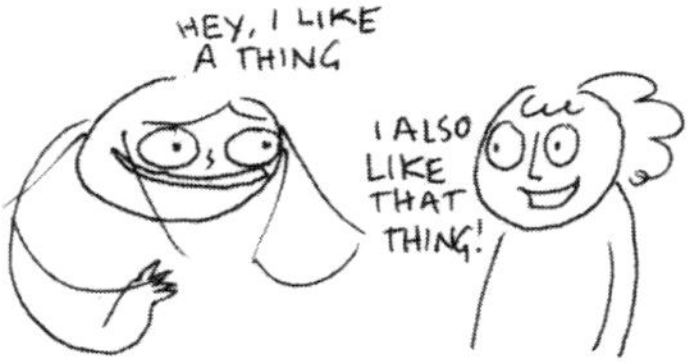
HEY, I LIKE A THING
I ALSO LIKE THAT THING!

FIND PEOPLE WITH SIMILAR INTERESTS

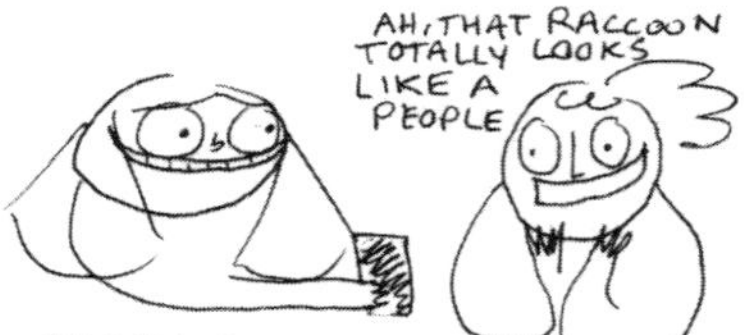
AH, THAT RACCOON TOTALLY LOOKS LIKE A PEOPLE

SHARE RELATABLE INTERNET CONTENT

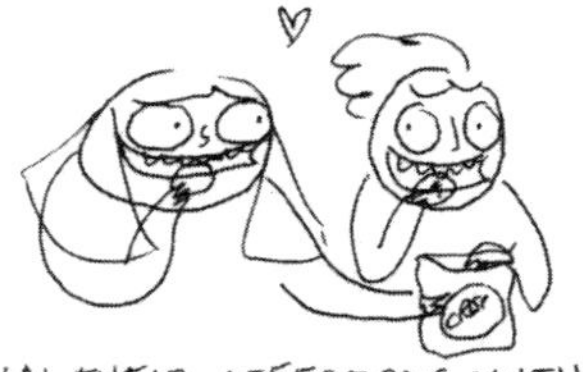

WIN THEIR AFFECTIONS WITH CHIPS

OR FAILING THAT

JUST BECOME A FREE WIFI HOTSPOT

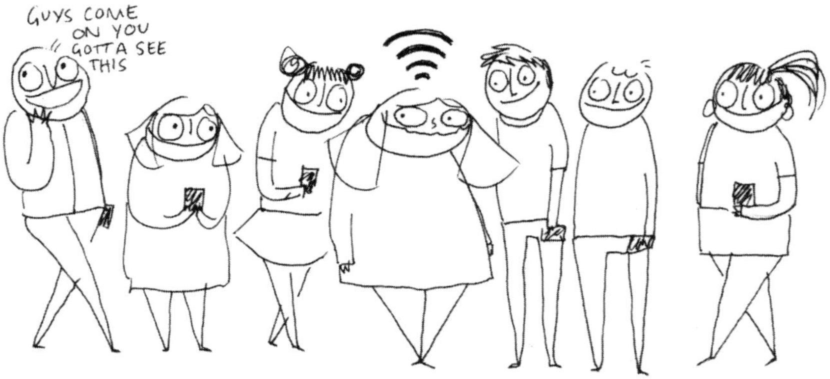
GUYS COME ON YOU GOTTA SEE THIS

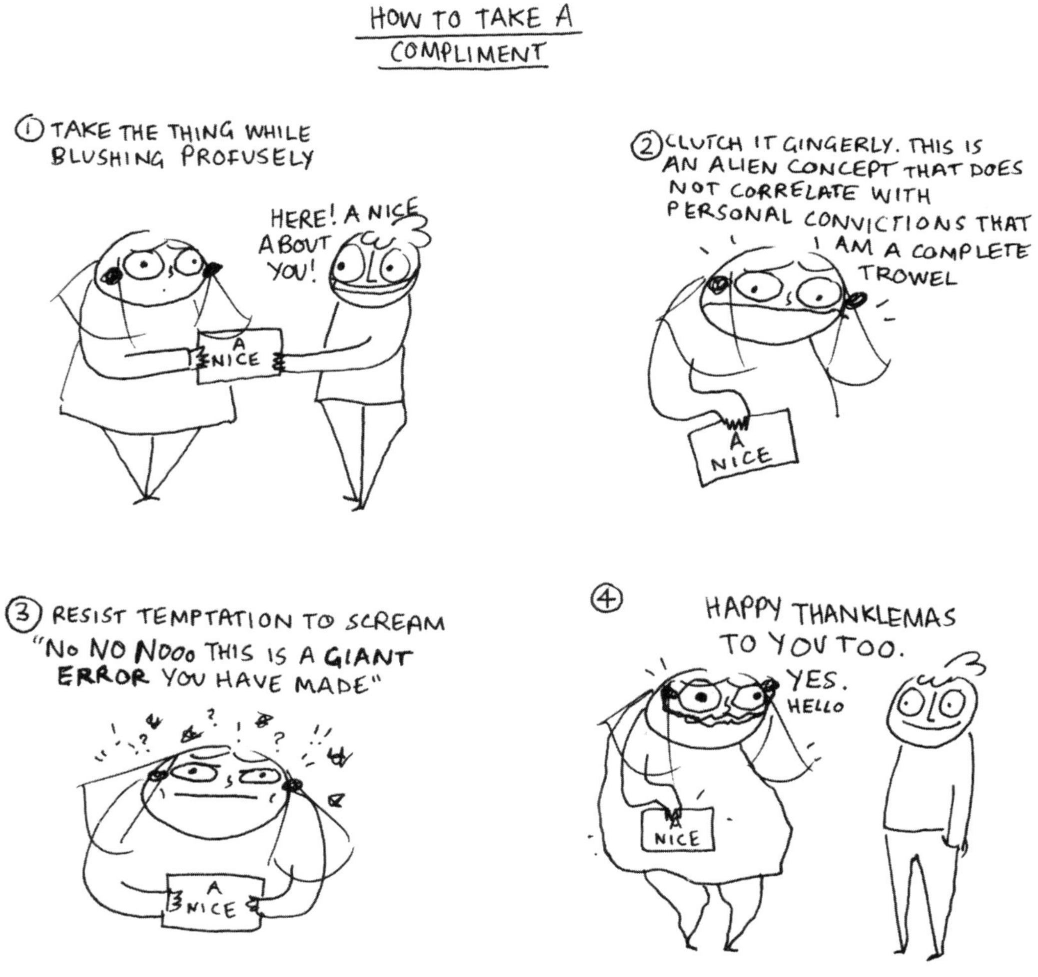
HOW TO TAKE A COMPLIMENT
① TAKE THE THING WHILE BLUSHING PROFUSELY
HERE! A NICE ABOUT YOU!
A NICE
② CLUTCH IT GINGERLY. THIS IS AN ALIEN CONCEPT THAT DOES NOT CORRELATE WITH PERSONAL CONVICTIONS THAT I AM A COMPLETE TROWEL
A NICE
③ RESIST TEMPTATION TO SCREAM "No NO Nooo THIS IS A GIANT ERROR YOU HAVE MADE"
A NICE
④ HAPPY THANKLEMAS TO YOU TOO.
YES. HELLO
A NICE

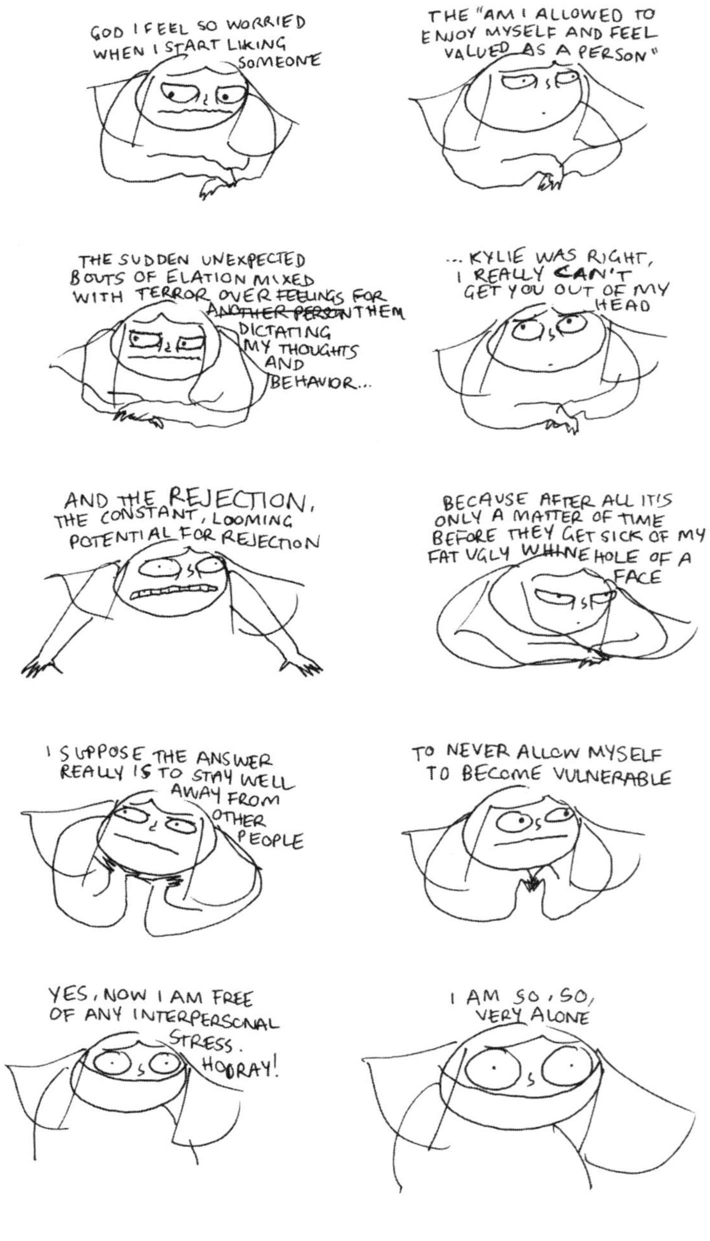
GOD I FEEL SO WORRIED WHEN I START LIKING SOMEONE
THE "AM I ALLOWED TO ENJOY MYSELF AND FEEL VALUED AS A PERSON"
THE SUDDEN UNEXPECTED BOUTS OF ELATION MIXED WITH TERROR OVER ~~FEELINGS FOR ANOTHER PERSON~~ THEM DICTATING MY THOUGHTS AND BEHAVIOR...
...KYLIE WAS RIGHT, I REALLY CAN'T GET YOU OUT OF MY HEAD
AND THE REJECTION, THE CONSTANT, LOOMING POTENTIAL FOR REJECTION
BECAUSE AFTER ALL IT'S ONLY A MATTER OF TIME BEFORE THEY GET SICK OF MY FAT UGLY ~~WHINE~~ HOLE OF A FACE
I SUPPOSE THE ANSWER REALLY IS TO STAY WELL AWAY FROM OTHER PEOPLE
TO NEVER ALLOW MYSELF TO BECOME VULNERABLE
YES, NOW I AM FREE OF ANY INTERPERSONAL STRESS. HOORAY!
I AM SO, SO, VERY ALONE

I'M NOT CLINGY

IT'S JUST MY EAR,
SHE IS TIRED

CAN I GO?

...NO

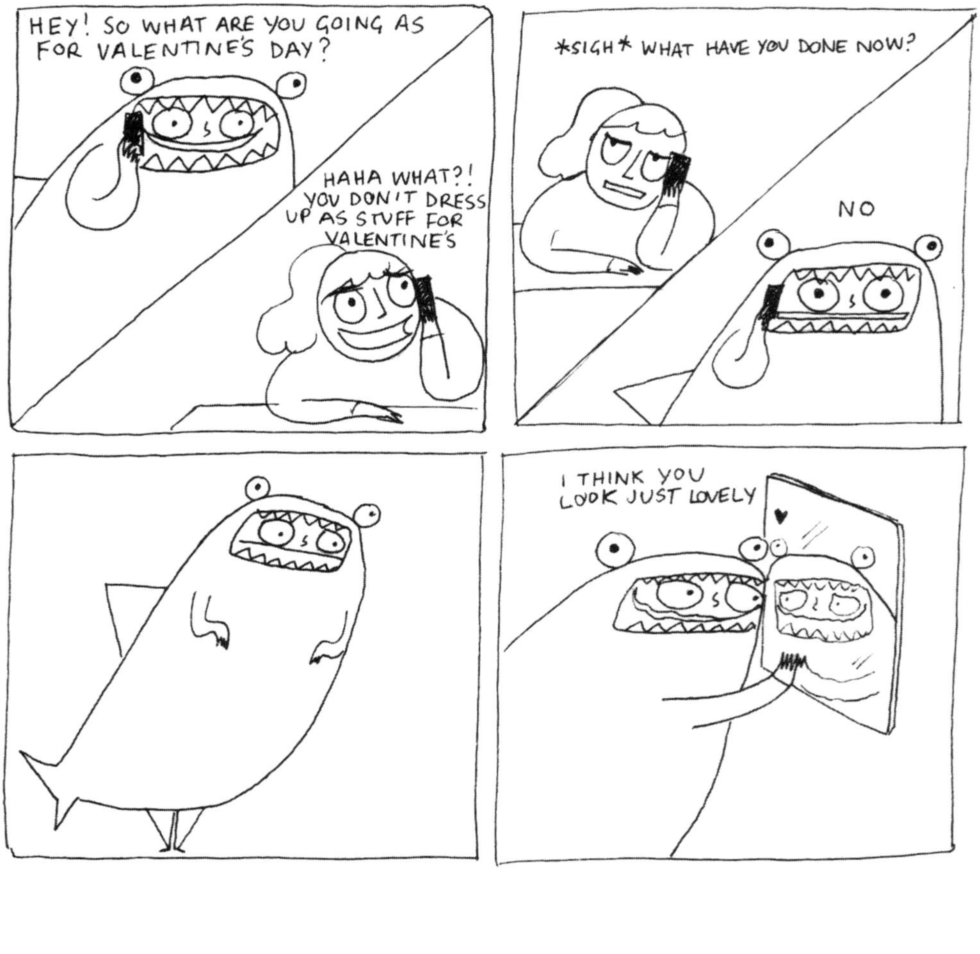
HEY! SO WHAT ARE YOU GOING AS FOR VALENTINE'S DAY?
HAHA WHAT?! YOU DON'T DRESS UP AS STUFF FOR VALENTINE'S
SIGH WHAT HAVE YOU DONE NOW?
NO
I THINK YOU LOOK JUST LOVELY

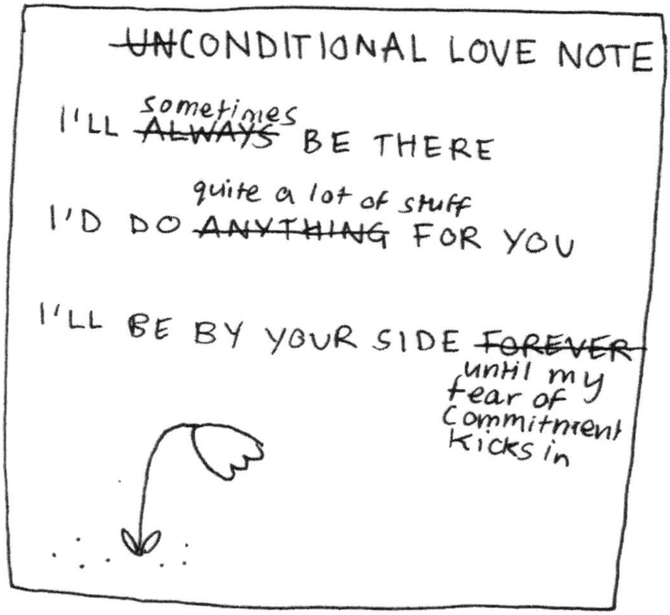
~~UN~~CONDITIONAL LOVE NOTE
I'LL ~~ALWAYS~~ sometimes BE THERE
I'D DO ~~ANYTHING~~ quite a lot of stuff FOR YOU
I'LL BE BY YOUR SIDE ~~FOREVER~~ until my fear of commitment kicks in

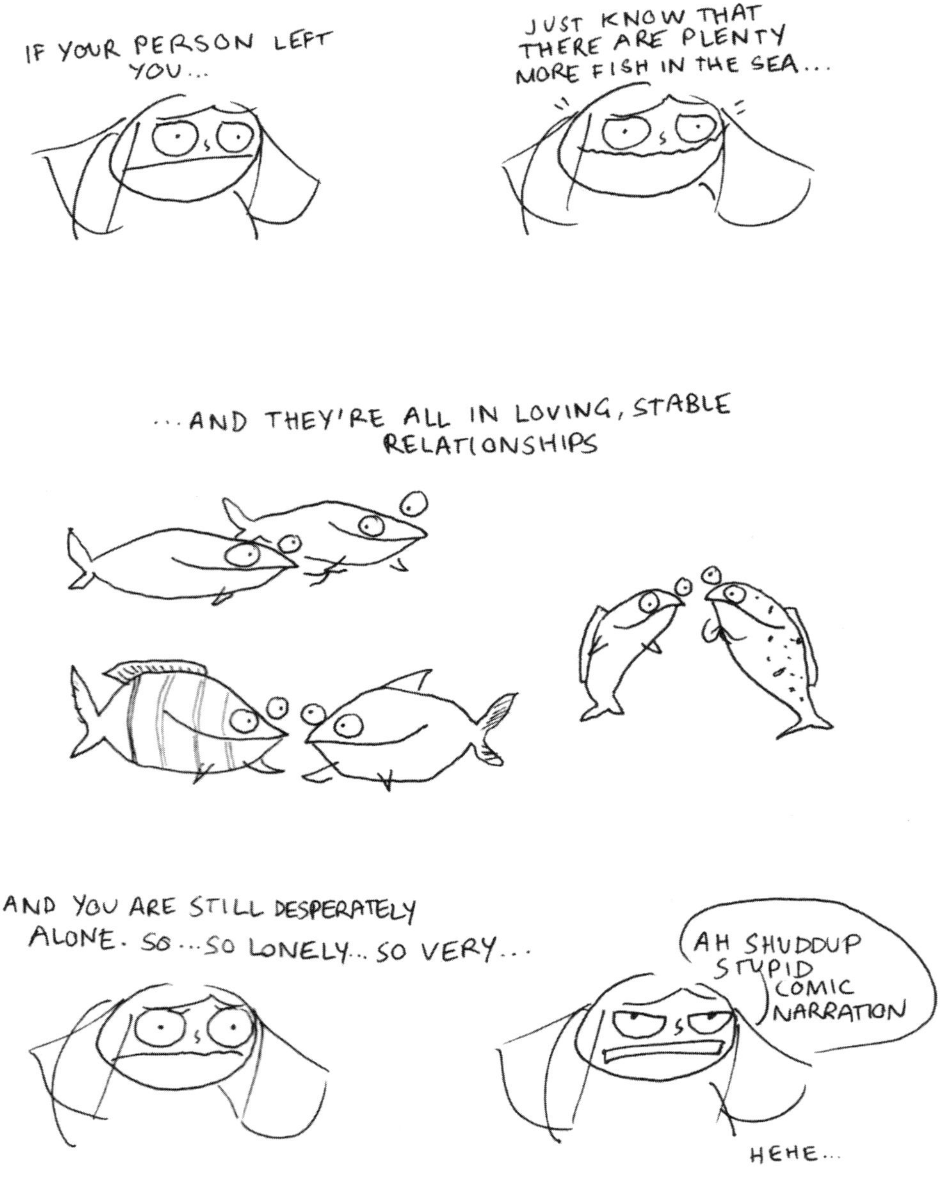
IF YOUR PERSON LEFT YOU...
JUST KNOW THAT THERE ARE PLENTY MORE FISH IN THE SEA...
...AND THEY'RE ALL IN LOVING, STABLE RELATIONSHIPS
AND YOU ARE STILL DESPERATELY ALONE. SO...SO LONELY...SO VERY...
AH SHUDDUP STUPID COMIC NARRATION
HEHE...

HEY
HEY
THE SEA
I MISS YOU
I ALSO AM HAVING A MISS OF YOU
THE SEA
HAHA
THE SEA
"HEY SHUT UP "THE SEA" YOU DON'T EVEN HAVE FRIENDS
YEAH, YOU PISS TANK FULL OF SALT
THE SEA
I COULD KILL YOU BOTH
YEAH GO ON THEN
THE SEA
THE SEA
WHEEEEE
THE SEA
SPLEP
FEEL THE WRATH
THIS IS A JELLY-FISH
THE SEA
THE SEA

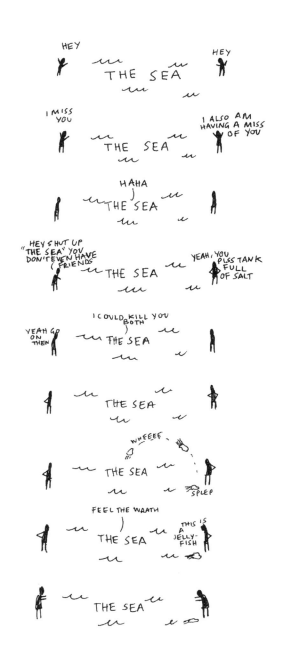

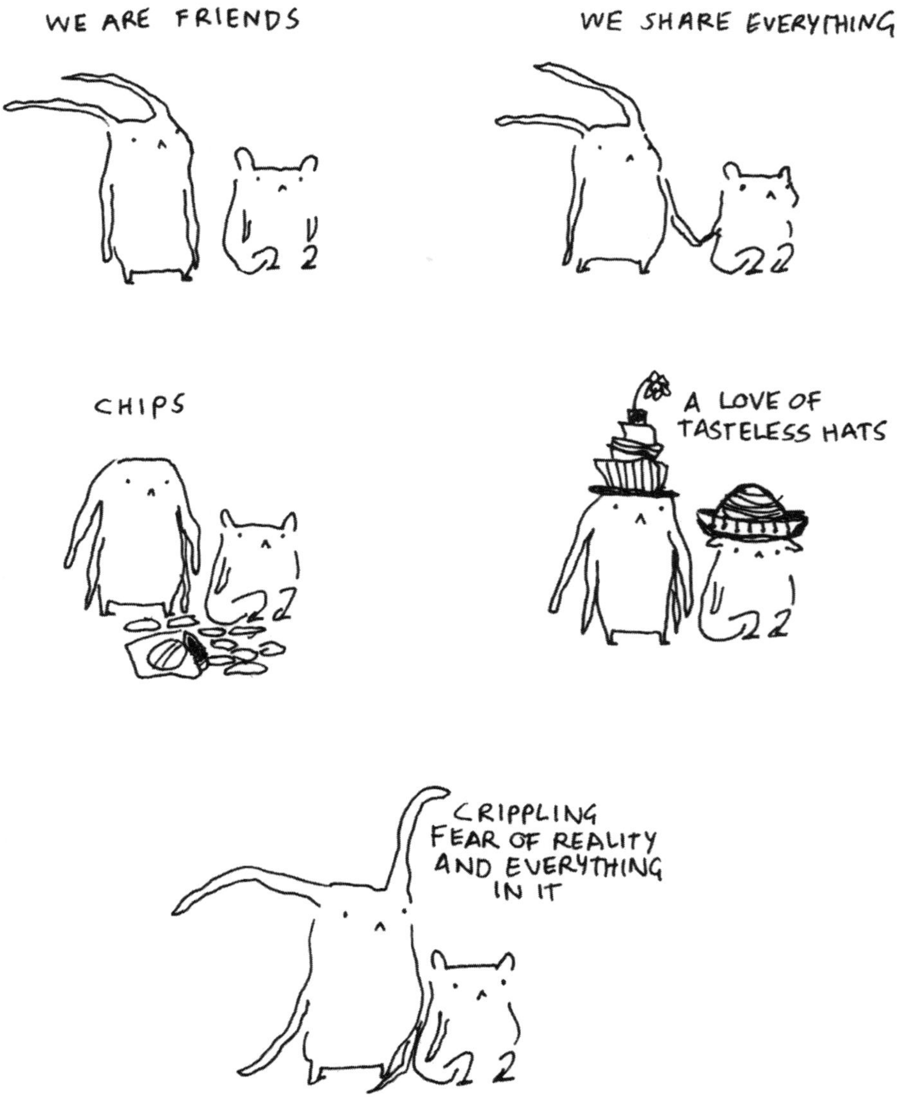
WE ARE FRIENDS
WE SHARE EVERYTHING
CHIPS
A LOVE OF TASTELESS HATS
CRIPPLING FEAR OF REALITY AND EVERYTHING IN IT

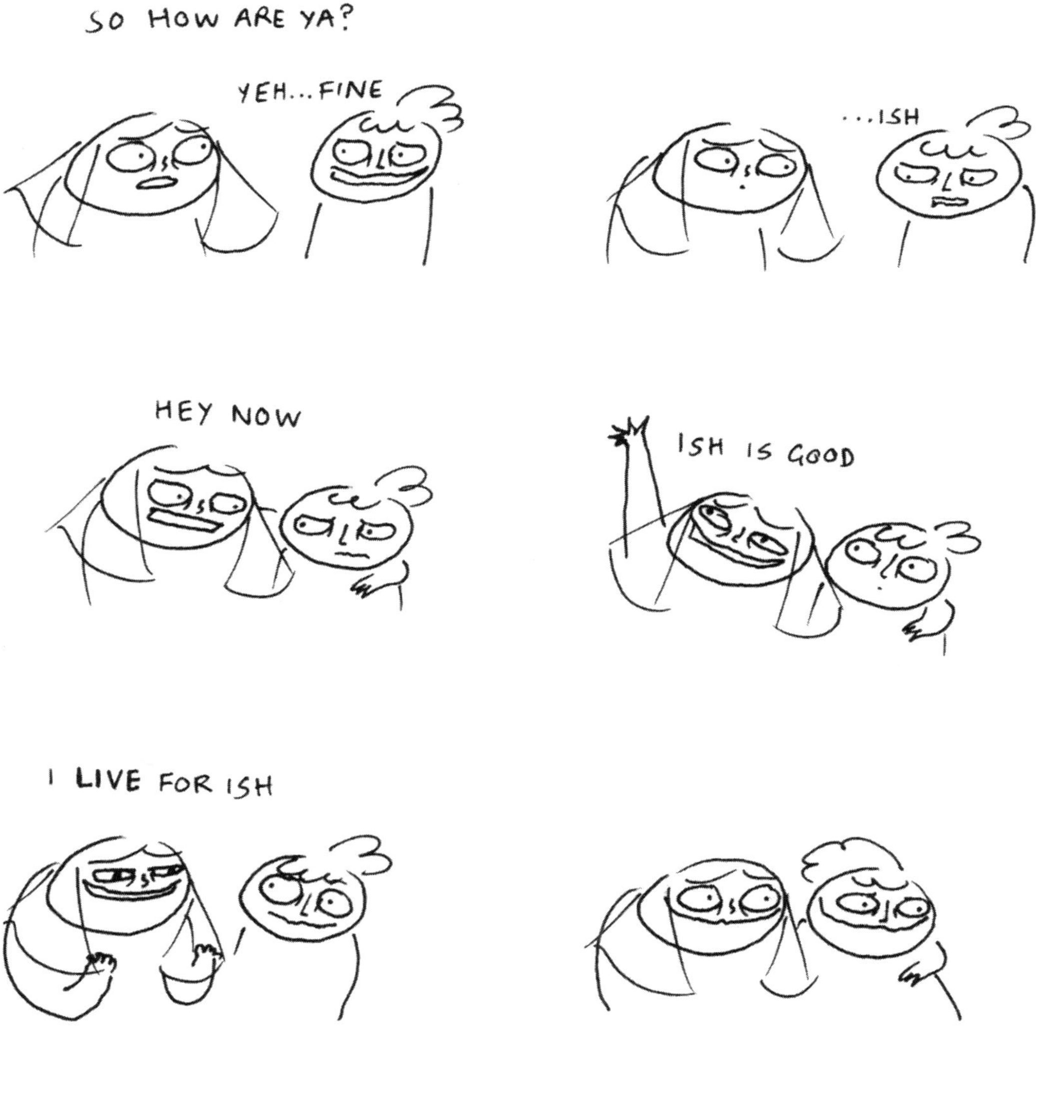
SO HOW ARE YA?
YEH...FINE
...ISH
HEY NOW
ISH IS GOOD
I **LIVE** FOR ISH

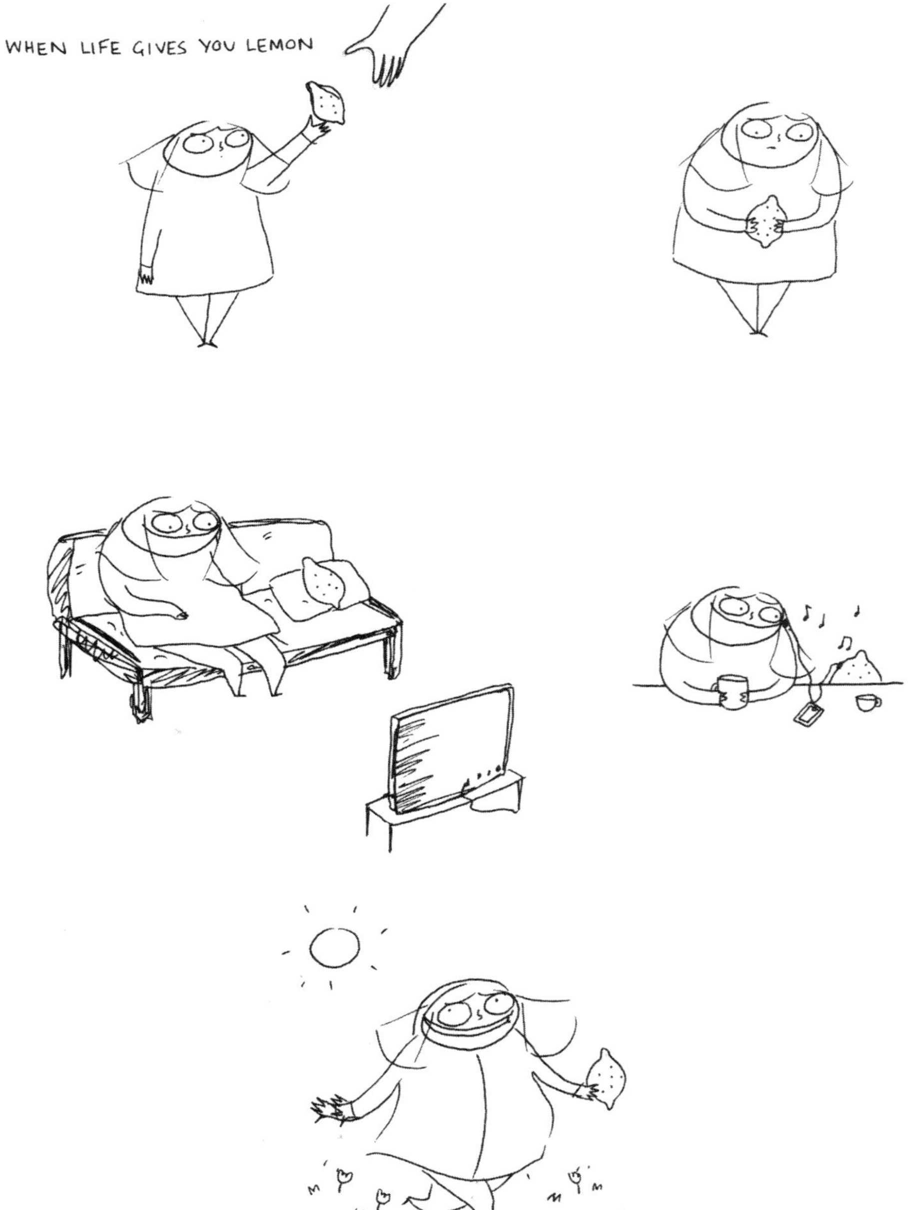
WHEN LIFE GIVES YOU LEMON

LEMONADE
RECIPE
?

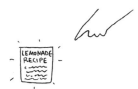

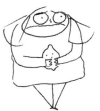

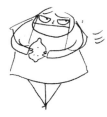

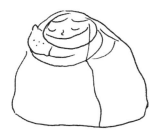

TYING UP LOOSE ENDS

OUTRODUCTION BIT

So yep, life's stupid sometimes. It's like someone handed you a nice yogurt and then said you can only eat the nice yogurt with a fork; incredibly fiddly, takes ages, you look like an idiot trying to work it out, AND it causes you to start making bad metaphors involving dairy products. Great.

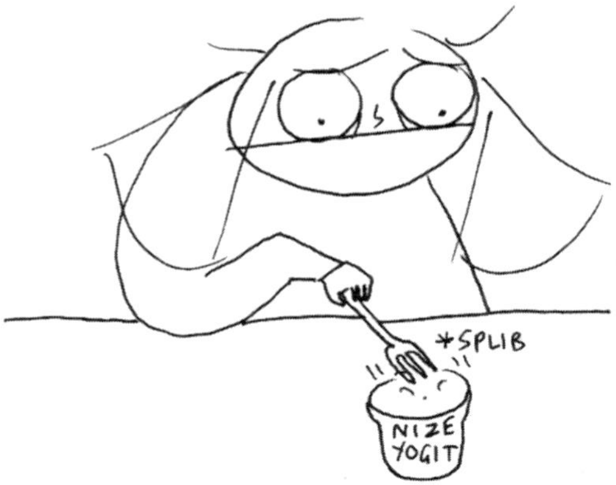
*SPLIB
NIZE YOGIT

I digress . . . this is the end of the thing you've been reading. And now you're going to go off and do something else. Maybe it's a good day and you're feeling on top of things and there's A Nice planned and existing feels relatively easy. Maybe it's a bad day, end of the world levels of bad even, a sad soggy salty pillow sort of time is occurring. Maybe you can't put your finger on what's going on but you know it's A LOT or maybe you're having no discernible type of day at all, floating about neither here nor meh. But we are doing it, in one way or another. Life's happening at us and we're all bob-bling along to our various degrees like the crying, laughing, very sentient potato weirdos that we are. I'm not actually that great at endings (again, see above with the whole life yogurt thing), but I'll leave this last drawing here, just in case you need it.

WHAT DID YOU
DO TODAY?

MANAGED

ACKNOWLEDGMENTS BIT

I would like to thank everyone at Orion and Trapeze who was crazy enough to say Yes and then help me bring this book to life and launch it (very skilfully) at the world with such dedication and enthusiasm, and in particular Emma Smith for editin' it and telling me when I have green pen on my face. A huge fuck-off sized thank you to Nicola Barr for being a relentlessly brilliant human and agent, and to Andy for making that phone call. Thanks also to Christopher Schelling and Patty Rice for all their hard work over in the US or "The States" as we call it in UK English.

I am incredibly grateful to everyone that has watched and heard and responded to me burping my art out online over the years in the most wonderfully kind and consistently supportive way, more than I am able to articulate in words actually so, if that is you: Know that you are just great and have this

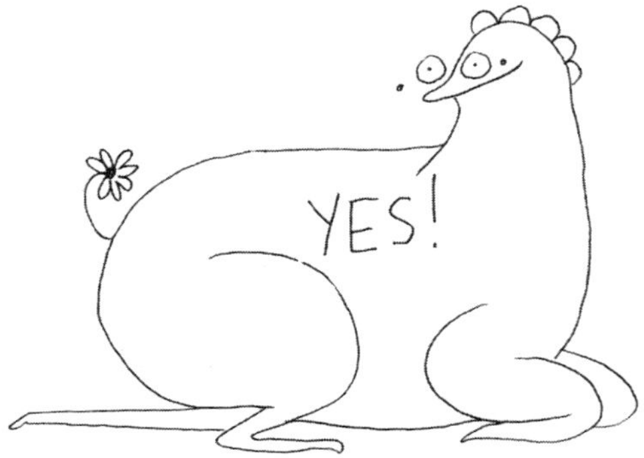
YES!

There are many (too many to list) NHS professionals and hospitals that have supported me through some extremely difficult years and hovered around with me on the brink until I've been ready to step back. It's a very long haul, but I am getting there; thank you.

There are a few brilliant people who listened to me moan and worry about this book most days for well over a year and continued to encourage the shit out of me when I needed it most; I think it will sound cool and mysterious to say YOU KNOW WHO YOU ARE so that is what I am saying and I will be yelling and pointing to this paragraph when I see you next.

I would like to thank my dog, Sadie, for tolerating me.

And finally my family, who are the funniest people I've ever met and have just been Getting It for so many years. Me being able to write this book is, in many ways, all of your faults. So yeah, thanks for that.